THE EVERYTHING®

Cheese Book

Dear Reader,

I can't remember a time I wasn't in love with one cheese or another. As a child I adored Longhorn Colby. As a teenager I explored the wonders of fondue. Somewhere along the way I fell in love with Sonoma Jack, and then, as an adult I began to love Brie. Now that I know so many more cheeses, these early ones feel like puppy love, but in truth, they were a springboard to jump into my exploration of hundreds and hundreds of delicious new cheeses. Every day I work behind the cheese counter, I watch someone fall in love with a cheese they've never seen or heard of before. It's a fascinating and engaging world that I feel lucky to share. If you love cheese, and even if you just like it a lot, you're in for a real treat.

Laura M. Martinez

The EVERYTHING® Series

Editorial

Publisher	Gary M. Krebs
Director of Product Development	Paula Munier
Managing Editor	Laura M. Daly
Executive Editor, Series Books	Brielle M. Matson
Associate Copy Chief	Sheila Zwiebel
Acquisitions Editor	Kerry Smith
Development Editors	Jessica LaPointe
	Brett Palana-Shanahan
Production Editor	Casey Ebert

Production

Director of Manufacturing	Susan Beale
Production Project Manager	Michelle Roy Kelly
Prepress	Erick DaCosta
	Matt LeBlanc
Interior Layout	Heather Barrett
	Brewster Brownville
	Colleen Cunningham
	Jennifer Oliveira
Cover Design	Erin Alexander
	Stephanie Chrusz
	Frank Rivera

THE
EVERYTHING®
CHEESE
BOOK

From Cheddar to chèvre, all you need to select and serve the finest fromage

Laura Martinez

A
Adams Media
Avon, Massachusetts

To my husband, David, and our cheese-loving kids,
Jen, Dave, Theo, Alex, Tatiana, Margo, Chris, and Clay. You
inspire me every single day. Thank you.

An Everything® Series Book.
Everything® and everything.com® are registered trademarks of F+W Publications, Inc.

Published by Adams Media, an F+W Publications Company
57 Littlefield Street, Avon, MA 02322 U.S.A.
www.adamsmedia.com

ISBN-10: 1-59869-252-6
ISBN-13: 978-1-59869-252-5

Printed in the United States of America.

J   I   H   G   F   E   D   C   B   A

Library of Congress Cataloging-in-Publication Data

Martinez, Laura.
The everything cheese book / Laura Martinez.
p. cm. – (Everything series)
ISBN-10: 1-59869-252-6 (pbk.)
ISBN-13: 978-1-59869-252-5 (pbk.)
1. Cookery (Cheese) 2. Cheese–Varieties. I. Title.

TX759.5.C48M3786 2007
641.3'73–dc22
2007010846

This book is available at quantity discounts for bulk purchases.
For information, please call 1-800-289-0963.

Contents

Cheese with Sweet and Savory Foods / 173

Acknowledgments

A special thanks goes to Juliana Uruburu, for helping cheese choose me, but more importantly, for her incredible generosity in sharing her cheese and cooking wisdom; to Porsche Combash, for putting me behind the cheese counter (not to mention her incredible support and fantastic food wisdom); to Mariko Hayashi, Kate Hill, Alma Avalos, Barbara Cushman, Wendy Robinson, and the entire cheese-department crew for being such great cheese teachers and cheese pals; to Sara Wilson of The Pasta Shop for her support; to Sara Feinberg for her amazing good energy; to Ali who assumed I could do this; to Ahmed for his jokes; and to the Lindas: Sikorski, Hughes, and Jones, for always being happy to share their vast knowledge of food. A very special thanks goes to Maggie Gosselin of the Center for Urban Education about Sustainable Agriculture (CUESA) who asked if I'd write about cheese; and to Kerry Smith of Adams Media who asked the same thing.

I am indebted to Liam and Cindy Callahan who graciously invited me to visit Bellwether Farms and allowed me to stand in whey with them; to Bob, Lynn, and Jill Giacomini and Monty McIntyre of Pt. Reyes Farmstead Blue for graciously telling their story and allowing Alma and me free rein of the place. We milked a cow! Thanks also go to Jennifer Bice of Redwood Hill Creamery and Farm, who seems to delight in opening up her creamery and farm for the curious; to Donna Pachecho of Achadinha; and to Javier Salmon of Bodega Goat Cheeese. And special thanks to Michael Zilber, who dropped everything when Alma and I showed up unannounced at Cowgirl Creamery. Mark Todd and Daniel Strongin, cheese resource and marketing consultants, provided excellent advice on beer, packaging, and cheese professions, and so many wonderful people from the American Cheese Society extended offers of help. I only regret I didn't have time to take you all up on it. And where would any of this be without the Tasters' Group? Thank you, everyone, for dropping everything, anytime, to sip and taste everything I put in front of you. But most of all, thank you, David, for your love and my room, and thank you, kids, for everything.

Top Ten Things You Should Know about Cheese

1. Cheese makes you smile. It's true, just saying "ee" makes the corners of your mouth turn up. Not to mention your delight in eating it!

2. Cheese can be made from any kind of milk. The most common milks used for cheese come from cows, goats, and ewes.

3. Raw milk cheeses are legal in the United States if they are aged more than sixty days. That's enough time for any harmful bacteria to die.

4. Artisanal cheese is made according to traditional, handmade methods that date back thousands of years.

5. White wine is easy to pair with cheese, but red wine has tannin that can clash with salty cheese. But almost all beer pairs well with cheese!

6. Hard nuggets of older cheese can be scraped of mold and grated for cooking and toppings.

7. Some cheeses melt better than others. When cheese is made from cooked curds, the fat doesn't separate and puddle when melted.

8. Not all cheese browns when heated. Fresh mozzarella will not brown on a pizza, but it will melt.

9. On average, one ounce of cheese has seven grams of fat.

10. Always bring cheese to room temperature before you eat it. That way, the aromas and flavors will be at their best.

Introduction

▶EVERY DAY IN AMERICA, people are discovering new and interesting cheese. Twenty-five years ago, except in a few rare instances, the only kinds of cheese Americans could buy were factory-produced cheeses made in huge quantities, and then cut and sealed in plastic before being shipped to the store. Up until recent years, the cheeses available to most Americans were American cheese, bright orange Cheddar, cold-pack cheese, Havarti, Monterey jack, mozzarella, processed cheese, provolone, and Velveeta. And unless you traveled to small pockets of America or abroad, you may not have had a chance to taste anything like Peluso's teleme, Vella Dry Jack, or fresh chèvre. But thanks to a few pioneering American cheese makers and chefs who wanted local sources of French cheeses, the seeds of an American cheese revolution were planted in the early '80s.

At first it was just a matter of making a few select handmade cheeses and fresh chèvre, or fresh goat cheese. But as those cheeses caught on, cheese makers started branching out, making cheeses like crottins, and people who loved cheese started looking for sources of new and unusual cheese. At the same time, innovative retailers started importing more specialty cheeses from Europe, and soon a handful of cheese counters with rotating stocks of a couple hundred handmade specialty cheeses popped up in Michigan, New York City, and the San Francisco Bay Area. Today there are dozens of wonderful cheese counters all over the country, stocked with a hundred or more different types of cheese, all sitting patiently in their spots, surrounded by a flurry of anxious and hurried customers and cheese mongers taking them through tastings and talking about fruity aromas; tangy sharpness; and long, nutty, buttery flavors. These stores have cheese covered in green furry mold; soft, downy sorts of cheese; cheese that looks like it's grown a wrinkled hide; cheese in large flat wheels and small squat cylinders; and some cheese that looks almost exactly like the cheeses you're used to seeing, only different. All of this is terrific news for cheese aficionados, but even better, it's fantastic news for people eager to explore the exciting range of flavors and aromas of artisanal, handmade cheese.

But how does someone used to eating three or four standard cheeses begin? *The Everything® Cheese Book* is here to help you. Through this book you'll learn to identify the types of aromas and flavors you respond to, then the textures you're after, and voila! You've found at least one new cheese to enjoy. From there you'll find another, and then another, and soon you'll have discovered an entirely new world of food to love. Really, it's that simple!

Along the way, this book will help you learn a little about how cheese is made, what difference it makes to use milk from different animals, and whether you should be concerned about eating cheese made from raw or pasteurized milk. Then you'll realize there are thousands of variations in cheese-making methods, and all lead to slight variations in aroma, texture, and flavor. You'll learn what it takes to run a good cheese counter and how to buy cheese, and then you'll spend some real time savoring certain aromas, textures, and flavors. You'll travel the world through cheese, be nourished through cheese, laugh about cheese in the media, and learn to care for your cheese at home. You will learn to pair different kinds of cheese with wine, champagne, beer, and spirits; you'll incorporate cheese into every meal; you'll pair different cheeses with sweet and savory food; you'll melt and grill your cheese; you'll use cheese as an ingredient; you'll design stunning platters and plates of cheese; you'll consider turning your cheese hobby into a way of life; and soon you'll be planning every trip around cheese. Really, what could be more fun? Enjoy!

Chapter 1

Cheese Then and Now

It may seem slightly foolish to begin with the idea of cheese as a part of early civilization, but few would dispute the significant role domesticated animals played in allowing hunters and gatherers to become herders and farmers. And where there are herds of animals there is milk, and where there is milk, almost always there is cheese. Sheep and goats were among the first domesticated animals, and though the discovery of cheese making is not documented, most food historians believe humans learned to make cheese fairly early on in their existence.

Cheese in Ancient Times

Milk separates into curds and whey when it spoils, or when it encounters an enzyme or chemical that causes it to separate. This separation is the first step in making cheese. In ancient times, dried animal stomachs were often used as vessels, and most likely held milk. Animal stomachs contain chymosin, a form of rennet. So, when someone carried milk in the lining of an animal stomach, instead of souring, it curdled and became a mild-tasting cheese. No doubt the same person tasted it, didn't die, and cheese, a new food, presented itself to people. This may have happened by 7000 B.C. Certainly it occurred by 3000 B.C.

The Cradle of Cheese

Cheese was probably first produced along a strip of land between the Tigris and Eurphrates Rivers, in what is now Iraq. Around 7000 B.C., people herded cattle and goats, and archaeological digs have produced some evidence of processes that could have made cheese. It may be simply wishful to think some of the first cheese was made in Switzerland, but interestingly, around 6000 B.C., along the banks of Lake Neuchatel, Switzerland, people were making pottery with drain holes, which could be the earliest evidence of vessels used to drain the whey from curds. Again, there is no indisputable evidence of cheese making then, but the animals and tools were there.

FACT

Rennet is a broad term used to refer to substances that make milk curds coagulate. Throughout history, many different forms of rennet have been used: enzymes from animals, plant extracts, and fungus extracts. Today, manufactured enzymes are also available. No matter what type of rennet is used, most cheese makers today buy rennet in liquid or powder form from dairy-supply companies.

By 5000 B.C. many people throughout what is now the Mediterranean and the Middle East had shifted from nomadic to domesticated life and maintained herds of sheep and goats. Two thousand years later, in 3000 B.C., the Sumerians, who were the earliest settlers of Mesopotamia, recorded their activities on clay tablets, using pictures, and within these tablets are descriptions of twenty different types of cheese. While King Shoulgi ruled the Sumerians, cheese making was included as part of the records on food production, and clay tablets have been found that record an eight-year cheese history. In the beginning, 8 liters of cheese were made in one year. Eight years later, 63.3 liters of cheese were produced. This first real evidence of cheese in civilization certainly seems sophisticated enough to suggest that cheese-making procedures were already advanced beyond any beginning stage. From there, cheese making branches out all along the northern tip of Africa, and into southern Europe.

The Egyptians definitely knew about cheese. An excavation of King Horaha's tomb, dated at 2300 B.C., revealed the remains of cheese. Cheese was sold at markets in Babylonia, and in 1600 B.C. King Hammurabi II established a Code of the Amorite to regulate taxes on dairy food, including cheese.

Cheese in Ancient Europe

The Basque claim that some of their cheese recipes are 4,000 years old, which means cheese making began in that area around 2000 B.C. And, cheese appears among some of the first writings about ancient civilization. According to Homer's *Illiad*, the serving woman Hecamede healed Prince Machaon's Trojan War wounds with a mixture of wine and grated goat's-milk cheese. And Pliny the Elder, a first century B.C. scholar, soldier, and author of numerous volumes chronicling wars between the Romans and Germans, credits a twenty-year cheese diet for the Iranian prophet Zoroaster's eloquence. The earliest days of Rome included cheese; in fact, separate kitchens were devoted to perfecting the art of making, smoking, and ripening it.

Cheese Spreads Across the Globe

As civilization progressed in the form of Greek colonies, the Golden Age of Athens, Alexander the Great, Hannibal, the rise and fall of Carthage, and the birth of Christ, cheese not only survived, it also became a dietary staple throughout the Mediterranean, North Africa, the Iberian Peninsula, the British Isles, and most of what is now called Europe. The only area it did not survive in was China, and for that some credit can probably be given to Confucius, who believed and taught that spoiled food was unhygienic. He likely viewed soured milk as spoiled milk. Since the Chinese did not have ready access to fresh milk or preserved milk products, some believe this was the beginning of a historically high number of Chinese with lactose intolerance.

European Cheese Takes Shape

From most accounts, the centuries between A.D. 200 and A.D. 600, the Dark Ages, were mostly ones of meager survival, and certainly not a time when it was safe to graze animals and produce food without fear of destruction. During this time, cheese followed a couple of different paths, one associated with war, the other with peace. It fed the Barbarians—the Goths, Visigoths, Vandals, Gepids, Alemanni, and Franks, who survived primarily on cheese, meat, and milk while they plundered the continent—and it fed the monks, who quietly retreated to their monasteries where they spent lots of time growing and producing food. In fact, Benedictine and Cistercian monks, who saved many people from starvation during these years, became such extraordinary cheese makers that many of their recipes are still made today.

The world of food owes a huge debt to Benedictine and Cistercian monks. Not only are they extraordinary cheese makers, they also are renowned winemakers. Throughout the centuries, they've planted hundreds of thousands of acres of grapes all over the world for winemaking. Many of these vineyards originated in Burgundy, Bordeaux, Champagne, and the Loire Valley.

By A.D. 1000, over five hundred Benedictine and Cistercian abbeys had been built in Europe, all of which became cheese-making facilities. Both orders followed dietary restrictions that required periods of fasting, or omitting certain foods, such as meat. These fasts often lasted for months at a time, and by turning to cheese as compensation for meat, the monks discovered that very pungent or meaty aromas and flavors could be achieved if, while aging, cheese was dipped in brine. This discovery led to the development of washed-rind cheeses, in which the formed cheese is washed in a brine solution that washes away mold and bacteria and introduces a specific bacteria that will improve the cheese's flavor. At times the monks were also restricted from using animal rennet, and this led to their discovery of fig, thistle, and various other plant extracts as curd coagulants. Hundreds of European cheeses originated this way; among the best known are Brie, Maroilles, Muenster, Roquefort, Pont-l'Eveque, and Port Salud, all named after European abbeys. Benedictine monks were also instrumental in creating traditional Basque-style sheep's-milk cheeses—low, round wheels with rustic brown rinds and dense interiors with hints of fruit and nut flavors.

FACT

It's common knowledge that many historical exchanges of payment were really forms of bartering. Perhaps wool was traded for onions, or grapes for wine. But cheese was actually recognized as a form of currency in the 1100s. In both Switzerland and Scandinavia, you could pay your bills with wheels of cheese.

The Medieval Period

Following the Dark Ages, as Europe was refashioned under Charlemagne, cheese became a royal delicacy, and for the next thousand years, from A.D. 800 to A.D. 1800, hundreds of new cheeses were developed, first in Europe, and then in European colonies.

The first indication of cheese regaining its presence outside of the monasteries is around A.D. 800, under Charlemagne. Apparently he was something of a gourmet, and when he visited abbeys where Brie and Roquefort were made, he declared both so sumptuous that he insisted on their regular delivery to his meals. It was during this same time, in A.D. 879, that Gorgonzola was first made in Italy's Po region. Then, in the 1100s, Gruyere was made in Switzerland, and the Jura region (the mountains between France and Switzerland) became home to Beaufort, Comte, and Emmental cheese. Cooperatives dairies, using milk from several herds to make large or multiple wheels of cheese formed in France, Switzerland, and Italy, and in Italy, the first large wheels of Parmigiano-Reggiano were born.

In France, tenant farmers who paid rent in wheels of quintax (115 pounds of cheese) started hiding cheese to avoid payments. In secret they drew milk from second milkings and made cheese for their own homes. This was the first reblechon, a cheese made from the *rebloche*, or second milking. By the 1300s, it took 1,500,000 sheep to produce enough cheese for Spain, and the need for access to northern pastures for almost twice that many sheep by the mid-1400s is one of several reasons Spain ousted the Moors.

The Renaissance

During the 1500s cheese was made throughout Europe, and had become so readily available in enough variety that by the end of the next century people began changing their minds about what type of milk they preferred their cheese to be from. For example, up until the 1600s sheep's-milk cheeses were most common in England, but then, during Elizabethan times, people developed a preference for cow's-milk cheese. This shift in demand led to a complete change in English dairy farming, and by the end of the 1600s, almost all English cheeses, the ones we know today, were made from cow's milk: caerphilly, Cheddar, Cheshire, Gloucester, Stilton, and Wensleydale, to name a few.

After the Renaissance

During the 1700s and early 1800s, European cheese had a brief decline in popularity. Some of the decline was the result of sugary desserts becoming popular, but it also occurred because people realized that some foods, including cheese, had lead added to them, and that ingesting lead was dangerous. In 1820 Frederick Accum, a German chemist, published "A Treatise on Adulterations of Food, and Culinary Poisons," wherein he revealed that red lead was responsible for giving a rich orange color to Gloucester cheese.

In France, however, none of this seemed to make a difference. Cheese was a star in Brillat-Savarin's 1825 *Physiology of Taste*, in which he wrote, "… a dessert course with no cheese is a beauty with only one eye." And a wheel of Brie de Meaux won the award for best cheese in the world during a dinner at the Vienna Congress toward the end of the Napoleonic Wars.

QUESTION?

Was Wensleydale ever made from sheep's milk?

Wensleydale cheese was invented by French Cistercian monks from the Roquefort region of France. They modeled it after cheeses like Cantal and Laguiole, both cow's-milk cheeses, so it's unlikely it was ever intended as a sheep's-milk cheese. When the monks settled in the town of Wensleydale and began making cheese, they named the cheese after their new town.

The New World Makes Cheese

Paul Kinstedt, in his book *American Farmstead Cheese*, provides a detailed account of the influence of European cheese makers settling in the Americas. They brought cows, goats, and sheep with them, and established small dairies up and down the East Coast, in Mexico, and in Canada.

Kindstedt describes the American industry of cheese making, beginning in the Massachusetts Colony of Puritans from East Anglia, England, who settled in North America between 1629 and 1640. East Anglians were known for their cheese making, especially of hard, Cheddar-style cheeses for export, and seeing a need to supply the New World, including the plantations in the South and the West Indies with cheese, they quickly set up a robust cheese-making industry. The industry spread to Rhode Island and Connecticut during the 1700s, and as East Coast cities such as Boston, Providence, Hartford, New York, and Philadelphia grew, their cheese found new markets. Then in the 1750s, the industry expanded to Vermont, New Hampshire, along the Hudson River Valley, and into Wisconsin. By the time of the American Revolution, some cheese makers were making 13,000 pounds of cheese annually, or on average, slightly more than 36 pounds per day. Almost all of the cheeses were hard, Cheddar-style cheeses that lasted long in shops and traveled well. Exports to Canada, the South and the West Indies continued to grow, and in 1829 almost a million pounds of cheese and butter were shipped from Vermont's Champlain Valley to New York City.

Cheese Goes Commercial

Until the mid-1800s, cheese making was essentially taking place the same as it had been for hundreds, sometimes thousands of years (depending on the type of cheese). All cheese was made from fresh, raw milk, and mechanization was virtually unheard of. Some new curd-cutting knives, and better cheese presses that reduced hand labor were introduced in the 1830s, but milking was still done by hand and for the most part cheese making was a handmade process. The industrial revolution of the mid-1800s, however, changed everything for cheese.

Refrigerated railroad cars used in the 1840s gave cheeses their first climate-controlled, long-distance rides. Then in 1850, a Frenchman, Louis Pasteur, discovered that bacteria in liquids, such as wine and milk, died when exposed to heat. By 1857, specific methods of pasteurization (named after Pasteur) were adopted for milk, and soon, almost all the milk intended for cheese was pasteurized first, which was a revolution in and of itself.

The first U.S. compulsory pasteurization law was passed in 1908, requiring all cow's-milk products to be made from pasteurized milk. Almost 100 years later, this law remains the standard, and has been amended to allow cheeses made from raw milk if they are aged more than sixty days before consumption, as it is believed pathogens can't survive in aged cheese.

Pasteurization opened new doors for large-scale cheese making, as the process killed bacteria otherwise difficult to control in large, mechanized settings, and minimized the risk of infections previously attributed to pooling and storing milk. This meant larger pools of milk could be used safely, and that emerging industrial mechanization could be employed without risking the growth of unwanted bacteria in raw milk. Meanwhile, all sorts of machines aimed at reducing hand labor were being rapidly invented, and cheese factories began steadily replacing small, handmade cheese operations with larger, more mechanized ones. Two more inventions especially contributed to the industrialization of cheese making. In 1870 a Danish man, Christian Hansen, developed a way to extract animal rennet without having to dry the stomach lining of the animal in question. He went on to found an internationally successful company, "Chr. Hansen," that today supplies cheese makers and food producers with enzymes, bacterial cultures, and related products. And, in 1899, an acidimeter test was developed for measuring the acidity of whey, which helped cheese makers figure out when to introduce rennet to whey to achieve optimal coagulation.

Different Directions

The industrial revolution meant very different things for cheese making in the United States and Europe. In the United States, cheese makers embraced science and mechanization by building hundreds of cheese factories. Science and industry had their effects on European cheeses as well, but instead of mechanizing most cheese production, Europeans found a way to produce some cheeses for large commodity markets while preserving hundreds of handmade cheeses as well.

In the United States

In 1851, the father and son team of Jesse and George Williams built the first U.S. cheese-making factory, and in a single season produced more than 100,000 pounds of cheese. By 1866, there were more than 500 cheese factories in New York State alone. The largest cheese market in the world was established in Little Falls, New York, where cheeses from more than 200 factories were sold.

Out west in California, Portuguese and Swiss dairy farmers working for David Jacks (a successful land owner and dairy farmer in Monterey County) developed Monterey jack in 1882, and in 1900, the Marin French Cheese Company, in Marin, California, began making Camembert.

Paul Kindstedt, in *American Farmstead Cheese*, gives an account of how the sudden growth of American cheese factories created a glut of cheese, and prices dropped. The response at some cheese factories was to cut costs by, for example, skimming cream to make butter and producing low-fat cheese. Not sure that local consumers would approve, the cheese was shipped to England with no mention of the difference in fat. When the English complained, lard was added to the cheese instead of cream. Lard, however, doesn't have the staying power of cream, and quickly went rancid, thereby toppling the American cheese export industry, which went from 148 million pounds in 1881 to almost nothing the following year.

FACT

The first American version of Limburger cheese, known for its pungent odor, was made in the 1890s by Emil Frey in New York, who created Liederkranz in Limburger's honor. Today the Wisconsin Cheese Group distributes American Limburger cheese that is made in Wisconsin.

The lesson learned was to give the consumer exactly what he or she expected, which was just the right setting for a man named James L. Kraft, who, in the early 1900s, discovered how to chemically prevent cheese from ripening. By 1916, his invention was patented; then in 1917, the U.S. Army bought Kraft's cheese in a can.

Meanwhile, population growth in the Northeast, especially New York, along with the stunning collapse of cheese exports to England, forced many dairy farmers to find new and cheaper land, and by 1900 Wisconsin had become the cheese dairy center of the United States. Farmstead cheeses were a thing of the past, and with the help of J. L. Kraft, Americans embraced the standardized, nonaging, imitation of Cheddar cheese that quickly became known as American cheese.

In Europe

The first cooperative dairy in Northern Europe was established in 1856 in Norway, and throughout Scandinavia, processes for making Gouda, Edam, Jarlsberg, and Havarti quickly became standardized enough to produce vast quantities of each cheese every year. A shift was seen from small, individual cheeses that ranged in color, texture, aroma and taste, to standardized products with uniform colors, textures, and moisture content.

Interestingly, not all countries agreed with this trend, and in 1955 Italy became the first European nation to adopt the *Denominazione di Origine Controllata* (D.O.C.) thereby protecting traditional cheese making under the Ministry of Agriculture and Forests. Through the Ministry, cheese-making consortiums were authorized to regulate several dozen cheeses according to breed of animal, milk type, feed, place of origin, and cheese-making techniques allowed. Asiago, Fiore Sardo, Gorgonzola, Parmigiano-Reggiano, Pecorino Toscano, and Taleggio are some examples of the most famous D.O.C.-protected Italian cheeses.

People have been tracking cheese eating for hundreds of years. Over a period of 150 years, from 1815 to 1965, French cheese eating grew phenomenally. In 1815 people were eating about 4½ pounds of cheese per year, and by 1964 they were eating 23⅓ pounds of cheese per year! Today the French consume about 52 pounds of cheese a year, whereas Americans eat only 31 pounds of cheese each year.

Switzerland followed suit, protecting Appenzeller, Emmental, Gruyere, and raclette, among others, and in 1979, France adopted the *Appellation D'Origine Controllee* (A.O.C.) for the same purpose. Beaufort, Brie de Meaux, Camembert de Normandie, Chaource, Comte, Epoisse, Fourme d'Ambert, Livarot, Muenster, reblechon, and Roquefort are among the most well known of the protected French cheeses.

Then, in 1981 Spain adopted cheese protection under the *Quesos con denominacion de origen* (D.O.) to protect, among others, Cabrales, Idiazabal, Manchego, Mahon, Roncal, and Zamorano.

Today's Cheese Revolution

Shortly before World War II, the Maytag family (of Maytag appliances) began working with an Iowa State University professor to produce blue cheese from a herd of Holstein cows they had had for about twenty years. E. H. Maytag, the son of the founder of the appliance firm, spearheaded the effort, and before long, the company began producing Maytag Blue, an artisanal, farm-stead blue cheese aged in caves. The cheese was quickly accepted and to this day continues to have a loyal following.

Cheese in the 1980s

Not much happened outside of industrial cheese making for the next forty years, but in 1981 Laura Chenel (the originator of the American Chevre), then in her twenties, decided she wanted to live on her own farm in Sonoma, California. She bought goats for milk, tried to make cheese, hired a cheese maker who made fresh chèvre (fresh goat's-milk cheese), and then apprenticed herself to Jean-Claude Le Jaouen, a French dairy scientist. In no time she returned from France to make excellent fresh chèvre, delicate bloomy-rind Chabis, and rounder Cabecous, and began selling her cheeses to restaurants like Chez Panisse, the landmark restaurant run by Alice Waters in Berkeley, California.

Meanwhile, Mary Kheen of Cypress Grove Farms in Humboldt County was going through similar diary experiences. She purchased and raised a herd of dairy goats, learned how to make cheese, and then began producing the now award-winning Humboldt Fog, a slightly aged goat's-milk cheese layered with vegetable ash and covered in a bloomy rind. Laura's and Mary's experiences set an example for others who wanted to make cheese, and soon artisan cheese makers began popping up beyond in California, in Vermont, along the Eastern Seaboard, in Wisconsin, and elsewhere. Many of them relied on help from Ricki Carroll, an English-trained cheese maker who sold cheese-making equipment and offered advice. In 1983, Professor Frank V. Kosikowski thought the interest in artisanal cheeses was widespread enough to found the American Cheese Society, so that, annually, cheese makers could meet to exchange information and encourage one another.

Cheese in the 1990s

Alice Waters and other chefs became enthusiastic about the wealth of emerging artisanal cheeses, and soon fine restaurants in large metropolitan areas began offering cheese courses. And as Americans traveled abroad and fell in love with European cheese, they became eager consumers of similar cheeses at home. Farmers' markets provided a venue for new cheese makers to test their wares, and the wine industry, which by now was flourishing in California, laid the foundation for those wanting to make and market handmade, artisanal food.

FACT

The "Real California Cheese" campaign is so successful that California cheese production increased 609 percent between 1983 and 2004, and is responsible for a 48 percent increase in U.S. cheese consumption between 1994 and 2003.

A whole series of campaigns fueled America's cheese revolution. For example, the California Milk Advisory Board started its "Real Cheese from Happy Cows" campaign, which has been recognized by management schools as one of the most successful marketing campaigns ever.

The New Millennium

In the early 2000s, Atkins Plan dieters allowed to eat cheese began looking for new and interesting cheeses to satisfy their palates. New information came to light on the influence on people of the hormones and antibiotics in animal feed, leading some to seek more natural forms of milk and milk products, including artisanal cheese. The number of people enjoying gourmet food began growing almost daily, and the epithet "foodie" became something to aspire to. Cookbooks, Web sites, cooking shows, and real-food advocates found larger and larger audiences. It became common for specialty food stores to install cheese counters with imported and domestic cheese, where people trained in cheese could offer tastes and educate people about new products. And as all this was going on, several hundred artisan cheese makers all across America began making cheese. In Vermont alone, over 100 different farmstead cheeses are now being made, and at the 2006 American Cheese Society meeting in Portland, over 900 American artisan and farmstead cheeses were judged and shown.

Chapter 2

It's All about the Milk

If you stop ten people on the street and ask them what cheese is made of, you're likely to get ten different answers, and probably, only a few will say milk. In this day and age, when so much of our food is manufactured, it's hard to believe a single ingredient could make something as interesting and complex as cheese, but it's true. Cheese is made from milk, and that's what this is all about.

The Animals

Try a quick experiment. Pour three different milks, whole, 2 percent, and skim, into three clear glasses, and hold them to the light. They vary considerably in their appearance, don't they? The whole milk is more opaque, is a creamier white, and looks thicker than the other two. The skim milk has some translucence to it, and seems to have a hint of blue. It swirls like water and looks thin. The two-percent milk is in between these two in color and density. Now imagine pouring three new glasses: one cow's milk, one sheep's milk, and one goat's milk. All three not only taste different, they also have different amounts of fat and protein, and behave differently when made into cheese.

FACT

The rather unlikely water buffalo has proven over time to be a consistently good producer of milk, certainly more adaptable to different climates and easier to deal with than the camel, yak, or reindeer, and today *mozzarella de bufala* mozzarella is made with water-buffalo milk.

How the Animals Differ

Cow's, goat's, and sheep's milk are each made up of water, fat, protein, lactose, and minerals. The first and most important differences between the three are in the percentages of these ingredients, particularly fat and protein. On average, sheep's milk is higher in fat and protein than cow's and goat's milk, goat's milk is lower in protein than cow's milk, and cow's and goat's milk have about the same percentage of fat.

Water, Fat, and Protein in Animal Milk

Animal	Water	Fat	Protein
Cow	87 percent	3–5 percent	3–4 percent
Goat	89 percent	3–4 percent	3–3.5 percent
Sheep	83 percent	6 percent	5–6 percent

Milk Protein

During cheese making, much of the water is drained from milk, and most of the fat and protein stay with the curds (this is explained in detail in Chapter 3). The curds are what make the cheese, and the higher the percentage of protein, the firmer the curds are and the faster they coagulate. This means that more cheese can be made from milk with high protein counts than from milk with low protein counts. So, sheep's milk, at 5–6 percent protein, makes up to twice the amount of cheese as cow's or goat's milk. The type of protein is also important. Milk protein is casein, and at the molecular level, there are alpha-casein and beta-casein molecules. These molecules coagulate differently. Alpha-casein molecules are firmer and more solid, while beta-casein molecules are more fragile. Not only does this contribute to how much cheese can be made from a set amount of milk, but it also contributes to the texture of the curd. Beta-casein molecules produce a fragile curd that is flakier in texture. It turns out that sheep's and cow's milk are both high in alpha-casein molecules, while goat's milk is higher in beta-casein molecules. This is partly why it takes more goat's milk to make cheese and why goat's-milk cheese has some flakiness to its texture.

Next time you're in a cheese store, have the cheese monger cut a Chevrot or a crottin open for you to taste. Note the lovely resemblance to a sparkling geode. Then take a look at the inside and see how it flakes. This is the way goat's-milk curds naturally solidify.

Milk Fat

The type of fat in milk is also important. Different fats create different aromas and flavors, and these three animal milks have different fat molecules, which contribute to different tastes. For example, fat molecules in sheep's and goat's milk are mostly short fatty acids, which create strong aromas and flavors. Cow's milk is mostly made up of long chains of fatty acids that are sweeter and milder in flavor. And cow's milk is the only one of the three that contains cryoglobulin, which is a sticky whey protein that effectively creates the clusters of fat that cream is made from. As milk cools from the temperature of the cow, these fat clusters rise to the surface and can be skimmed off for cream, or reincorporated into the milk. When reincorporated, the milk is whole, and contains all its original butterfat. Neither sheep's nor goat's milk can be skimmed in this way because without cryoglobulins, the fat rises to the surface very slowly, over several days, and the milk would likely spoil before the cream could be skimmed.

Milk Production

Finally, one of the most important differences between cows, goats, and sheep is how much milk they produce. On average, a cow will produce from eight to twenty quarts of milk per day. A goat will produce three to four and a half quarts per day, and a sheep will produce about one quart of milk per day. With cows producing two to four times as much milk as goats, and eight to twenty times as much milk as sheep, it's easy to see why cow's-milk cheese is the most plentiful, followed by goat's-milk cheese.

QUESTION?

What is homogenized milk?
Homogenized milk has been spun in a centrifuge or stirred very quickly to permanently combine the fat with the water and proteins of milk. When cheese is made with homogenized milk, it is usually very creamy, but interestingly it is also whiter in color. This is because red corpuscles are released from the milk when spun in a centrifuge. The red corpuscles stick to the sides of centrifuge instead of remaining in the milk. Without red corpuscles, the milk's natural color is less yellow, and whiter.

So far, you've read about cows, goats, and sheep in general terms, but different breeds also differ in percentages of fat, types of protein, and production of milk they usually offer. For example, on average, Holstein cows produce more milk per day than Jersey cows, but Jersey cow milk has a higher fat content than Holstein cow milk. Among the goat breeds, Nubians and La Mancha goats have higher butterfat, but they produce about the same amount of milk per day as other milking goat breeds.

Animal Husbandry

Animal husbandry, the agricultural practice of breeding and raising livestock, plays a very important role in milk production. Generally speaking, healthy, content animals produce nutritious, flavorful milk, and unhealthy or discontented animals produce milk that is inferior in nutrition and flavor.

Animals can be pasture fed, grain fed, and silage fed, and some diets are supplemented with vitamins, minerals, antibiotics, and hormones. Unless animals are moved, pastures are available only at certain times of the year, so often pasture-fed animals also eat grains, and many farmers grow grain and create their own mixture of grains to supplement lean pasture months. Silage is made up of edible farming byproducts and can range from crushed grape skins to a mixture of grains, seeds, grasses, and other byproducts. Animals without access to pastures are usually fed a combination of grain, silage, and supplements of vitamins and minerals. All of these diets directly influence the flavor and nutritional content of cheese.

FACT

In Italy, Parmigiano-Reggiano can be made from Holstein or Red Cow milk, but of approximately 270,000 cows, only about 1,000 are Red Cows. Red Cow's milk Parmigiano-Reggiano is stamped as such and prized for its more elastic texture, which is the result of the milk's unique protein composition.

Living conditions and terrain also affect the milk. Animals under stress, that is, under conditions that require them to work too hard for their food, will produce less milk with fewer vitamins and minerals. Where food is readily available and terrain is natural to the animal's habitat (pastureland for cows, hillsides for sheep, and either or both for goats), the milk is more plentiful and more nutritious. Sweet grasses and spring flowers can be tasted in the milk and then the cheese, as can the aromas of crowded barnyard conditions.

Finally, milk is also affected by the seasons. As animals move in and out of lactation and graze on spring, summer, fall, and winter diets, the amount of fat and protein changes dramatically. Fat levels drop in summer, rise in the fall, and peak in early winter. Proteins do the same, so cheese made from fall milk will be higher in butterfat and protein than cheese made from milk in the summer.

Farmstead and Artisan Cheese Makers

One of the key things that sets farmstead and artisan cheese makers apart from other cheese makers is the milk they use to make their cheese. By definition, farmstead cheese makers make cheese from the milk of their own herds. Artisan cheese makers make cheese from the milk of local herds, and both make cheese mostly by hand, using traditional cheese-making techniques that date back hundreds, sometimes thousands, of years. As a result, most farmstead and artisanal cheese is produced in small batches from relatively small herds.

Farmstead Operations

Farmstead cheese makers usually have self-contained operations. They often breed animals as well as operate dairies where they sell milk, and, of course, also run creameries where cheese and sometimes yogurt is made. None of these operations take precedence over another because the three must work together to make the best milk and the best cheese. Farmstead cheese makers are involved in every aspect of animal husbandry: diet, treatment of illnesses, breeding, and milking, and in every aspect of cheese making: milking; transportation of milk to the creamery; handling milk; cutting curds; and forming, salting, and aging cheese. Normally, farmstead cheese makers also handle the retail end by selling directly from their creamery or at farmers' markets, but some are large enough to work with wholesale distributors. Often milk production is postponed during breeding and pregnancy, and cheese making is halted during this time too.

Artisan Cheese-Making Techniques

Many farmstead cheese makers also consider themselves artisan cheese makers because they use traditional, handmade cheese-making techniques. The difference between the two lies in where the milk comes from. The advantage of artisan cheese makers is that they do not necessarily have to spend time and energy caring for their own herds of animals. Nevertheless, they work closely with local dairies to obtain milk to produce some of the most flavorful and complex cheeses in the world. By knowing the animals' diets and living conditions, artisan cheese makers are able to bring out the best aromas, flavors, and seasonal changes of the milk in their cheese.

Part of the art of making cheese is in understanding which starter cultures, spores, rennets, and curd-cutting techniques produce which results. Cheese makers generally keep this knowledge close to the chest, and depending on the milk production, time of year, feed, and other mysterious factors, they will adjust which techniques they use.

One way to enhance the creaminess of cheese is to minimize the agitation of milk before it is made into cheese. Recall how cream rises to the surface of cow's milk. If this cream is agitated too much, the fat will separate from the whey and protein; in effect, it is churned out of the liquid. By working closely with dairies and creameries, both farmstead and artisan cheese makers minimize the amount of agitation the milk receives during pumping and transportation, thereby keeping the cream fully able to reincorporate without requiring excessive mechanical intrusion.

Raw and Pasteurized Milk

Raw milk is milk that has not been pasteurized and contains all of its original bacteria, minerals, and enzymes. Raw milk is commonly used to make cheeses all over the world, and almost without fail produces cheeses that are more complex in aroma and flavor, and that have longer tastes. That is, the initial taste is different from the finish taste, which makes the experience of eating the cheese all that more delightful. People who are able to do side-by-side comparisons of the same type of cheese made from raw and pasteurized milk often find the pasteurized version lacking in substantive, bold tastes, which has led many cheese lovers to seek out raw-milk cheeses whenever they can. In addition, some believe that raw-milk bacteria and enzymes are helpful digestive aids and argue that lactose-intolerant people are able to digest raw-milk cheeses without their usual difficulty. Also, people who aim to maximize their vitamin and mineral intake also seek raw-milk cheeses.

What Is Pasteurization?

Pasteurized milk is milk that has been heated to a degree that kills most bacteria, and stops some enzyme processes. Pasteurized milk is required for young cheeses sold in the United States, and is commonly used in cheese making in many parts of the world. Those in favor of pasteurized-milk cheese value the safety of having harmful pathogens eliminated, and to offset the reduction in taste, cheese makers often go to extra lengths to allow flavors and aromas to develop in pasteurized-milk cheeses through different processes, rinds, and various techniques of adding herbs, spices, or flavorful coatings.

There are several ways to pasteurize milk for cheese. One is to heat it for thirty minutes at 145°F, and another is to heat it for fifteen seconds at 161°F. The low-heat (145°) method is often called vat pasteurization because the milk is slowly heated in vats. In the high-heat method, milk is passed through a mechanism resembling a radiator that heats the milk quickly. The higher-temperature method can give cheese a cooked flavor.

Raw Milk Versus Pasteurized Milk

The controversy over raw and pasteurized milk has people of strong opinions in both camps. As mentioned earlier, up until the early 1900s, all cheese was made from raw milk. Pasteurization was not available until the late 1800s, when French microbiologist Louis Pasteur discovered that milk bacteria were killed when the milk's temperature was raised to a certain point, then quickly cooled to prevent spoilage. In 1908, the United States passed the first compulsory law requiring milk from cows to be pasteurized. Since then, milk pasteurization is credited with dramatically lowering the incidence of typhoid fever, scarlet fever, diphtheria, and tuberculosis in the United States.

In France and many other European countries, young and aged raw-milk cheeses have been made for centuries and continue to be made and legally sold throughout Europe. Raw-milk cheeses have not been associated with high incidence of disease in Europe, most likely because raw-milk cheese makers, whether they are making young or aged cheese, must pay extra attention to the type of bacteria that develop in milk at different temperatures, and need to routinely test for bacterial counts. Sanitation conditions must be held to the highest standards to avoid the introduction of bacteria that can develop in unheated milk. Also, raw milk needs to be made into cheese immediately to avoid fluctuations in temperature or possible contamination.

The bottom line is that in the United States today, milk intended for young cheeses (those that will age less than sixty days before being sold), must be pasteurized, and raw milk may only be used for cheeses that age longer than sixty days. This applies to all cheeses sold in the United States, whether made here or imported. Also, many U.S. doctors advise people with special dietary needs and pregnant women to avoid raw milk cheeses as a precautionary measure. As you begin to explore the world of cheese, you'll want to take some time to taste different raw- and pasteurized-milk cheeses and decide for yourself.

Regional Pooling

Long before the days of large dairy herds, people were making very large wheels of cheese, weighing 40, 50, 80, 100, and up to 220 pounds. Larger wheels not only simplified the cheese-making process (it's easier to make one large wheel than several small wheels), but also served as a way to efficiently preserve large quantities of milk in the form of cheese that could be stored for several years. The milk for these large cheeses has to be available within a short period of time, usually twenty-four hours before cheese making begins. Clearly, a lot of animals are needed to produce milk for these wheels, so early dairy farmers began pooling the milk from different herds to make these cheeses.

But other, smaller cheeses have also benefited from regionally pooled milk. Morbier, a French cheese from the lower Jura region, is made in two parts. One part is morning milk, from which raw-milk curds are formed into hoops and covered with a layer of vegetable ash. The second part is evening milk, from which raw-milk curds are put on top of the vegetable ash, the entire wheel is salted and drained, and then it is aged in caves where it develops a natural, briny rind, lending it a hint of delightful piquancy. With multiple herds to draw from, many wheels of Morbier can be made at the same time.

FACT

Pooled-milk cheeses are quite famous. They are made in huge sizes, so that all of us may enjoy them. Gruyere normally weighs about 85 pounds, Emmental weighs close to 220 pounds, and Parmigiano-Reggiano weighs between 70 and 80 pounds.

Milk for Lots of Cheese

On average, Americans eat slightly more than 31 pounds of cheese per year, far more than small cheese makers can provide. Most of the nation's domestic cheeses are made in California and Wisconsin, in large cheese-making facilities supplied by large dairies.

The milk for these cheeses comes from large-scale dairy farms and is almost exclusively cow's milk. These dairies milk cows twice a day in large sheds, sometimes on carousels, and the milking is done mechanically. Some cows graze on pastureland, but weather conditions and practical considerations mean that all return to the sheds twice a day for milking. Many dairy farms house cows in long sheds, and some even provide water beds for the cows to sleep on. They are fed mixtures of hay and grain supplemented by fiber, vitamins, and minerals.

Cows don't have to be told to drink water. They instinctively know what's good for them. On average, a cow drinks thirty to forty gallons of water every day. Perhaps it has something to do with eating fifty to sixty pounds of feed every day.

After cows are milked at the dairy, the milk is pumped into refrigerated holding tanks and kept cool while being gently agitated so the fat does not separate. Then the milk is pumped into insulated milk tanker-trucks and driven to the cheese makers. The milk is pasteurized, and then the process of large-scale cheesemaking begins.

Chapter 3

The Art of Cheese Making

How do you transform a glass of milk into a wheel of cheese? Do you wave a magic wand? Do you let it sit on the windowsill for a month? Or is it something that would happen anyway, without anyone interfering? The answer is all about science and art, and in cheese making, the two make a delicious pair. In the world of food, cheese stands out as one of the most aesthetically elegant products of skillful science and creative imagination.

Cheese Making as an Art and a Science

Simply put, cheese making is the science of converting a glass of milk into a block of cheese. Taken a step further, cheese making is the final step in a process that begins with the transfer of sunlight energy into plants; the transformation of that sunlight energy and plant nutrition into milk; and the transformation of sunlight energy, plant nutrition, and animal nutrition into cheese: a natural energy bar high in protein, fat, vitamins, and minerals.

The holes in Swiss cheese are called eyes. Many other cheeses have eyes. Next time you're at a cheese counter, take a look at the sprinkling of small holes in Havarti, or the eyes of a Gouda that's been aged for more than a year. These cheeses begin with mesophilic starter cultures (cultures that thrive at room temperature) that contain CO_2.

Fortunately, nature and the animals take care of the first two parts of the cheese-making process. All a cheese maker has to do is transform liquid milk into a solid. How do they do this? Basically, by repeatedly conducting a scientific experiment under carefully controlled conditions, with different variables such as milk type, time of year, types of starter cultures, types of rennet, and how the curd is cut, worked, formed, and aged. Wonderfully, it's these same variables that make room for art, and successful cheese makers have learned how to use them with the restraint and creativity needed to produce some of the world's most exquisite tastes.

Starter Cultures, Coloring Agents, and Spores

Left alone, raw milk will spoil and become cheese-like, but the results are uneven and unpredictable. Because pasteurization kills most bacteria, pasteurized milk will not spoil in a way that produces cheese. As a result, starter cultures are used to introduce helpful bacteria that spoil milk in a controlled way before it is separated into curds and whey.

Starter Cultures

One of the first steps in converting milk to cheese is taking advantage of lactose. As milk ages, the lactose it contains turns into lactic acid, which in turn allows desirable and undesirable bacteria to develop. By using starter cultures to promote the development of lactic acid in fresh milk, cheese makers are able to control against harmful bacteria and promote the growth of beneficial microorganisms. Two families of starter cultures are used to make cheese, mesophilic cultures and thermophilic cultures, both available in freeze-dried form from dairy-supply companies. Mesophilic cultures thrive at room temperature while thermophilic cultures require higher temperatures.

FACT

Not all starter cultures come freeze dried. Long before freeze-drying was available, cheese makers carefully preserved milk from one day to be used as starter cultures for the next day. This method is still used and is called using a mother culture.

Mespophilic cultures work best in moderate temperatures (50°–108°F), and are used when making fresh, bloomy-rind, soft, semisoft, and washed-rind cheeses. Thermophilic cultures survive at higher temperatures (68°–125°F), and are used when making semihard, hard, and cooked-curd cheeses, such as mozzarella, Gouda, and Swiss. Some cheeses are made with a combination of mesophilic and thermophilic cultures. For example, Swiss cheese varieties use both cultures. They use thermophilic cultures to produce the right texture, but they also take advantage of a specific mesophilic culture that contains carbon dioxide. During aging, the carbon dioxide gas creates eyes, or holes, in the cheese.

Coloring Agents

Natural cheese color ranges from creamy white to buff and reflects the type of milk used. Goat's milk produces the whitest cheese, cow's-milk cheese is naturally cream to butter colored, and sheep's-milk cheese tends to have yellow, buttery tones. Even with this range, cheese makers have found it fun and interesting to experiment with different colors of curd.

One of the most successful and widely used food dyes is an extract of the seeds of the annatto tree, *Bixa orellana*. Grown in the tropics, the seed is commonly used for coloring dishes such as Spanish rice. You'll find annatto listed as an ingredient in cheeses that have been made for hundreds of years, like Mimolette, and in newer cheese products like Velveeta.

The beautiful French cheese Mimolette is one of the most famous cheeses colored by annatto. The cheese is aged in balls about eight inches wide and high, and coated with salt. After eighteen months of turning and aging, the salt and the curd develop into a natural buff-colored rind, forming a hard ball that looks almost impenetrable. However, when sliced open, a bright orange paste is revealed, making the entire cheese appear to be a brilliantly colored cantaloupe.

Natural colorings are also added to the rind of cheeses. For example, Drunken Goat, a semisoft cheese from Spain, is rubbed with red wine while aging. The result is a gorgeous purple rind set against a white goat's-milk cheese. It's a wonderful treat on a hot summer day. In the United States, the FDA allows the milk of some cheeses to be bleached and the curd to be colored by specifically approved natural and artificial food dyes.

Spores

When starter cultures are introduced, mold spores can also be added to produce rinds and molds. This technique is often referred to as seeding the starter culture. The two most common types of mold spores added to cheese are *Penicillium candidum* and *Penicillium roqueforti*.

Bloomy-rind cheeses have white, green, floral, and/or grey rinds that look a bit like velvet. Some cheeses like Bries and Camemberts have pure white rinds, while others, like Selles-sur-Cher and Valencay have bloomy rinds grown over layers of vegetable ash. Either way, the bloomy rind is the result of a mold spore called *Penicillium candidum*. In France, *Penicillium candidum* occurs naturally in aging caves, and these spores are harvested and reproduced for cheese makers around the world. The spores arrive in freeze-dried form and are added directly to the milk along with starter cultures, coloring agents, or both. Nothing happens to the curd right away, but while the cheese is aging it literally blooms with a soft, velvety white mold.

ALERT!

Not all blue cheese is called Roquefort. The name "Roquefort" is controlled by the *Appellation D'Origine Controllee of France*.

In France, some bloomy-rind cheeses are not inoculated with *Penicillium candidum* during the starter-culture phase. Instead, the cheeses are aged in rooms or caves that have been used for this purpose for decades, some for hundreds of years. Only one kind of cheese is aged in each cave or room, as the mold is part of the room and forms on the cheese without being introduced in any other way. To some, the results are indistinguishable from cheeses inoculated during the starter-culture phase.

The mold you see in blue cheese is grown by *Penicillium roqueforti* spores, which come in many varieties. Almost all blue cheeses are made with a strain of this spore. Again, these spores occur naturally in the caves of Roquefort, France, and are harvested, reproduced, and distributed worldwide in freeze-dried form. *Penicillium roqueforti* works differently than *Penicillium candidum*. Instead of growing a bloomy white rind on the outside of the cheese, it grows a bluish green mold inside the cheese.

Curds, Whey, and Rennet

Once milk has the necessary level of lactic acids, and spores have been added, it is ready to separate into curds and whey through the use of rennet.

Curds and Whey

The basic properties of milk are water, protein, fat, sugar, vitamins, and minerals. Curds and whey are the result of separating the water and sugar, or whey, from the protein and fat, or curd. The separation happens by introducing an enzyme, commonly known as rennet, which acts on the milk protein, or casein molecules. These molecules are naturally attracted to water, but when rennet is introduced they lose their hold on water and instead accumulate around fat. The result is a gelatinous, coagulated curd, surrounded my milky water or whey, all of which will eventually become cheese.

Whey is rich in water, sugar, vitamins, and minerals. Some cheese makers use it to make ricotta, others use it to bathe the curd while it's being worked, and still others use it as feed for animals. Pigs are especially fond of whey, and pig farmers often buy whey from cheese makers.

Rennet

As mentioned previously, rennet is a term used by cheese makers to describe the enzyme responsible for separating curds and whey and causing the curd to coagulate. In fact, cheese makers have several different rennets to choose from. Rennet can be the same as the the enzyme chymosin, which occurs naturally in the stomachs of animal ruminants, or can be a derivative of vegetable enzymes, or can be an enzyme bioengineered from chymosin. Lemon juice and vinegar can also be used as rennet.

Chymosin or Animal Rennet

As mentioned in Chapter 1, it's most likely cheese was discovered in ancient times when people stored fresh milk in pouches created from animal stomachs. This milk would have encountered the enzyme chymosin and curdled within a matter of minutes or hours, depending on the strength of the rennet and temperature of the day. The same people must have also realized that milk stored in other containers soured before it curdled, and must have come to the conclusion that something within the stomach lining was responsible for curdling milk in a way that created cheese.

These ancient people must have also figured out that not just any stomach lining would do to make cheese, and that in fact, the fourth stomach of an unweaned calf, kid, or lamb produced the best results. The enzyme chymosin was not identified until modern times, but regardless, once other containers were available to make cheese, cheese makers knew they still had to dry and scrape stomach linings to produce a powder that curdled milk. Today, animal rennet can also be obtained by extraction from animals.

Bioengineered Rennet

In 1989, the U.S. FDA granted "generally recognized as safe" (GRAS) status to genetically engineered rennet, which is created by inserting a calf's prochymosin gene into a microorganism. The results are difficult to distinguish from pure animal rennet, and bioengineered rennet can be used to successfully make both soft and hard cheeses.

Vegetable Rennets

Vegetable rennets are derived from extractions of plants such as stinging nettle and thistle, and from fungus fermentation. These rennets are successful in producing soft and semisoft cheeses, and are commonly used to produce vegetarian cheeses.

Lemon Juice and Vinegar

Lemon juice and vinegar can be used to create curds for cheeses that do not need to age such as *queso fresco*, *fromage blanc*, and cottage cheese (also referred to as "rennetless cheeses"). This technique has also been around for thousands of years.

QUESTION?

Why are cows called ruminants?
Ruminants are animals that chew their food, and then after it's been swallowed, it is essentially chewed again by the action and enzymes of several stomachs. To accomplish this feat they have three to four stomach chambers. While their food passes through each chamber, it is digested and chewed. Cows, goats, and sheep are all ruminants, as are deer, camels, water buffalo, and a host of other plant-eating animals.

Work the Curd

Science and art come together in earnest when the separated curd is ready to cut, be drained of whey, and formed into the initial cheese shapes. Cheese makers refer to this stage as "working the curd."

Cutting the Curd

Cheese makers use long-handled knives and rectangular, stainless steel screens with evenly spaced vertical or horizontal wires to cut the curd. Generally speaking, the more the curd is cut, the more whey drains off, and the drier the cheese will become. In other words, the more surface area created on the curds, the more whey will drain. Also, uniformly sized and shaped curds will respond evenly to salts, herbs, seasonings, and aging techniques. Nonuniform curds may be moist in one part and dry in another, and will be subject to variations in aging and fermentation. In other words, curd cutting is one of the primary cheese-making processes that will determine the cheese's final moisture and texture.

FACT

Curd-cutting screens are also called harps. The harps are pulled through large vats of curds, much like the blade of a mixing machine, to provide clean, even cuts. Some harps are small, like the blade of a paddle, and others are several yards square. It all depends on the size of the milk vat.

Soft cheeses such as Brie, Camembert, and Chevrot are very moist, cheeses, and are aged less then sixty days. If these curds are cut at all, they are cut just a few times by a long-handled blade drawn vertically, then horizontally, through the curd. After this, the curd is ladled into molds.

Semisoft to semihard cheese curds are cut and drained, then sometimes cut again, all to achieve the desired texture and moisture.

Cheddar cheese is made by Cheddaring. *Cheddaring* is actually a verb, from which the name Cheddar cheese is derived. Cheddaring involves cutting the curd, stacking it, cutting it again, restacking, and cutting again until the desired level of moisture and texture is achieved.

Bathing and Cooking the Curd

After the curd is cut, some curds are bathed in water or whey, or cooked. Curds bathed in water produce very clean, light flavors. The curds for some Cheddars, certain styles of Monterey jack, and some mountain cheeses, are rinsed in some of the drained whey, which imparts a creamy, sweet flavor to the cheese.

Pasta filata cheeses (such as mozzarella) are named after the process of dipping the curd into hot baths of water, whey, or both, much like pasta is cooked. The process makes the curd elastic, after which it is stretched and pulled, like taffy. As one example of this process, mentioned previously, mozzarella di bufala is made in Italy with water-buffalo milk. The curd must be able to stretch to one meter (or thirty-nine inches) before being taken from hot baths. Then it is stretched again, spun into balls, and immersed in brine.

Very finely grained cheeses, such as Gouda, Gruyere, and Emmental, are the result of the curds being heated to shrink the curd size and consolidate the texture.

The Necessary Salt

The next step involves salting the curd. Aside from adding flavor, salt is a critical component to the cheese-making process.

Salt Reduces Moisture

Cheese is ready to eat when it has the right flavor, moisture, and texture profile. Achieving the right balance of moisture and solids is one of the final and most critical stages. Left alone, a block of curd will lose only about 60 percent of its moisture. During aging, too much moisture can lead to unwanted bacteria or fermentation. However, if salt is added to the curd, additional moisture is drawn out, and a naturally balanced and safe aging cycle can proceed.

Salt Creates Surface Rinds

Surface-ripened cheeses such as Parmigiano-Reggiano develop a rind of dehydrated cheese, which in turn protects the rest of the cheese from being penetrated by unwanted bacteria or other organisms. Surface rinds are created by salting the curd, and either packing and rubbing wheels of curd in dry salt while they age, or immersing wheels in brine for a few days or weeks.

Salt Keeps the Cheese Clean

If you've ever had salt water splashed on an open cut, you know how much it stings. The sting is created by the cleansing power of salt to rid a cut of germs. Likewise, salt in cheese acts as a major deterrent to the development of unwanted bacteria, which in turn allows cheeses to enjoy long, graceful periods of aging.

Salt Enhances the Flavor

Finally, salt has a significant effect on the flavor of cheese, not only because it enhances the flavor of the curd, but also because it melds with the curd to create microbe and enzyme activity that, in turn, create the very special flavors unique to cheese.

How Salt Is Applied

There are three basic methods of adding salt to curds. Curds can be dry salted before being pressed into forms, or dry salted after being pressed into forms. Curds can also be immersed in brine, and it's not uncommon for cheese makers to use a combination of these techniques to produce their cheese. Coarse salt is most commonly used because it absorbs gradually. If applied before pressing the curds into forms, it is sprinkled on evenly cut pieces of curd, stirred into the curd, and reapplied until the desired amount is incorporated. If applied after pressing, salt is sprinkled on the outside surface of newly formed cheeses and serves to draw the moisture to the cheese's surface, where it forms a brine, some of which evaporates, and some of which is reincorporated into the cheese. When salt is applied through brine, the curd is immersed in a bath of brine for anywhere between a few hours and up to several days. During this time, the brine bath is carefully monitored and modified to allow for the appropriate exchange of things being leached from the curd (primarily lactic acid and calcium), and things being added to the curd (salt and desired microbes).

Forms and Applications

Cheese forms are a defining factor in cheese making. Different shapes and forms affect the amount of moisture a cheese will retain, and the amount of time a cheese has to reach its peak. While in their forms, curds can also be pressed to release the whey.

Different Cheeses Have Different Forms

A French Chevrot, for example, is about 2 inches high and 2½ inches wide, and weighs a few ounces. It gets its slightly conical shape from a per-forated form. The curds are ladled into the forms, and then kept in a drain-ing room with carefully controlled temperature and humidity. Once set, the Chevrot is removed from the form, and then air-dried in an aging room.

A wheel of Montgomery Cheddar, on the other hand, weighs about 60 pounds, stands about 16 inches high, and is about 18 inches wide. This cheese is made to age at least 14 months. After Cheddaring, the curd is ladled into cheesecloth-lined buckets, the size and shape of the final block of cheese. There the curd is pressed and drained for 2 days (it is removed, rewrapped, and reformed after 24 hours) before it is fully formed. Then the cheesecloth is removed again, and the block of cheese is wrapped with linen and sealed with lard, or a flour-and-water paste, before being aged.

Lots of cheeses are flavored with herbs and spices. These can be added at different times, but generally they are added when the curds are just beginning to collect into their finished form. Just before the curds are placed in molds, herbs and spices are sprinkled in.

In between these two extremes are all sorts of variations, but every cheese goes through a stage during which additional whey drains off and the final cheese shape begins to be formed, followed by an application of material that will maintain the cheese's shape while it ages. The Chevrot mentioned earlier is part of the natural rind family, and as it ages it will develop a natural, buff-colored rind that has a brainy-textured surface. Other applications range from paraffin wax, to rings of bark, to wrappings of leaves, to coatings of herbs and spices, to vegetable ash, to thin paper. The exception is blue cheese, which does not receive or develop a rind. Instead, the curds are hooped into rounds, then needled to produce air pockets for the blue mold to develop inside and out.

How Cheese Is Aged

As cheeses age, they bloom with the essence of everything that's come before: the sunshine collected by plants, the plants themselves, the water and air of the environment, the animals producing the milk, milk treatments, starter cultures, molds, and the techniques of the cheese maker. But far from simply storing a finished product in a room until it's magically declared done, cheese aging is an art form in and of itself. If the carefully cut, drained, pressed, and molded curd were allowed to sit in one place, it would form large wet and dry spots, and the flavors would pool toward the bottom.

Role of the Affineur

In France, cheese agers hold the title *affineur*, which means they are the ones who carefully select the appropriate conditions for each type of cheese to age properly. They select a room or cave with enough air circulation, the right temperature, humidity, and mold spores (if necessary). Once the cheeses are in the aging room or cave, the *affineur* tends to them regularly to assure an even distribution of moisture and rind development. An *affineur* regularly checks that all conditions will promote the development of the desired cheese. To walk into a cheese-aging room is to be surrounded by row after row of highly stacked wheels of cheese, each tagged with their date of entry into the aging room, and all at different stages of ripening.

Here, perhaps more than anywhere else, is where different rules governing food production come into play. In France, a cheese-aging cave or room is devoted to one cheese, and only that type of cheese will be aged in that cave or room. Many of these rooms are filled with spider webs and are very cave-like, but, as mentioned earlier, these rooms hold the mold spores that contribute to the cheese. Sometimes, instead of seeding their milk during the starter-culture phase, the French allow the cheese to bloom with mold while being aged. In the United States, however, cheese makers are required to age their cheese in sterile conditions, and aging rooms must be washed quite regularly. While this allows different cheeses to age side-by-side, it also requires the step of seeding during the starter-culture phase.

FACT

Most people believe the crunchiness they experience in Parmigiano-Reggiano or an aged Gouda is salt. In fact, the crunch comes from a breakdown of amino acids that happens while the cheeses are aged. These crystals do taste salty, but this is because of the salt added to the curd prior to forming and aging.

Neal's Yard

One of the most famous aging rooms is Neal's Yard, a cheese warehouse in London, England, that distributes artisanal and farmstead cheeses from England and Ireland. The facility is specially designed to continue the aging process of cheese once it arrives, and the warehouse works closely with its cheese makers to be sure each cheese is sold at its peak.

Goudas

Some cheeses, like Goudas, are aged for several years. During this time, carbon dioxide gas from the starter cultures forms eyes, or holes in the cheese. Some amino acids also break down and form small crystals. If you compare a young Gouda, say six months old, to a four-year-old Gouda, you'll notice that the young Gouda is fairly smooth and uniform in texture and doesn't have the crunch of the amino-acid crystals. The four-year-old Gouda will be riddled with small holes formed by gases and subsequently filled by these amino-acid crystals.

Blue Cheeses

Recall that blue cheeses don't develop a rind. This makes the task of aging blue cheese a little different. As mentioned, hoops are used to collect and solidify the curd during the forming stage. After much of the whey has been drained off, the forms are removed, and holes are punched into the wheels with long metals needles or spikes. This allows air to work with the *Penicillium roqueforti* spores to create the beautiful blue-green molds on the inside and outside of the cheese. To keep the wheels from degrading or turning to mush, they are turned quite regularly. Many blue cheeses are aged for two months or more before being ready to eat.

When the Grubb family began making their award-winning Irish Cashel farmstead blue cheese, they used Mrs. Grubb's knitting needles to perforate the wheels of cheese. Fortunately, Mr. Grubb is a retired engineer, who's since invented a machine that automatically perforates several wheels at a time with long needles.

Hand-Rubbed Cheese

For the artisan cheese maker, aging can also be a time to flip and rub their semisoft to hard cheeses with olive oil, or homemade wine, or a mixture of herbs, spices, and/or oils. While their cheeses age, you'll see them in the aging room, rubbing the surfaces with the utmost care.

Chapter 4

How Cheese Is Classified

To the delight of cheese lovers worldwide, there are hundreds of cheeses to get to know. However, unless you can describe the type of cheese you're looking for, it can be more difficult to find new varieties to enjoy. Luckily, this problem is solved by cheese classifications. This chapter will acquaint you with the language and meaning of cheese classifications—by texture and moisture content, by rind, by cheese-making method, by milk type, by butterfat percentages, and by region. As you expand your cheese repertoire, you'll put these terms to good use.

Texture and Moisture Classifications

The inside of the cheese is often referred to as the paste, and in general terms this means all the cheese that is not part of the rind. The paste can show different layers of aging (often cheese ages from the outside in) and artisanal cheeses often have cores of paste that are firmer than the surrounding paste. Texture and moisture classifications are used to describe the different types of paste found in cheese.

Soft

Buttery, custard-like, silky, oozing, and spoonable: In a word, soft cheeses are voluptuous. Their ooziness is the result of minimally cut curds that retain 40–70 percent of their moisture, the fact that these curds are ladled into molds, and short aging cycles. They are made in a variety of sizes, from small, individual, or one-meal servings, to wheels eighteen inches across. Soft cheeses have the feel of a firm pillow when young. They age from the outside in, and mature soft cheeses will feel a bit squishy at their peak. Their flavor is heightened and extended by aging, making young cheeses lighter and milder, and mature cheeses full-bodied and more flavorful.

FACT

Most soft cheeses are aged less than sixty days. As mentioned previously, in the United States, raw-milk cheeses must be aged more than sixty days, so almost all soft cheeses sold in the United States are made with pasteurized milk.

Two of the most famous soft cheeses are Brie de Meaux and Camembert de Normandie, both French A.O.C.-protected cheeses. However, there's a wonderful array of soft cheeses from all over the world, and many cheese makers specialize in making these elegant treats.

Semisoft

Mild, friendly, milky, creamy to strong, aggressive, ripe, and rich, semi-soft cheeses run the full gamut of flavor profiles. Two techniques, washed curd and washed rind, distinguish them from soft cheeses.

Washed-curd cheeses have their curds bathed in whey or water before being pressed into molds. They are usually made in relatively large wheels, have a buttery mouthfeel, and sometimes are dotted with irregular, small holes, referred to as an open texture paste. Some of the most famous are Monterey jack, Colby, and Havarti.

An Epoisse is a washed-rind soft cheese from Bourgogne, France. Wheels of Epoisse have a deep, orange rind, and are usually exported in small, round, wooden boxes that serve both as packaging and containment. Not only are they washed in brine, but also they are given a good dousing of cognac. When opened, they exude a strong, pungent aroma that is carried over to the cheese's rich and enticing flavor.

Washed-rind cheeses are said to originate with monks who developed them to eat during long, meatless fasts. By washing the curds in brine, the monks learned to coax out cheese's earthy, more rustic, and pungent qualities. These earthy, rustic qualities are reflected in their cheeses' rind, which develops into a deep orange to rust color. The results are some of the cheese world's most famous stars, prized for their complexity and fullness of experience, such as Muenster, Pont-l'Eveque, and Port Salud.

Semihard

Eatable, sliceable, and wonderful to cook with, semihard cheeses are neither soft nor hard, and, as you might expect, they are a little bit harder than semisoft cheeses. The distinction between semisoft and semihard cheeses is important because the difference in moisture (semihard cheeses have less moisture) means semihard cheeses easily break into chunks, can be cut into cubes, and can be sliced and grated. Many different cheese-making techniques produce semihard cheeses, but they have in common a significant loss of moisture while their curds are cut and pressed, a generous addition of salt to absorb more moisture, and attention on the cheese maker's part to creating a relatively smooth and even-textured cheese. Their flavors range from mellow and subtle to spicy and sharp. Cheddar, Swiss, Gruyere, pecorino, Asiago, fontina, and raclette are among the most familiar names from this category.

Hard

The distinction between semihard and hard cheese can be a fine line, but hard cheeses are generally those that are significantly drier, more aged, sometimes crumbly, and often thought of as cooking cheese. Many people are surprised, however, when they take a moment to taste some of the truly magnificent hard cheeses such as Parmigiano-Reggiano, aged Comte, aged Asiago, or aged Gouda. With the exception of Parmigiano-Reggiano, all of these cheeses have younger and slightly different cousins that fall into the semisoft or semihard category. But when they've reached their full potential through aging, they give off fruity, almost candy-like aromas. They are complex in taste, starting out on the tongue with bright flavors, and ending with stronger, smokier, and denser flavors. In addition to being essential ingredients in the kitchen, they make ideal table cheeses as well.

Au Naturel to Waxed Rinds

Cheese rinds are another important clue as to how a cheese is made, and rind categories are common terms in cheese circles.

Natural Rind

Natural-rind cheeses are those that grow rinds on their own, without any addition to the cheese. On a Chevrot (a young goat cheese), for example, a buff-colored rind grows and takes on a wrinkled appearance over a matter of weeks. This rind is the "oldest" part of the cheese, as aging occurs from the outside in. Underneath the rind is a thin, creamy layer of slightly less aged cheese, followed by a flaky, drier core.

QUESTION?

Are there any older cheeses that develop a natural rind?
Yes, there are lots. Some of the best known are Cantal, Stilton, Mimolette, and Parmigiano-Reggiano. Because of their age the rinds on these cheeses need special care as they grow. *Affineurs*, or cheese agers, tend to them for months and sometimes years.

Bloomy Rind

Bloomy-rind cheeses are those that bloom with white, green, floral, or grey mold while they age and are almost exclusively seen on young cheeses. White molds are the type seen on Brie-style cheeses. Green blooms often go along with white molds when a coating of vegetable ash is applied to the outside of a cheese. The ash and accompanying mold adds complexity and a hint of smokiness. Floral blooms literally bloom with bright yellows, light greens, white, and grays. Tomme de Savoie is one of the most well known floral bloomy-rind cheeses.

According to Steven Jenkins, author of *Cheese Primer, tomme* refers to a "hunk, round, or piece." But in the cheese-making world, people have been using this term to refer to cheeses made from the milk of several herds. The best way to think of this kind of cheese is to combine the two definitions: "a round of cheese made from the milk of several herds."

Herbaceous Rind

Herbaceous-rind cheeses are layered or rubbed with leaves, herbs, or grasses before or during aging. Leaves usually add a woody flavor or, in the case of Hoja Santa goat cheese from Texas, the leaves covering the cheese provide a minty sassafras flavor. Herbs may be added to bloomy-rind cheeses or rubbed into the rind of other cheeses as they age.

Washed Rind

Washed-rind cheeses are those that have been immersed in salt brine, then allowed to form pale orange to deep russet–colored rinds. Without fail, this process adds pungency and depth to the cheese.

Wrapped Rind

Wrapped cheeses are banded, for instance with bark, or wrapped with linen to help hold their shape for storage and serving. Cheeses banded or wrapped in bark always take on the subtle flavors of the bark. L'Edel de Cleron is a soft, bloomy-rind cheese ringed in bark. The bark gives it a woody, mushroomy taste. Montgomery's Cheddar and Keen's Cheddar, both made in England, are two of the most well-known bandage-wrapped cheeses. The bandages protect the cheese while it ages and give the rind an aroma of aged linen.

Wax-Coated Rind

Wax-coated cheeses are generally coated in clear or colored paraffin. Wax does not directly affect the flavor of cheese and is used simply as protection. Famous wax-coated cheeses are Goudas, Asiagos, and many pecorinos.

Plastic-Wrapped Rind

Plastic-wrapped cheeses don't really have a rind. Most often they are small pieces cut from larger pieces and then wrapped in plastic. Some cheese makers shrink-wrap cheese in plastic envelopes, thereby protecting the cheese in an almost inert state. There are differing opinions on plastic- and shrink-wrapping cheese. Some feel plastics and shrink-wrapping robs a cheese of some complexity, while others value the added shelf life and ease of storage.

Making Cheese, from Ladled to Cave-Aged Methods

A third way to classify cheese is according to how it is made. All different cheese-making techniques come into play here, and these classifications provide important clues about how a cheese will look, smell, feel, and taste.

Fresh

Fresh cheeses are those intended to be eaten right away or preserved in brine. Bright to creamy white, with a milky, almost soft taste, they are sold in bulk or in small packages. They are high in moisture, and some crumble easily. Fresh chèvre, ricotta, *fromage blanc*, and feta are all fresh cheeses.

Pasta Filata

As mentioned previously, pasta filata are cheeses made to stretch. After the curd has set, it is heated in water or whey, and then stretched and pulled until the desired amount of elasticity is obtained. This creates a resilient cheese for cooking and melting, though it is often eaten as is. Like fresh cheeses, pasta filata cheeses are bright to creamy white, sold in bulk or small packages, and have a fresh, milky taste. Mozzarella is the best-known pasta filata cheese.

Soft-Ripened or Mold-Ripened Cheese

Soft-ripened or mold-ripened are two ways to refer to soft cheeses that ripen quickly and develop bloomy or washed rinds and silky, creamy interiors. Their ripening is evident from the growth of mold. As mentioned earlier, these cheeses mature within weeks.

Brine-Cured Cheese

Brine-cured cheeses is another way to refer to cheeses like feta that are cured in a bath of brine until eaten. The brine helps feta maintain its creamy, salty flavor.

Pressed and Unpressed Cheese

Pressed cheeses are made by forcing whey from the curd with weights, and unpressed cheeses drain whey without being pressed. Both can be uneven or smooth and uniform. Pressed cheeses like Ossau Iraty and Petit Basqueboth sheep's-milk cheese, are made in large quantities, but they retain their rustic outward appearance and are made according to recipes developed hundreds of years ago. Unpressed cheeses like the Italian Pecorinos are also often rustic and made according to hundred-, sometimes thousand-year-old recipes. Both pressed and unpressed cheeses are often buttery and nutty, and have a long, complex flavors.

FACT

String cheese is pasta filata cheese. It gets its stringy texture from being pulled over and over while the curd is fresh, much like taffy is pulled. But next time you have a piece of whole or part-skim mozzarella, try pulling it apart like string cheese. You'll quickly realize that someone simply changed the shape of a piece of cheese and gave it a new name.

Cheddar

As mentioned previously, Cheddar cheese is made from Cheddared curds. The technique of cutting the curd, stacking it, cutting it again, restacking it, etc., is called Cheddaring, and is responsible for this cheese's name. Cheddars are most often made from cow's milk. White Cheddars are the color of the paste and don't have additional coloring. Orange Cheddars are colored with annatto seed extract and, in some cases, with artificial food dyes. Cheddars range from mild to sharp and are one of the world's most popular eating cheeses.

Swiss

Swiss cheese gets its name from its country of origin, Switzerland, and has come to mean a large family of cheeses, all of which are made with cooked curds and cultures that will produce enough carbon dioxide to create eyes, or holes. Blocks of Emmental, a Swiss-style cheese, are huge, some weighing up to 220 pounds, but are still hand rubbed and tended while they age. Swiss cheeses have tangy, buttery tones and are commonly eaten in sandwiches and used as cooking ingredients. Appenzeller, Emmental, Gruyere, and Jarlsberg are all common Swiss cheeses.

Gouda

Goudas are also made from cooked, tightly knit curds. A traditional cheese type of Holland, they are high in butterfat, which goes hand in hand with preserving rich summer milk to be eaten during a long, cold winter. Goudas are often made in 20- to 30-pound wheels and coated with thin paper or wax. Cheese makers in Holland aim for uniformity of color, texture, and taste, and look to different aging techniques to obtain a range of flavors. Young Goudas are mild and bright. Aged Goudas take on tones of caramel and butterscotch as they age.

QUESTION?

How is processed cheese made?
Processed cheeses are compiled from other cheeses rather than made from curd. In the United States, processed cheeses must contain certain percentages of moisture and fat, depending on the type of cheese they are emulating.

Blue Cheese

Blue cheeses are grouped together only because they are easily recognized for their blue-green mold, lack of rind, and common techniques for aerating during aging. However, blue cheeses represent a stunning array of tastes, textures, aromas, subtlety, and sharpness. Stiltons, for example, are made from hand-ladled curd into 17-pound wheels, and are aged for at least 3 months. Others, like Irish Cashel blue, are made from hand-cut curd into 3-pound wheels, and aged for at least 3 months. Wisconsin's Roth Kase Buttermilk Blue, on the other hand, is hand-hooped and aged at least 2 months.

Granas

Granas are cheeses with thick rinds, usually well aged, and always intended for grating and cooking as well as eating. They are big cheeses, both in size and taste, and most are dotted with the crunch of dissolved proteins. Grana Padano and Parmigiano-Reggiano are two famous granas from Italy.

Every Milk Is a Different Category

Now that you are becoming acquainted with the world of cheese, you can start to distinguish between the milks used to make different cheeses. Though not an official cheese classification, milk type certainly is important in determining flavor.

Cow's Milk

By far, cow's-milk cheese is the most common. Cow's milk is readily available for large commodity cheeses produced on a big scale, and for smaller, and more specialized cheese makers as well. When you smell cow's-milk cheese, it will be milky and somewhat sweet. This is the nature of cow's milk, and since most of us are accustomed to drinking milk from cows, it will smell the most familiar of the different kinds of cheeses. When you taste cow's-milk cheese it will also taste familiar, but stop for a moment and let a piece of cheese rest on your palate. Note the sweetness, and perhaps the hint of fruitiness. This is the classic cow's-milk taste.

Sheep's Milk

Sheep's-milk cheese is second to cow's-milk cheese in popularity and availability. It's made almost anywhere sheep are raised, and often is associated with mountain or monastery cheese. Sheep's-milk cheeses are often associated with buttery, nutty flavors. When made well, sheep's-milk cheese is one of the most complex in flavor profiles, as it can start out almost as sweet as cow's milk and end with nutty tones. Bries, Goudas, fetas, and mountain cheeses commonly are made with sheep's milk.

Goat's Milk

Goat's-milk cheeses have grown in popularity by leaps and bounds over the past twenty years. Once rarely found outside of Europe, they are now being made by large, commercial dairies as well as small artisan cheese makers. Laura Chenel, who (as mentioned previously) started making fresh goat's-milk cheese (fresh chèvre) in California in the late 1970s, is credited with popularizing fresh chèvre, and by example, encouraging many other American cheese makers to begin experimenting with goat's-milk cheese.

FACT

Many people in the cheese world refer to all goat's-milk cheeses by the French word for goat, *chèvre*. Fresh chèvre is most common and means a fresh goat's-milk cheese. A chèvre is a general reference to any number of cheeses made from goat's milk. You'll also hear the term *natural-rind chèvre* used to refer to Chevrots and crottins, which are fresh chèvres aged about thirty days until they develop a natural, buff-colored, wrinkly rind.

Goat's milk is used to make all kinds of cheeses: fresh, natural rind, washed rind, semisoft, semihard, Goudas, and blues. What sets goat's-milk cheese apart from the others in taste is a lemony brightness of flavor, followed by a tang.

Other Animals and Blended Milk

Throughout the world, wherever animals are milked, cheeses have been made from their milk. Water-buffalo cheese comes in fourth to cows, sheep, and goats in popularity of cheeses, and cheeses have also been made from camel's milk and from the milk of other mammals.

Lots of different cheese is made from the blended milk of different animals. Cow and water buffalo milk goes into mozzarella di bufala; cow, goat, and sheep milk go into the Spanish Iberico; and Italian Robiola-style cheese often combines milk from cows, goats, and sheep, or just two of the animals. Also, Greek cheeses such as feta and Manouri are blends of sheep and goat milk.

Dry, Nonfat, and Part-Skim Milk

The use of dry and nonfat milks for cheese making is mostly the province of commodity cheese makers who produce nonfat and lowfat cheeses. The absence of fat is offset by emulsifiers that act to bind the curd and give it the body of a higher-fat cheese. In addition, mechanized cheese-making processes help produce the smooth texture of a higher-fat cheese.

Powdered milk is often used to make cheese powder. Cheese powder, in turn, is used in lots of prepared foods like macaroni and cheese, cheese-flavored chips, sauces, and dressings. Sometimes natural food coloring, like the extract of annatto seed provides a bright orange color, and other times the color comes from carotene or artificial food dyes.

Part-skim milk is commonly used in many cheeses that are made with both morning and evening milk. For example, a wheel of Parmigiano-Reggiano is about 80 pounds, and with small herds, it requires two milkings to fill a vat with enough milk for a wheel of cheese. Before the evening milk is added to the vat, the cream is skimmed from the morning milk, thereby rendering it a part-skim milk. Some Gruyeres and Swiss cheeses are made in a similar fashion.

The Amount of Butterfat

People often talk about the fat content of cheese, and those who watch their diet worry about the percentages of fat they read on a cheese's label. In France, bloomy-rind cheeses are classified by butterfat: 45 percent, 60–65 percent, and 70–85 percent. At 85 percent fat, it seems you might be better off eating a stick of butter than cheese. But don't let the percentages scare you. These percentages are calculated on the basis of the percentage of fat in the dry matter only, not in the cheese as a whole. Recall that cheese has a lot of moisture. Luckily, this moisture creates some balance for all that butterfat.

Forty-Five Percent Butterfat

A 45 percent butterfat cheese is called a single-cream cheese. The word "cream" is used instead of butterfat. Single-cream cheeses have about the same amount of butterfat as the original milk. Camembert is the most commonly known 45 percent butterfat cheese.

Sixty to Sixty-Five Percent Butterfat

Sixty to 65 percent butterfat means you're dealing with a double-cream cheese, meaning cream has been added to the milk during the cheese-making process. Many Bries are double-cream cheeses.

FACT

Because the percentage of butterfat is an important indicator of how a cheese is made, several European countries have traditionally labeled their cheeses with this notation. You'll find it most common on cheese from France, Italy, and Spain. All three use the French term of measurement "matiere grasse," or its abbreviation, "m.g."

Seventy to Eighty-Five Percent Butterfat

Seventy to 85 percent butterfat denotes a triple-cream cheese, meaning two helpings of cream have been added to the milk during the cheese-making process. Triple-cream cheeses are famous for their decadence, and you'll find strong hints of other wonderful dairy foods in their taste: whipped cream, ice cream, and creamy butter.

One Hundred Percent

One hundred percent butterfat is butter, and technically not cheese. It comes from separated milk, but not through the process of curd setting.

Cheeses from Around the World

If you divided the world up by type of cheese, you'd draw some interesting borders, primarily along geographic, instead of political, boundaries. For example, the French cheese Comte, comes from the French Comte region, which borders Switzerland. This region is mountainous, with snowy, cold winters, and pastures are normally found on the approach to peaks. Spring-time brings sweet spring grasses and fields of flowers, and herds of dairy cattle are brought up from lower altitudes to graze. Just over the border, where Swiss Gruyere is made, the geography and animal husbandry prac-tices are virtually identical. And as you probably suspect, or know, Comte and Gruyere are very similar semihard cheeses. Both are made from raw cow's milk, their curds are cooked and pressed, they develop eyes and natu-ral rinds while aging, they are made in large wheels, and they have fruity, nutty tones.

Do some geographical comparison for yourself. Compare a northern California crottin with a Loire Valley French crottin. Compare an aged Comte and an aged Gruyere; and a northern Italian Fresh Asiago with a Wisconsin Monterey jack. Have fun with it, and soon you'll think of the world according to cheese boundaries. What could be better?

Gruyeres are normally more assertive in flavor than Comtes, and when tasted side by side they are clearly distinguishable from each other. How-ever, these cheeses are the product of their geography more than their nation. Likewise, many Mediterranean cheeses from different countries have striking similarities, as do cheeses from northern Italy and Switzerland, and from the Netherlands. Because of this, many experts refer to cheeses in geographical terms: alpine cheeses, Pyrenees cheeses, cheeses from the Netherlands, and so on.

Chapter 5

Where to Buy Cheese

Perhaps you've just tasted some amazing cheese in a restaurant, or read a gripping article about a new cheese, or just returned from travels that led you to some particularly exquisite cheese. Now you'd like to buy some of this great stuff. For the new American cheese enthusiast, the joys of cheese discoveries can be tempered by some frustration in the difficulty of finding a good U.S. cheese outlet, but don't worry; cheese selections are growing throughout the nation. With a little bit of sleuthing, you'll have no trouble.

Specialty Foods Stores

One of the first places to look for cheese is in a specialty food store. Cheese inventories are expensive and fragile, and optimally, the inventory turns over very quickly (within a few weeks). Because of this, you're most likely to find well-stocked cheese counters in stores that bring customers in for all sorts of different foods, stores located in large metropolitan areas with a large customer base.

When specialty food stores invest in cheese, they usually purchase large refrigerated cases, then fill them to overflowing with delicious cheese. In addition, they have staff trained to care for the inventory of cheese, to understand product classifications, to know how to help you with your selections, and to teach you how to pair cheese with many different beverages and foods. These stores often have full cheese counters, and because their inventories are diverse, sometime the owners of these stores can off-set the risk of investing in cheese by stocking items they know will sell quickly and well.

Cheese stores are specialty food stores with an emphasis on cheese. They are common in Europe, especially in France, where it's difficult to find a town without one (though who would try?). They are few and far between in the United States, but whenever you have a chance, visit one!

Specialty food stores often pair cheese with other foods, and take advantage of certain promotions, like food themes, cooking styles, foods from certain countries, and special menus, to bring in new and interesting cheese. For example, The Pasta Shops in Oakland, and in Berkeley, California, regularly promote foods from different countries. During their Spanish food promotion, for example, they carry a large and varied stock of Spanish cheeses.

Cheese Counters

Have you ever stood in front of dozens and dozens of different types of cheese? Have you seen narrow stacks of Brie wedged between creamy rounds of Italian Robiolas, and the tiered haystacks of natural-rind chèvres cascading around the base of Basque country mountain cheese? How about 75-pound wheels of Parmigiano-Reggiano, cracked open to reveal craggy insides, or an entire section of mottled-green blues? The aroma of this combination is nutty, yeasty, and downright cheesy, and there's a cheese monger standing on the other side, asking if you have any questions, or perhaps if you'd like to taste something. Truly, it's an experience no cheese lover should live without.

FACT

Even without full cheese counters, many stores carry a nice selection of carefully chosen cheeses. Scout around; you may be surprised at the stores in your area that have a small but wonderful cheese selection tucked in a corner.

If you've found a cheese counter, what's next? Don't be shy. Remember, you are not alone in discovering the delights of cheese. Whoever has opened that cheese counter is as excited about cheese as you are. So take a look around, and keep in mind the following:

- **Are there large wheels of cheese around?** If so, the store sells enough cheese to sell whole wheels, which means their inventory turns over pretty quickly.
- **Is the counter staffed?** If so, the staff should offer advice and tastings.
- **Do the cheeses look fresh and ready to serve?** On what day were they wrapped? Ideally, they should have been wrapped no more than four or five days earlier.
- **Is there a cheese wire behind the counter?** If so, they cut cheese to order, which is wonderful when you want a specific amount.

- **Does it seem like the cheeses have enough air circulation?** Remember, cheese is alive, and for optimal taste it needs to have a little bit of breathing room.
- **Is the cheese case clean?** No doubt you'll see a bit of mold here and there, which is normal, but you shouldn't see too much of it.

Satisfied with the counter? Then strike up a conversation with the cheese monger. Ask about the cheese you're looking for, or ask about a certain category of cheese. Ask to taste some of the merchandise, and ask for advice on selecting cheeses for certain pairings, meals, parties, or a picnic. What you want to know is whether or not the person behind the counter can guide you through sampling and choosing cheese, and if they can, you want to establish a relationship with that person, just as you would with a seller of fine wines.

Dairy Farms and Creameries

One of the best resources Americans have for obtaining gourmet cheese is American artisan cheese makers, whose numbers grow steadily every year. Although not all cheese makers have a retail outlet at their creamery or farm, if they do, seize the opportunity to see what it takes to produce this most enjoyable food.

Next time you're in Seattle, stop by Beecher's in the Pike Street Market. Here the process of Cheddaring goes on almost continuously behind large plate-glass windows, and you can see Beecher's Flagship Cheddar cheese-making process in action.

The easiest way to find out about visiting a creamery or farm is on the Internet, and most are concentrated in dairy country: the Northeast (Vermont, New York, and Connecticut), the northern Midwest (Wisconsin and Michigan), California, and northwest Oregon and Washington. Most cheese makers have a Web site where you can find directions, visiting hours, and phone numbers to call for more information. To find local cheese makers, be sure to check the Web sites of dairy organizations in the region, and ask your local cheese monger. Or, as you'll learn later in this chapter, you can find cheese makers at local farmers' markets.

Sometimes creameries and farms are on the same site, and sometimes they are separate. Farms are where the animals are housed and cared for, and where the milking takes place. As mentioned previously, milk processing and cheese making happen in creameries.

There are lots of good reasons to visit a cheese-making creamery or a farm. If the chance of petting a Nubian goat isn't enough to get you there (these goats are especially curious and friendly), then think of it as a chance to see how the animals are cared for, what they eat, and whether they prefer to laze about a barn or nibble grasses on a pasture. Think of seeing hot-tub sized pools of milk (don't jump in!), miles of stainless-steel piping and trays, and rooms stacked high with freshly made cheese (pure heaven).

Depending on the size of the operation, you might also find yourself chatting with the owner, the cheese maker, or the breeder of the herd. These knowledgeable and cheese-passionate people can describe all aspects of cheese making, and once they know you are a true tyrophile (cheese lover), you're apt to hear a bit of their philosophy on life too.

Farmers' Markets

Twenty-five years ago, farmer's markets were few and far between, but today they are so common, books are being published as guides to seasonal and heretofore unusual produce that people would tend to find only at such markets. Just as interest in specialty food has blossomed, so has interest in fresh and seasonal produce and locally farmed animals. People turn to farmers' markets for fresh, organic, and handmade products. Almost every large city in America has a farmers' market, as do many smaller cities and towns. When you are traveling, you can rely on farmers' markets to be great places to visit and find unusual and locally made gifts to enjoy or take home.

Farmers' markets are ideal places for cheese makers to sell their wares. Not only can they see how people respond to their cheese, but also they can test prices, showcase new cheeses, and gain a presence in the community, all things that help popularize their cheeses.

If you're looking for new and interesting cheese, then first thing Saturday morning, grab a basket, get yourself over to your nearest farmers' market, and see if any is around. If you don't see any, ask the bread sellers, honey makers, or yogurt makers if they know of anyone making cheese.

FACT

From April to September, a special cheese market is held every Friday in Alkmaar, Holland, at the site of a cheese "Weigh House," a hub for Dutch cheese exports going back more than 400 years. Hundreds of cheese wheels are lined up for everyone to see. Similar markets are held in the towns of Gouda, Bodegraven, and Woerden.

You can also use the farmers' market as a place to pair seasonal foods with cheese. For example, in the summer you can pair ripe stone fruits such as peaches and nectarines with fresh sheep's-milk ricotta, or fresh basil and heirloom tomatoes with fresh mozzarella, or a slice of crottin with a fresh, sun-warmed fig.

Supermarket Cheese Selections

None of the enthusiasm for specialty foods has escaped the notice of supermarkets. As the number of specialty food stores grows, so do specialty-food selections in supermarkets.

This past year Safeway dedicated thousands of square footage to organic foods, and Wal-Mart is also carrying organic foods. Nationwide, perhaps the largest supermarket gourmet-cheese presence is at Whole Foods. The company has a national cheese buyer, each store has a cheese counter stocked with several hundred cheeses, and each counter is staffed with a knowledgeable and helpful cheese staff. Local, high-end supermarkets are also good sources of cheese, as often they have built their business around high-end specialty food, and even if they don't have a cheese counter with a dedicated cheese monger, they often have a robust selection of very good cheese.

Finding cheese at a supermarket has its advantages too. You can do much of your other food shopping at the same location where you shop for cheese, and sometimes the cheese will be priced lower than the cheese you find at smaller stores. This is because the retailers who buy large quantities of cheese can sometimes negotiate lower wholesale prices, and these savings can be passed along.

Annual cheese festivals are held throughout the United States. Be sure to check out the Arthur Cheese Festival in Arthur, Illinois; the Artisan Cheese Festival in Petaluma, California; the Great Wisconsin Cheese Festival in Little Chute, Wisconsin; the Maine Cheese Festival in Rockport, Maine; and the American Cheese Society's Festival of Cheeses, held at the site of their annual conference each year.

High-volume cheese buying should translate into high cheese turnover, which means the cheese should be on sale at its peak. However, recognize that caring for hundreds of pieces of cheese is a labor-intensive process, and unless the supermarket is staffed for it, it's not likely anyone is flipping, rotating, and caring for the cheese on a daily basis. Instead, supermarkets will often choose relatively durable cheeses that arrive in their for-sale packages. The cheeses are inspected, then offered for sale. Or if cheese arrives in a large block or wheel, quantities are cut and wrapped every few days. At a supermarket it's easier to find excellent aged Cheddar (a fairly durable cheese) than it is to find a decent pyramid of natural-rind chèvre. Choose your supermarket cheese with attention to the conditions and staffing of the store, and check the packaging dates. In other words, choose your cheese with care.

Cheese in Cyberspace

Can't find a cheese counter, a specialty food store, a farmers' market, or a gourmet section in a supermarket? Don't despair. If none of these are available, or you're short on cheese-shopping time, give the Internet a try. Quite a few high-end cheese stores have Internet sites through which you can order cheese.

Unless you are willing to sort through all the things that pop up on an Internet search for "cheese," you'd be wise to find these stores through a narrower search, such as "cheese and food," or "specialty food cheese." Several reputable sites are listed in Appendix B under "Cheese Resources." One of the biggest advantages to ordering cheese online, besides the convenience, is gaining access to a wealth of information about cheese. Most cheese retail Web sites offer indexes of cheeses, accompanied by a short description of each cheese, recipes, and pairing ideas. Many also have archives of articles and news releases about individual cheeses. From these sites you can find links to cheese-discussion blogs, and to all sorts of informative dairy-industry Web sites.

Internet sites are also great if you want to send cheese to someone as a gift. They offer tried and true selections of well-paired cheeses to send as gifts. That is, they know which cheeses ship well, which to pair with certain foods, and how to package the cheeses effectively. In addition, most Internet sites have fun and useful cheese accoutrements for sale, such as cheese boards, cheese slicers, wires, and aprons and hats with a cheese theme.

FACT

Cheese is often the subject of food blogs, Internet sites where people post information and their opinions about food. Type "cheese blog," into a search engine and go from there. You will also find interesting results under "food blog."

What the Internet can't do for cheese lovers is offer a wide selection at low-cost, or a chance to taste before buying. Most of these Web sites offer a dozen or so cheeses that ship well, and mostly these will be harder, durable cheeses. If they offer softer and more fragile cheese, then they will recommend overnight shipping during the warm months of the year. Unfortunately, in this kind of situation the cost of shipping can exceed the price of the cheese. There's no alternative to being able to taste before buying, so buying cheeses on the Internet is sometimes less than ideal, but the Internet is very helpful when you want to order cheeses you already know.

Chapter 6

How to Buy Cheese

So far, you've read about cheese history, different milks, cheese making, and cheese classification, but unless you intend to set up a cheese-making facility in your spare bedroom or basement, your next step is to be standing in front of a cheese counter, ready to buy some cheese. But wait a second, there are a hundred cheeses or more. How do you choose one? Don't worry. You're here because you like food and you're open to a world of new tastes. Take a deep breath (ah, the aroma!) and plunge in!

What's It For?

Asking what cheese is for might sound like a silly rhetorical question. "To eat," you might reply. But stand in front of a cheese counter and take a look. There are a dozen different blue cheeses, and pile after pile of firm-looking cheeses with rough-hewn rinds. There are stacks of chopped white cheeses, and quite a number of beautifully wrapped small cheeses. There are fresh cheeses in buckets, and stacks of cheeses resembling well-worn building blocks. Tucked in and among the cheeses are small jars of preserves, logs of salami, boxes of crackers, and bags of nuts. Behind the counter you see huge, beckoning wheels of Gruyere, Cheddar, and Gouda.

So the first question you should ask yourself is why you're here. Not in a philosophical sense, of course. In the world of cheese, this is a very practical, matter-of-fact question. Why are you here to buy cheese? Is it for a snack? Is it because someone asked you to bring cheese to a party? Is it to put on a platter, or for a meal, or an ingredient, or to melt? Or is it to begin building your cheese knowledge and vocabulary? Begin by answering this question, and you'll start to easily find your way.

Instead of string cheese for lunch, try packing half-a-dozen bocconcinis. These small, fresh mozzarella balls will be fine out of refrigeration for several hours (in moderate temperatures), and you'll enjoy their light, fresh taste. Perfect combined with fresh fruit!

Snacks

Snacks are a cheese lover's best friend. A small morsel of cheese can satisfy your taste buds, take away that edge of hunger, and provide protein, vitamins, and minerals. Any cheese makes a good snack, so ask yourself if you're in the mood for something heavy or light, flavorful or mild, filling or not, or perhaps, something decadent or unusual. A good cheese monger can point you to new and unusual cheeses you might want to try, and these are always fun to snack on. Perhaps the Brin d'Amour, a sheep's-milk cheese from Corsica, coated in herbs from the island, is at its most nutty, creamy, and flavorful peak. A small sliver will be expensive, but a wonderful opportunity to taste something unique. For lighter snacks, think about the small chèvres, or a half-dozen fresh mozzarella bocconcinis, or a sliver of fresh Asiago. In Italy, people often snack on crumbled Parmigiano-Reggiano. Try some, or some bits of another grana.

ALERT!

Don't be afraid to substitute cheeses. With so many cheeses in the world, many have different names but are really quite similar. Work with your knowledge of classifications: textures, rinds, techniques, milk, and butterfat, and you'll find excellent substitutes.

Parties and Platters

It's terrific news when someone asks you to bring cheese to a party. First, you don't have to cook, and second, you get to visit the cheese counter! However, when asked, take the opportunity to ask the host or hostess what else is being served and when they plan to serve the cheese. Then you can confidently use the following platter guidelines to select an assortment of cheeses that will complement other flavors.

Platters are an ideal showcase for cheese. They can be served as part of any meal, before or after a meal, or for a snack. To get you started, an array of platter ideas is offered in Chapter 17, but here are some simple ideas to follow. First, decide if you want the cheeses to stimulate or satisfy everyone's appetite. If intended to stimulate taste buds before a meal, stay light and bright. If intended to satisfy after a meal, go with heavier, more full-bodied cheeses.

You can also choose cheeses that complement each other or contrast with each other. Or you can choose by region, or milk type, or cheese type. Do you want the creamy sweetness of cow's milk, the nutty, buttery tones of sheep's milk, or the delightful lemony tang of goat's milk? Perhaps a combination of the three will do. Another fun thing to do is serve one or two fairly traditional cheeses, like a rich, complex Cheddar with a rich, double-cream Brie, and then add something seasonal and unusual. Most of all, have fun grouping cheese. The more combinations you try, the better your cheese instincts will become.

Meals, Ingredients, and Melting

Cheese is the perfect food to make or round out a meal (later in this book you'll find over a hundred different recipes with cheese). But here you need to be fairly specific when looking for a cheese. If the cheese is the main body of a meal, you can choose the cheese first, then find complementary foods to accompany it, but if it's an ingredient or something to be melted, only certain cheeses will do. A good cheese counter will have a number of different cheeses that can be used almost interchangeably in cooking and melting, so spend a few moments with the cheese monger and tell them what you're cooking. If it's pasta, she might offer several different types of hard, Italian grating cheeses. If it's pizza, he might offer several different flavor profiles of melting cheeses. If it's dessert, there are numerous light cheeses that go well with fruits, honey, or other desserts. You get the idea. If you start with a recipe or an idea for a meal, look for the cheese it calls for, and then be open to new possibilities. Your cheese knowledge will grow exponentially, and next time you prepare the same dish or something similar, you might find yourself asking a whole new question: What other cheeses can I use here?

What Will the Cheese Be Eaten With?

The importance of this question cannot be overstated. Everyone's palate is influenced by other food and drink, and when choosing a cheese to complement other food and drink, this fact must be taken into account. That's not to say you shouldn't experiment, but when you do, you'll quickly learn that some flavors cause others to lengthen or shorten. In general, flavors should lengthen each other, or enhance each other. This makes all the food seem more complex and enjoyable. Some cheeses, like a firm, earthy, Spanish goat cheese, for example, will be a wonderful complement to a meal of lentils and lamb. But what if you served that wedge of Emmental you've had in the refrigerator instead? Close your eyes and imagine the tastes on your tongue. Even better, buy a small wedge of the aged, Spanish goat cheese, and taste it with your meal. Then taste the Emmenthal with the same food. You'll see that the Spanish goat cheese complements and lengthens the flavors of the lentils and lamb, while the other cuts the flavors off and finishes them too quickly.

QUESTION?

What's a cheese monger?
The phrase *cheese monger* comes from "monger," or peddler. Successful peddlers were always knowledgeable about their wares, and so are cheese mongers, the people available to assist you at a cheese counter. Rely on them to know their cheeses, work with you on your choices, provide tasting and advice, and to handle the cheese they sell well.

Several chapters of this book are devoted to pairing cheese with other foods, wine, beer, and spirits, but your cheese monger should also be able to help you through this. The important thing is to think about pairing your cheese with other foods and beverages so that all the flavors and aromas complement each other.

Look Inside and Out

Once you've narrowed your search to certain types of cheeses, it's time to look them over. Recall how much time and attention the cheese maker paid to creating the curd texture, balancing the moisture content, and giving the cheese a protective rind. These are the very things to look at when choosing a cheese.

The Rind

First, take a look at the rind. Unless you're looking at a fresh cheese, or a blue cheese without a rind, the rind should be absent of excess moisture or gooeyness. Also, unless it's a washed-rind cheese, avoid rinds with pink mold, as this indicates the cheese has ammoniated, or gone bad. Large cracks in the rind should also be avoided, as they let in air and release moisture. Then inspect rinds according to their classification.

Natural rinds should be buff colored, have a brainy texture, and evenly surround the cheese. Soft natural rinds indicate young cheeses, and hard natural rinds indicate older cheeses. These cheeses often bloom with a light dusting of white or green molds, and this is perfectly natural.

White bloomy-rind cheeses should look like pillowy velvet. Some, especially those with layers of vegetable ash, also develop bluish-green and dark, almost slate gray molds. Don't shy away from them. These molds indicate the cheeses are in their prime. Herbaceous rinds are harder to judge. The herbs or leaves sometimes mask the cheese, but look for freshness and an absence of extra mold.

FACT

Soft cheeses packed in wooden boxes swell as they age. A young soft cheese will not touch the edges of its box. An aged soft cheese will touch the edges and be puffy on top. Unless the rind has turned pink, there is a strong ammonia smell, or both, this expansion indicates healthy and delicious ripening.

Washed-rind cheeses take on the colors of sunset. Sometimes they are a dusty orange, or a pinkish orange, or a deep, russet orange. All of these colors indicate healthy, washed-rind cheeses. Avoid cheeses with large areas of discoloration.

A wrapped or dry cheese rind should be consistent in color, relatively unblemished, and uncracked. If the color varies dramatically, that is, if the cheese is much lighter or darker in one area than another, then it's possible the cheese sat too long on one side or somehow developed too much moisture in one spot. Blemishes can also indicate trouble, though not always. Some cheeses naturally develop blemishes, but for the most part they are scattered all over the rind. If a cheese has one or many blemishes that look out of place, again, it may have been mishandled, and the taste could be off. Cracks will also affect the taste of cheese. They let air in and moisture out, allowing molds to develop quickly and cheese to become dry. Avoid any cheeses with large cracks, or ask for a wedge from another part of the wheel.

Waxed cheeses often show a bit of mold on the outside, and when covered in paper too, the paper can be torn or scrunched up. None of these things indicate the cheese has gone bad. The wax coating is very effective in protecting the cheese, and unless the wax has been significantly damaged, these cheeses should be fine.

Inside the Cheese

The next most important thing to look at is the inside of the cheese. All cheese should be available to view on the inside, and you should never hesitate to ask a cheese monger to cut a cheese open for view. Generally speaking, you are looking for signs of health on the inside of the cheese. Here, you are interested in how the cheese is classified according to moisture and texture. Colors should be clean and unblemished, textures should be uniform or progress according to the aging cycle of the cheese, the cheese should have the appropriate amount of moisture, and it should look inviting. Think about looking at a road cut into a hillside. The hillside reveals a story of sedimentary layers, or the stresses of temperatures, or turbulent, volcanic energy. A cheese is just the same. When cut open, its past is revealed and it tells you whether the cheese has endured any significant stresses. Fresh cheeses should be uniform in color and texture and not have a story to tell. After all, they are fresh! Soft cheeses will have different layers of aging, but should always have a creamy heart. Semisoft and semihard cheeses should be relatively uniform in color and texture, and absent the kind of granularity seen in aged cheeses. Hard cheeses should be very firm but not too crumbly, and you will often see pockets of granularity in the eyes.

Blue cheeses should have the intended amount of blue-green mold throughout the cheese, should not be overly weepy, or losing a lot of moisture when cut. It's normal for many blue cheeses to ooze or weep some moisture, but if they weep too much they can become quite salty. Blue cheeses, as a rule, should also be smooth and creamy or crumbly in texture, as opposed to granular or grainy. If they are grainy, something may be wrong with the cheese. Perhaps it's suffered rapid changes in temperature, or has sat too long on one side or another. It still may taste fine, but the texture is not up to par. Often, very granular blue cheeses are also quite salty.

ALERT!

The strong smell of ammonia in cheese indicates the growth of unwanted bacteria. Pungent washed-rind cheeses sometimes smell slightly of ammonia. If you're not sure, unwrap the cheese and let it breathe for about fifteen minutes. Then examine it for excessive puffiness or gooeyness. If the smell has dissipated and the cheese is relatively firm, it is probably okay.

Is It Soft or Firm?

Cheeses are meant to be touched. While you don't want to handle unwrapped cheeses at a cheese counter, it is perfectly okay to pick up wrapped cheeses and inspect them. If you want to handle an unwrapped cheese, ask your cheese monger for some assistance. Regardless, how a cheese feels will also reveal something about its health and taste. All cheese continues to age until cut. Because of this, young, soft cheeses continue to ripen. The younger they are, the firmer they are. Similarly, the softer they are, the more aged they are. So if you're looking for an especially ripe Camembert, just by gently (very gently) squeezing it, you can tell if it's too young or just right. Likewise, all the texture and moisture classifications of cheese help you to know if a cheese feels right.

Ah, the Aroma

Cheese and pungency go hand in hand, and a cheese's smell is another important indicator of its health and taste. Think about how well you taste food when you have a cold. Not very well, right? That's because our taste buds need the help of our olfactory senses to register taste. We need to smell what we eat in order to taste it, and smells reach us in two ways. First, they reach us through the nose; then, after we've taken a bite, they reach us through our sinuses in the back of our throat. We'll get into the world of cheese tasting in the next chapter, but for now we'll talk about how we perceive cheese before we've taken a bite: through our nose.

Remember, we're still standing in front of the cheese counter, having thought through what we're buying cheese for, and whether it needs to be paired with other food or drinks. We've examined it from the outside, looked at its insides, and given it a soft, gentle squeeze. So far, everything's gone well. Now, bring that piece of cheese close to your nose (not touching your nose, please!), and take a deep breath. What do you smell? A bit of freshness, a hint of mold, something buttery, grassy, like mushrooms or almonds or wool? These are all smells from lighter cheeses, those that will brighten and titillate your palate. But suppose you picked up a washed-rind or bandage-wrapped cheese. None of those descriptors would be working for you. Instead, your eyes might be watering and you'd be thinking "Gym socks?" Don't be alarmed; most people recoil at these strong smells. After all, no one likes the smell of gym socks. But think about how these cheeses were made. Cheese microorganisms have mixed with the microrganisms of brine, linens, or both, and grown. The rinds are not intended for eating; they are on the outside of the cheese, protecting the inside, and these aromas are the exact aromas they are supposed to give off.

Cheeses to avoid are those that smell truly funky, or (as mentioned previously) like ammonia. When you smell it, you'll know these cheeses have aged beyond their prime.

Cheese That Doesn't Break the Bank

With so many wonderful cheeses it's tempting to go a bit wild, especially when you've just begun to experience all the new textures, aromas, and tastes. Gourmet cheese comes at a price. With an understanding of the factors that drive the price up, you can make economical choices and still enjoy a wide array of wonderful cheeses.

The first thing to consider is how the cheese is made. Like any other product, intensive hand labor is more expensive than mechanized labor. Handmade, artisanal, and farmstead cheeses are expensive because almost every aspect of cheese making, from animal husbandry to retailing, is done by hand. Still, many people want to support these cheese makers and are willing to pay a few extra dollars a pound for their wonderful products. After all, without artisan and farmstead cheese makers, there wouldn't be any artisanal and farmstead cheese. But know that when you are buying these cheeses, you are paying for all the time, attention, and care that go into them. If price is your most important consideration, then you'll want the bulk of your cheeses to be produced on a more commercial, and less expensive, scale.

Unique ingredients also drive up the price of cheese. One of the best examples is Brin D'Amour, a true storybook cheese. Brin D'Amour is made from Corsican sheep's-milk cheese. The milk is used in a raw state, rather than pasteurized, cut into a smooth-textured curd, and then formed into small rounds. After the curds have been pressed and drained, the cheese is coated with herbs from the island, the same herbs the sheep have fed on, and then the cheese is aged. During aging, the scent of the herbs mingles with curd, and the cheese develops a soft, green mold rind, unique to Corsica. As you can imagine, there is no other taste like it in the world, nor can it be made anywhere else. So, yes, it is one of the most expensive cheeses around.

Transportation drives up the cost of cheese: the farther a cheese travels, the more it costs. This does not mean that all cheeses from out of state or out of the country will cost more than a local or domestic cheese.

Other currencies also contribute to the cost of cheese. Right now, the dollar is weak compared to the euro. This means that cheese from Europe is more expensive to buy wholesale, and that cost is also reflected in retail prices. So how can you still enjoy wonderful cheeses without breaking the bank?

First, buy artisanal and farmstead cheeses locally. You'll often find these cheeses at farmers' markets and specialty food stores, and you won't have to worry about the added costs of transportation.

Second, look for very good cheeses that are produced for large markets. Goudas are an excellent example. The Dutch have long prized cheeses with uniform tastes, textures, and end results, and this has allowed widespread mechanization of Gouda production. As such, Goudas are excellent, relatively low-priced cheeses.

Bries are another good example of cheeses that are produced for large markets. French Bries are made by French companies in American dairies. The same procedures are used here as in France, but in the United States you can obtain the product without the added costs of transportation and currency exchange. One very popular cheese made this way is Fromage D'Affinois, a double-cream Brie with an incredibly silky, creamy taste, and at a relatively low price.

Many domestic cheese makers also produce wonderful commodity cheeses at excellent prices. Wisconsin Cheddar, Colby, and Monterey jack are widely known, and cheese makers throughout the United States make these cheeses. To experience these at their best, look for cheeses without added emulsifiers, artificial dyes, or additives.

Chapter 7

How to Taste Cheese

Learning to taste cheese is simple. It's a matter of learning to recognize certain aromas and flavors, learning to recognize when and where different flavors arise, becoming familiar with flavors associated with different types and ages of cheese, and developing a way to describe what you see, smell, feel, and taste. What could be more delicious?

Develop Your Palate

Sweet, sour, salty, spicy, toasted, roasted, fruity, and nutty; these are all familiar terms we use to describe flavors. We know when something is sweet, it tastes like sugar or candy. Sour makes our mouths pucker, salty tastes like salt, spicy means big aromas or heat, toasted is bread or nuts fresh out of the toaster or oven, roasted evokes pleasing aromas of meat or vegetables, fruity tastes like one or another familiar fruit, and nutty tastes like nuts. It's pretty simple, really.

The word *flavor* is derived from the Latin word *flatus*, meaning breath, or the act of blowing. Flavor is defined by Webster's as "a sensation obtained from a substance in the mouth that is typically produced by the stimulation of the sense of taste combined with those of touch and smell."

Foods and spices all contain flavors we've learned to recognize and describe. It gets a little trickier when foods and spices are combined. When they blend well they enhance each other and create entirely new flavors that are more difficult to describe. So it is with cheese. Alone, cheese curds are relatively bland, but every single part of the cheese-making process enhances and builds on their aromas and flavor.

Flavor

In 1825, Jean Anthelme Brillat-Savarin, a French author dedicated to the pleasure of food, wrote the *Physiologie du Gout* (later translated into English as *The Physiology of Taste*), a series of gastronomical meditations on how the senses perceive food, and though many people have written about food since then, Brillat-Savarin's description of taste is difficult, perhaps impossible, to surpass:

> *Whoever eats a peach, for example, is first of all agreeably struck by the smell emanating from it; he puts it into his mouth, and experiences a sensation of freshness and acerbity which invites him to proceed;*

but it is not until the moment when he swallows, and the mouthful passes beneath the nasal channel, that the perfume is revealed to him, completing the sensation which every peach ought to cause. And finally, it is only after he has swallowed that he passes judgment upon his experience, and exclaims, "Delicious!"

Whether you're eating a peach or tasting a cheese, all these sensations are happening in your palate, moving through your nose, going over your tongue, traveling along your olfactory nerves, and registering as taste.

Aroma

You smell most food before you taste it. Whether it's the smell of onions and garlic simmering on the stove, or a steak on the barbecue, or a chocolate bar, you know what you're about to enjoy without putting it in your mouth. This is because your nose perceives food by smelling it through the vapors and gases, or aromas, food gives off. The aromas give off hints about what you're about to eat, and most aromas likely played an important role for hunters and gatherers who came across new things to eat. Once they knew that bitterness was an indicator of poison, or that a rotten smell was an indicator of food that could make them sick, simply by smelling something first, they could decide whether or not it was good to eat. And so, as you train your palate to recognize different cheeses, don't forget that your nose plays a critical role in perception of taste. You will smell cheese long before you eat it, and after you've come to know several different types of cheeses, you'll recognize them by their smell.

FACT

When you take a bite of food you unconsciously smell it with your nose. Then, while you chew, vapors continue to travel to your nose, but they also begin to travel to your sinuses through your mouth. When you swallow, the aroma travels straight up the back of your throat to the sinuses.

While you eat, your nose is working overtime. Though it doesn't chew, it actively engages in every single bite by smelling the food as it enters your mouth. If you chew with your mouth open, your nose will remain engaged in the experience. If you chew with your mouth closed, as mentioned previously, the aromas will transfer to the back of your throat and travel up your sinuses to the olfactory nerves that perceive smell.

Basic Tastes on Your Tongue

In addition to being of vital assistance for chewing and swallowing, your tongue is also critical to tasting food. Most food scientists acknowledge different zones on the tongue that register different tastes. The front of the tongue registers sweet tastes, the sides register salt; just inside the salt zones are zones where sour tastes are registered, and bitter tastes are found at the back.

ALERT!

Be sure to taste cheeses in the right order. Start with mild cheeses, then progress to medium-bodied cheeses, and end with robust (strong) cheeses. By starting out mild, your palate will be ready for stronger and stronger tastes. And, the stronger the flavors, the more they will influence your palate, so reserve the big flavors for the end.

At the root of all foods are these four basic tastes: sweet, salty, sour, and bitter. Sweet tastes, since they are perceived at the front of the tongue, are the first you recognize. They are often fruity, and stand alone nicely even without many other tastes added. Think of how pleasing the taste of sugar, or honey, is, and you'll understand what this means. Salt is a basic taste, and when salt is present, other tastes are heightened. Just as sugar has a taste of its own, so does salt, but without salt, many other flavors stay flat and are perceived as bland, or without much taste. Sour or acidic flavors, are the bit of zing that refreshes, something everyone's palate needs. They wake up your senses. Bitter tastes are usually unpleasant, and because they are perceived at the back of the tongue, they are also the tastes that linger. Used in the right combination with sweet and sour tastes, however, they can stimulate your palate and appetite.

Cooks, vintners, and cheese makers have known for centuries that sweet tastes are enhanced by saltiness and sourness, and often, when devising recipes or designing new wines or cheeses, they seek new and interesting ways to balance these three flavors. When combined with sweet and salty flavors, sour flavors somehow retreat to the background and become almost a structural framework for all three to work together. For example, if you make your own spaghetti sauce, you probably use tomatoes and salt. The acid of tomatoes needs salt to bring out the roundness of the tomato flavors. But next time, add a teaspoon of sugar, and then taste the sauce. Do you taste the difference? The acid of the tomatoes has retreated to the background, and acts more like a basic ingredient, with other ingredients swirling around it. This is the balance brought on by combining sweet, salty, and sour tastes together.

How to Approach Your Cheese

When you were buying cheese in Chapter 6, you learned to look at the cheese first, then to smell, it, then feel it, and finally taste it. The same principles apply here, but now we'll go past the rind, and deal with only a slice of cheese at a time.

Look First

First, take a look at the slice of cheese, and take note of how many different areas there are to taste. Some cheeses, like Cheddar, are mostly paste, and that's all you need to try. Others, like Chevrots, have three areas important to taste: the rind; the layer just under the rind that is more aged; and the middle, or heart of the Chevrot, which has the least amount of aging. You'll want to taste each of these areas separately, and then together to get the full experience of this cheese. Also look for areas of dryness or excessive moisture, and make sure you taste from a piece that you will buy. If it's too wet or dry, ask to taste a different piece.

Smell Second

Next, hold the slice of cheese near your nose and breathe deeply. Note what you smell. Is it fruity, milky, nutty, or sweet? These are hints of what you'll taste first, the forward part of the cheese. Or, if you smell overpowering pungency, be prepared to take a very small taste, just in case the cheese has aged beyond its peak.

If tasting cheese at a cheese counter, make sure you taste from a fresh part of the cheese. If you taste from paste that's been wrapped in plastic too long, all you'll taste and smell is the plastic. It's okay to ask for the cheese to be refreshed before you taste. A good cheese monger knows how to guess if a cheese is approaching, at, or beyond its peak. Usually she will let you know what stage the cheese is at. And if either of you suspect the cheese is beyond its peak, she should taste it first.

Don't be scared to feel the cheese before you taste it. Pinch a small amount of the paste between two fingers and rub it around your fingertips. You'll gain important information about its texture, whether it is soft, crumbly, elastic, or granular.

Taste Last

It's been a long haul, working up to taste, but by now you have engaged all your senses that contribute to taste, giving you an acute awareness of what your nose is up to, what your eyes have seen, and how you will experience taste through your tongue.

This is how to taste: take a small bite first, and with your mouth closed, let the cheese rest on the tip of your tongue. Do you taste anything at this point? If you do, it is most likely the sweet flavors. Next, slightly open and close your mouth to let the aroma escape to your nose, then let the cheese slide toward the middle of your tongue and gently chew. Now you should taste the amount of salt the cheese has, acidic tastes, herbs and spices, and nutty tastes. This is the bulk of your tasting experience, what you perceive while the cheese is being chewed. Next, let the piece of cheese slide toward the back of your throat, note any strong tastes (hopefully not bitter ones) that emerge there, then let the cheese slide down your throat. Notice how the aromas kick off new sensations as they rise up the back of your throat? Now, breathe deeply, then open your mouth, and take note of all the tastes that linger and continue on in the cheese's aroma. Repeat the whole process once or twice, and the flavors will begin to talk to you.

Mouthfeel

Mouthfeel refers to how you experience the cheese paste on your palate, whether it is creamy, silky, chalky, gummy, buttery, or oily. As you chew, different cheeses feel very different in your mouth. Because of this, you can figure out how the cheese was made. For example, mozzarella will not coat your mouth; instead it is slightly rubbery and holds some shape as you swallow. This is because pasta filata cheese curds have been cooked and stretched, and chewing doesn't change the cheese's ability to stretch. Fresh chèvre coats your mouth cleanly. It is soft enough to be spreadable, and spreads around your mouth but doesn't linger. By nature, fresh chèvre is flaky and light. Buttery mouthfeels are often an indication of pressed and aged cow's- and sheep's-milk cheeses. A bite coats your mouth lightly with a buttery feel. Chalkiness, too much graininess, runniness, or excessive oiliness are all mouthfeels to avoid.

Starts and Finishes

Seasoned cheese tasters often talk about how a cheese starts and finishes, and how it feels in the mouth. As mentioned previously, the start of a cheese is how it begins on your palate, and the finish of a cheese is how it ends. The full experience, then, is the starting aroma and taste, the middle tastes, the feel of the cheese in your mouth, and the tastes that linger, after the cheese goes down. With starting tastes, your nose and the tip of your tongue are most involved, sensing taste through aroma and detection of sweetness. Often very mild and pleasing cheeses, like jack, Havarti, and young Goudas, have very sweet and lightly aromatic starts to them. They invite you in gently, and the flavors that follow unfold just as lightly.

As mentioned earlier, the finish is the aroma and the tastes that linger. People new to cheese tasting are often surprised to experience this for the first time. Ossau Iraty, a sheep's-milk cheese from the French Basque Pyrenees, is a spectacular example of a cheese with a long finish. It starts out slightly sweet, followed by buttery, hazelnut tones, and these are all pleasing enough to convince many people of the merits of this cheese. But moments later, as they swallow their first bite, they realize they are beginning to experience entirely new tastes. The butter melts, the hazelnuts are roasted, and the aroma dances back and forth across the palate, bringing the sweetness back to life. It's almost like getting two cheeses for the price of one.

FACT

That sweet taste you get with Monterey jack is intentional. Some of it comes from the curds being washed in whey before being placed in molds to form. The extra washing sweetens the cheese because whey has a lot of sugar, and this is a big part of why Monterey jack cheese has its initial sweet start.

A Vocabulary of Taste

As you develop your palate, you'll want to go beyond sweet, salty, sour, and bitter to describe the tastes of cheese. You'll want to describe hints of butterscotch and tones of hay. Maybe you'll taste spring flowers or onions. Here is a cheese-tasting vocabulary to get you started:

- **Milky:** sweet, creamy, lactic
- **Fruity:** sweet, citrus, berry, pear, apple, plum, apricot
- **Nutty:** hazelnut, almond, peanut, walnut, roasted, dry, salted
- **Herbaceous:** grassy, herbal, vegetable, floral, hay, straw, wheat, onion, artichoke, mushroomy
- **Spicy:** bright, cinnamon, nutmeg, vanilla, pepper, hay
- **Candy:** caramel, chocolate, butterscotch, toffee
- **Pungent:** overly salty, chemical, ammonia, stringent, barnyard, fermented, humus, burned, sour milk, wet wool

Taste Experiments

Now that you know what to look for, try a few experiments on your own. Taste conventional supermarket French Brie next to Brie de Meaux, and note where the flavors begin and end. Then try Kraft American Cheddar next to two-year-old American white Cheddar. Try a red-wax Gouda next to a six-month aged Gouda from Holland. Do a complete tasting of each and take notes. No matter which cheeses you prefer, you'll experience the difference between tastes that are short, those with one definitive taste and aroma, and tastes that are long, those that finish differently than they began.

Don't Let a Season Go By

Chapter 2 covered how the percentage of butterfat in milk changes with each season, and how the diets of animals change during each season of the year. The fun of this for cheese tasters is that your favorite cheeses change right along with the butterfat content and the diets, making them different experiences at each time of year. The best way to experience these seasonal fluctuations is to pick a favorite artisanal cheese, say a goat's-milk crottin, and taste it during the spring, summer, and fall. The crottin will be sweetest in the spring, when the goats have just given birth, are coming into lactation, and feeding on newly greened pastures. As the summer progresses, the butterfat content goes down, and the crottins become lighter, both in taste and texture. In fall, the goats begin to build up their winter stores of fat, and butterfat content goes up, making the cheese heavier, with nuances of savory fall grains. Finally, in late fall, the butterfat and flavors are at their creamiest peaks, making these crottins delightful holiday treats. But don't look for them again until spring; the goats will be taking the long winter months off for gestation and childbirth.

At a Restaurant

Restaurants are an ideal place to sample small selections of cheese, and more restaurants are incorporating cheese in hors d'oeuvres, salads, main courses, and dessert. Find a restaurant (or several) that makes an effort to use new and unusual cheeses in their menu and in cheese courses, and you've found yourself a quick and easy way to learn about new cheeses. The trick, however, is to let the cheese accompany a meal, rather than letting it dictate the meal. You'll also want to pair your beverage choices with the cheese (see Chapters 11 and 12), and then the entire experience will be one worth remembering.

When cheese is part of an entrée, it's been chosen by the chef to complement the tastes of the entrée, making your job very simple. You only have to savor the tastes of the cheese along with the other tastes in the food and enjoy.

Cheese courses are served as both hors d'oeuvres and desserts. Generally speaking, an hors d'oeuvre should liven your palate and get you ready to enjoy the meal. Light and bright cheeses make good hors d'oeuvres: some examples are fresh and young natural-rind chèvres, light Bries, fetas, mild Cheddars, lightly pungent washed-rind cheeses, and tangy, bright blues. Most of these cheeses have bright starting tastes and delicate finishes, making them ideal for priming your palate.

QUESTION?

What is a cheese steward?
A cheese steward is a specially trained and knowledgeable professional, most often found in fine restaurants or extensive cheese shops, who specializes in all things cheese. The cheese steward is often more informed than a regular waiter on pairing cheese with wines or other food items on the menu. The steward usually works directly with patrons on the floor of the restaurant or shop rather than in a kitchen.

Dessert courses are sweet and satisfying, they put a finish on a meal, and when cheese is a dessert course, you'll often see a selection of three or more cheeses with sweet, savory, and long finishes: pungent chèvres, highly aromatic washed-rind cheeses, complex and sharp blues, aged sharp Cheddars, and aged Goudas.

If you plan on eating the cheese course throughout your meal, make sure the flavors won't overpower other things you eat. Pair light food with light cheeses, and heavy food with earthy, robust cheeses. Don't be intimidated into thinking you have to order the smelliest cheese or eat large pieces. You are enjoying a lovely meal and your goal is to complement it, not overpower it. So nibble on the cheeses that enhance your experience.

In some countries, like France, cheese plates come out at every meal. This may seem like many rounds of cheese, but no one is expected to eat a lot of cheese or eat cheeses that don't go with other foods. The plate is simply there to enjoy if it feels right. Try this at home. Put three cheeses on a plate and bring it out at the beginning of a meal. By the end of the meal, the cheeses will be at room temperature and ready to enjoy.

Chapter 8
Cheeses of the World

If you were asked to guess about the geography and climate of a place, you'd be wise to choose cheese as your guide. Flat open countryside and alpine grasses usually mean cows, and hills with grassy terrain usually mean sheep. Where animals have to pick their way around rougher terrain and be resourceful in their diets, you'll find a lot of goats. Armed with this information, you'll travel the world with each new cheese you try.

The Netherlands and Scandinavia

Starting with northern Europe, cheeses from the Netherlands and Scandinavian countries are traditionally buttery and sweet, and almost all are based on centuries-old recipes that preserve spring, summer, and early autumn milk in the form of cheese for long, cold winters. For centuries, cheese has been an important trade commodity in this region.

The Netherlands

The Netherlands is made up of eleven regions, of which Holland is the largest. Cheese making began here during the eleventh century. The landscape is flat and filled with waterways that have supported a long history of trade and shipping. In the 1970s, the Dutch led the world in cheese exports, and because exporting cheese has been such an important part of their economy, cheese-making techniques have gravitated to those that ensure uniform cheeses, consistent in taste and texture, and able to travel long distances for lengthy periods of time: Goudas. Goudas are the most famous Dutch cheeses, of which there are young (less than one year old), medium (one to two years old), and aged (up to four years old) varieties. In the past decade or so, American stores have begun to stock a nice variety of young, medium, and aged Goudas, giving some Americans their first taste of the full range of Goudas that have been produced in the Netherlands for centuries. Edam and Leiden cheeses are also made in large quantities in the Netherlands.

Scandinavia

Of the Scandinavian countries, Denmark and Norway are best known for their cheese. Both have an abundance of seaports and enough flat pastureland to support large dairy industries. Denmark has the largest grazing lands in Scandinavia (in the nineteenth and twentieth centuries, acres of salty marshland were converted to agricultural use, thus contributing to the large areas available for grazing.). Cows are the principal dairy animal in Denmark, and both cows and goats are part of Norway's dairy history.

Cooperative farming methods are common in both countries. By pooling the milk of numerous herds, Scandinavian countries have created large signature cheeses such as Havarti and Jarlsberg. The first cooperative dairy of northern Europe was established in 1856 in Norway. Immigrating Trappist monks have also been influential, bringing with them recipes for Port Salud, Camembert, and Brie, and the fishing industry's methods for preserving and smoking fish have been adopted for smoking cheese.

FACT

The Norwegian "cheese," Gjetost, is not technically a cheese because it is not made from curds. Instead, whey from cow's and goat's milk is cooked until it develops a rich, caramel color. The results are sweet and nutty, and Gjetost is a traditional spread for breakfast toast.

As in the Netherlands, Scandinavia has pushed to implement consistent cheese-making techniques that produce cheeses uniform in taste and texture, and transport well. Danish Blue is called Danablu in Denmark. The cheese was developed in the early 1900s by Marius Boel who fashioned it after French Roquefort. It's become one of the most famous blue cheeses in the world.

Central Europe

As a country, France easily dominates cheese making throughout the world. Some estimate that French artisan cheese makers produce over 700 different cheeses. By taking advantage of different geographies and climates, they have perfected cheese-making techniques. Interestingly though, many Swiss, German, Italian, and Spanish cheeses are made with the same techniques used in France because the techniques have developed along geographical, rather than political, boundaries. In talking about central European cheeses then, it makes some sense to speak in terms of geographical regions, such as the Jura region, which spans parts of eastern France and western Switzerland. So, in true tyrophile mode, take a look at central Europe from the point of view of cheese.

Alsace

The Alsace region is in the northeast corner of France, along the Rhine River, and the cheese-making techniques of this region spread across the Rhine River into Germany, where the geography is made up of floodplains, low hills, forests, and rivers. Cows are the most common dairy herd, and Alsace is where the monks developed Muenster, a washed-rind cheese. Today Alsacian Muenster is a French name-controlled cheese (A.O.C.), although it is also made in Germany, where it is called German Muenster.

QUESTION?

What is cheese called in Germany?
Even with its geographical ties to France, the German language developed along Germanic, rather than Latin roots, and because of this cheese is called *kase* in Germany. In the Netherlands and Scandinavia, cheese is *kaase*.

The Jura

The Jura, just south of the Alsace region, runs lengthwise north to south along the southwest edge of Germany, the eastern side of France, and the western side of Switzerland. It is quite mountainous, and dairy herds of cows annually trek from the lowlands to Alpine meadows in summer, then back to the lowlands in the fall. Cheese making goes back to the eleventh and twelfth centuries of the Jura, and this is where some of the world's largest cheeses are made: 220-pound wheels of Emmental, and 80- to 90-pound wheels of Gruyere and Comte. French cheeses of this type are Beaufort, Comte, and Emmental. Swiss cheeses are Gruyere and Emmental, and the Germans also make an Emmental. Tomme de Savoie, reblechon, and Morbier are made just west of the Jura.

The Alps

South of the Jura, the Alps border France, Switzerland, and Italy. In Switzerland, this geography mimics the mountainous alpine meadows of the

Jura (up to a certain elevation), and along the slopes, you'll find Appenzellers, raclettes, Tete de Moine, and several Vacherins made with cow's milk. The same geography has produced Italian fontina, Asiago, and Gorgonzola, also made with alpine-meadow-fed cow's milk.

No cheese lover should miss tasting different wheels of Saint Nectaire, a cheese made throughout the Auvergne region west of the Alps. Handmade by dozens of cheese makers who age the wheels on straw beds in caves, each cave produces a unique strain of the same mold, thereby giving each wheel a slightly different aroma and taste.

Brittany and Normandy

The geography of northwestern France (Brittany, Normandy, and Picardi) is defined by the sea, low hills, and rich farmland supporting large herds of cows and sheep able to graze most of the year. As a result, cheese can be made for quick consumption, and some of the most famous bloomy- and washed-rind cheeses originated here. Camembert originated in Normandy, as did Pont l'Eveque and Livarot. Port Salud originated in Brittany, and throughout this region dairy farms and creameries continue to produce a wide assortment of fresh, soft, and semisoft cheeses.

The Loire Valley

The Loire Valley is dotted with castles, rivers, and rolling farmland. Though there are many herds of dairy cows, the cheese-making terrain has been given over mostly to goats, and from their milk, the famous French chèvres are made in two dozen named shapes. The most common shapes exported to the United States are Besace (beggar's purse), Bouchon (cork), crottin (horse's turd), Coeur (heart), Fleur (petals of a flower), Lingot (bar), and Pyramide (pyramid). These shapes were probably influenced by royalty enamored of gastronomy and the culinary arts. The flaky texture of goat's-milk curd lends itself more easily to being shaped than does cow's-milk curd.

The Basque Country

What better place to find hundreds of thousands of sheep than high rugged mountains flanked by miles and miles of sloping foothills? People on both the French and Spanish sides of the Basque country have been raising sheep and making cheese for thousands of years, and some say the sheep have nibbled most of the sharp edges off the rugged terrain. Certainly the cheeses are beautifully round in flavor, with tones of nuts, fruits, and olives, and clean, buttery mouthfeels. Basque cheeses are often made with 4,000-year-old recipes. In the United States you are most likely to find Petit Basque, Ossau Iraty, Idiazabal, Pyrenees with Peppercorns (a modern cheese), and French Brebis from the Basque Country.

You can have so much more fun in a country when you know a little of the language. When traveling in France, be sure to know what each milk-producing animal is called. Cows are *vache*, goats are *chèvre*, and sheep are *brebis*. And, most importantly, the French word for *cheese* is *fromage*.

The Mediterranean

Cheese making as we know it today originated near the shores of the Mediterranean Sea. All along its shores and stretching inland across Spain and Italy, you'll find a huge variety of world-famous cheeses of all milk types, with geographies to match. However, instead of the geographical links found in central Europe, here the sea separates countries. A quick look at Italy, Spain, and Greece will introduce you to the variety of cheeses you'll find there.

Italy

Traveling south from the Alps, where Italian cheese making is quite similar to Swiss and French cheese making, the next major cheese region stretches from Lombardy through the Veneto and into the Emilia Romano plains. Low foothills, long stretches of rivers and valleys, and a temperate climate make for an ideal countryside for cows. Three main cheese-making techniques have been perfected in this region: creamy blue Gorgonzola, washed-brine, soft Taleggio, and grana cheeses such as Grana Padano and Parmigiano-Reggiano. It's hard to imagine Gorgonzola and Taleggio were developed for anything other than elegant taste. However, it's easy to see the functionality of grana cheeses. Uncut, they keep for years and do not have to be refrigerated, but they too are spectacular in taste, bringing the flavors of the pasturelands forward in lovely, grassy fruitiness. All four of these cheeses remain in production, and three: Gorgonzola, Parmigiano-Reggiano, and Taleggio, are protected by the *Italian Denominazione di Origine Controllata* (D.O.C.).

FACT

Pecorino cheeses are so popular that many people think *pecorino* means *sheep* in Italian, which is not far from the truth. In Italy sheep are called *pecora*, so all pecorino cheese is sheep's-milk cheese. *Capra* is Italian for goat, and *vacca* is Italian for cow.

From Tuscany, south to the tip of Italy's boot, the geography is ideal for cows, sheep, and goats, but cows and sheep were the first to be established, and most of the cheese is made from their milk. All through central and southern Italy you'll find dozens of pecorinos, and four are protected under the D.O.C.: Pecorino Romano, Pecorino Sardo, Pecorino Siciliano, and Pecorino Toscano. The water buffalos of the Campania region are responsible for the milk of mozzarella di bufala, and cow's-milk mozzarella and provolone are both made throughout Italy.

Spain

The land south of the Basque country is still sheep's country in Spain, though large numbers of cow and goat herds dot the countryside. Throughout Spain you'll find hundreds of local, artisan-made cheeses reflecting the geography and primary dairy animals of each region. Some of the most well-known Spanish cheeses come from the interior region, which is a large plateau subject to sudden changes in climate and lots of wind. Sheep have fared best in this region, and from their milk, the famous cheeses Manchego, Ibores, and Zamorano are made. Manchego is controlled by the *Spanish Quesos Con Denominacion de Origen* (D.O.). In recent years Spain has become more lenient with its export trade, which is fantastic news for cheese lovers in the United States because more and more shops are importing and selling Spanish cheese.

QUESTION?

What are some Spanish words for cheese and milk?
In Spanish, cheese is *queso*. Milk is *leche*, cows are *vacas*, goats are *cabras*, and sheep are *ovejas*. Many Spanish cheese names begin with *queso* and finish with the name of the animal. For example, *queso de cabra* means goat cheese.

Greece

The geography of Greece is hilly and rugged, making it a difficult place to raise cows, so most of the dairy herds are sheep and goats, and most Greek cheeses are made from one or both of these milks. We can thank the Greeks for introducing us to feta, and with new cheese counters popping up around the United States, we are now becoming acquainted with the firmer Greek cheeses: Kasseri and Graviera, which make wonderful table and cooking cheeses. In Greece several cheeses are traditionally made in the pasta filata fashion. Their curds are bathed in hot water or whey, then stretched and pulled until they have an elastic quality to their texture. Haloumi, made on the island of Cyprus, is perhaps the best known of these, and wonderfully, it can be cooked directly on a grill without melting through.

The British Isles

Most of the cheese produced in the British Isles is made in England. The geography throughout England is fairly damp, with relatively mild winters and cool summers. There are low hills, some rocky outcroppings, but loads of good pastureland. Several thousand years ago sheep prevailed as the primary dairy animal, but during Elizabethan times in the seventeenth century, sheep's milk went out of favor and was replaced by a desire for cow's milk. Fortunately, the geography and climate are also conducive to cows, and since the seventeenth century, most English cheeses have been made from cow's milk. In the United States, Cheddar is certainly the most famous English cheese, but again, as more English cheese becomes available here, Americans are becoming familiar with other very famous and delightful English cheeses: Cheshire, Gloucester, Stilton, Wensleydale, and Lancashire, to name a few.

FACT

The word *cheese* has some interesting roots. *Cheese* has ties to both the Latin and Hindi languages. The Latin word *caseus* led to the Old English word *cese*, which led to the word *cheese*. And, *chiz*, originally a Hindi word meaning a thing, became an Urdu word meaning cheese. Urdu is the language of Muslims in India.

In recent years, several outstanding cheese makers from Ireland have made an impact with their cheeses: Adrahan, an aromatic, washed-rind cow's-milk cheese; Cashel Blue, a particularly creamy and piquant blue; and Durrus and Gubbeen, both washed-rind rounds of cow's-milk cheese.

The United States

In terms of geography, the United States might be the most diverse cheese-making country, and again, when considering cheese, it's easier to think about geographical regions instead of the United States as a whole. The Northeast, including New York, New Hampshire, Connecticut, and Vermont, with bitter cold winters and hot summers, was the first dairy region to be settled. The second major region is the northern Midwest, including Wisconsin, Michigan, and parts of the surrounding states. Again, this region has enormous swings in climate, from cold winters to hot summers, but, as in the Northeast, the pastureland is green in summer and enough feed can be grown to support dairy herds through the cold of each winter. The third major region is the West, with California leading, followed by Oregon, Washington, and parts of Colorado. Most dairy farming can be done in relatively temperate climates in the West, and many herds can feed on pastureland almost year-round.

Why do photographers tell people to say "cheese"?
Perhaps it's because the word is hard to say without moving your lips, but more than likely it's because the word "cheese" forces you to use the "eee" sound. Try saying "eee" without grinning. It's almost impossible. But really, wouldn't you rather say cheese?

The U.S. dairy industry started with cows, and cows continue to be the primary source of milk for most of the large, commercially produced cheeses, which are modeled after European favorites: Asiago, Camembert, Cheddar, Colby, Edam, Gouda, Gorgonzola, Havarti, Limburger, Muenster, mozzarella, Parmesan, and provolone. The United States also led the way in creating cold-pack cheese, which is several different cheeses processed together, and in creating spreadable cheese products with long shelf lives.

Over the past twenty-five years, artisan cheese makers throughout the country, but heavily concentrated in the Northeast, northern Midwest, and the West, have begun to make cheese from goat's and sheep's milk, and these cheeses have met with fantastic success. Instead of being uniform and produced for large commercial markets, they are mostly handmade and reflect the flavors of the regions where they are made.

The South Pacific

Australia and New Zealand are similar to the United States in their cheese-making past. Cheese making arrived to these countries through European settlers who brought sheep, cows, and goats with them, and in conformance with the trends of the day, cows became the primary source of their dairy industries when the countries were first settled. New Zealand went so far as to discourage any breed of cattle save the Freisan, whose milk is among the lowest in butterfat, but in recent years both Australia and New Zealand have begun to make artisan cheese. Most Australian cheeses come from Tasmania and are made from cow's and sheep's milk, and New Zealand is starting to produce artisanal Cheddars that compete well with others.

The Rest of the World

Portugal is one of the more isolated European countries, and Portuguese cheese making has also been isolated to meet the needs of only the local population. In the 1990s, however, Portugal voted to protect ten cheeses and begin exporting them throughout the world. Two that will no doubt begin popping up on American cheese counters are Sao Jorge, a hard cow's-milk cheese, and Serra da Estrela, a washed-rind sheep's-milk cheese.

FACT

St. George cheese, a hard cow's-milk cheese with a lemony tang, is made by the Matos family in Santa Rosa, California, who immigrated from Portugal. If you're in Santa Rosa, you should stop by the cheese-making operation for a visit. The family loves to tell people about its cheese!

Most of the cheeses produced in the Middle East are fetas, protected from heat with a salt brine. Mexican cheeses are mostly fresh, light tasting cheeses called queso fresco. Cheese is also made in South American countries, generally according to recipes adapted from Europe, and made with local dairy herds of cows, sheep, and goats. Very few Middle Eastern, Mexican, or South American cheeses are imported to the United States.

Chapter 9

Cheese Nutrition

Given cheese's long history, not to mention all its wonderful and varied flavors, it's hard to understand why so many people think cheese is something to avoid. Throughout history, as other foods became scarce, people needed and wanted the protein, fat, calories, and vitamins of a good cheese. Today the difference is not the cheese, it's in people's easy access to all sorts of other high-calorie proteins and fats. But with the right information, even the most nutritionally conscientious can always choose cheese!

Why Cheese Is Good for You

For optimal health, you need protein, carbohydrates, fats, and a full complement of vitamins and minerals. Combined with plenty of water and good exercise, a properly balanced diet goes a long way to ensuring your health. Milk and cheese are excellent sources of complete proteins (proteins that contain all eight of the amino acids humans need), calcium, potassium, and vitamins. And, though cheese does contain fat, and many people are concerned about limiting their fat intake, cheese contains fatty acids and saturated fats, both of which help our bodies absorb fat-soluble vitamins and regulate all sorts of biological processes. As a nutrient-dense form of milk, cheese is impossible to beat as a ready and easily accessible source of nutrition.

U.S. 2005 Dietary Guidelines for Americans

In 2005, the USDA issued new dietary guidelines for Americans that are intended to inform policymakers, nutrition educators, and health providers, who in turn counsel people on their diets. These guidelines are based on the latest scientific findings as recognized by government agencies, and though they are not without challenges; most of the challenges are focused on how to satisfy the dietary requirements rather than what the dietary requirements are. Two approaches are taken into consideration, the Dietary Approaches to Stop Hypertension (DASH) Eating Plan, and the USDA Food Guide. And while these two approaches differ in some areas, both recommend 2 to 3 cups of foods from the milk group every day. (One cup of milk is equivalent to 1 cup of yogurt or 1 to 2 ounces of cheese, depending on the cheese.)

Furthermore, studies show that many adults and children do not take in enough calcium, potassium, or vitamins, particularly vitamins A, C, and E. Calcium is needed for strong bones and teeth, it helps blood clot, and it assists in the way your nerves, muscles, and heart function. Potassium is essential to maintaining healthy cells, and, like calcium, it helps your nerves to function well. Vitamin A is important to the health of your skin and other membranes, and without vitamin C, you can develop scurvy and be vulnerable to a host of other diseases. Vitamin E is essential to absorbing other nutrients and maintaining good health.

Because Americans are often deficient in calcium and vitamins, and milk is such a wonderful source of both, the USDA has recommended, among other things, an average per-day increase of 1.6 cups of low-fat milk or its equivalent for women and 1.2 cups of low-fat milk or its equivalent for men, bringing the recommended total cups of milk per day for both men and women to 3 cups.

FACT

In 2006, the British Cheese Board released the results of a study in which 200 volunteers ate ¾ of an ounce of cheese one half-hour before bedtime. They were shocked to learn that Brie led to dreams of sunny beaches, Stilton led to dreams of battle, Cheddar led to dreams of celebrities, and after eating Cheshire cheese, people tended not to dream at all.

Nutrient-Dense Foods

Nutrient-dense foods is a recent phrase referring to foods high in nutrition and low in calories, and it's been coined as a way of contrasting it with the types of foods so common in the United States today: high-calorie, low-nutrition foods. The USDA is not alone in encouraging Americans to focus on nutrient-dense foods in their diets. The phrase has also become common shorthand among grassroots organizations promoting naturally healthy diets. Cheese is one of the original nutrient-dense foods!

How Different Are the Milks?

One of the most important things to remember about the nutritional quality of cheese is that it is a concentrated form of milk. Milk contains water, sugar, protein, fat, vitamins, and minerals, and when cheese is made, most of the water and sugar are drained off, leaving a concentrated block of protein, fat, vitamins, and minerals. Think of it as a small energy bar. The nutritional composition of cheese, that is, the percentages of protein, fat, vitamins, and minerals, depends partly on what type of milk is used, and partly on how the cheese is made. Before you think about nutrition and cheese-making methodology, take a look at the concentrations of protein, fat, and vitamins in different cow, goat, and sheep milks.

Protein

Sheep's milk has the highest concentration of protein, about 5 to 6 percent, and delivers the most protein per ounce of cheese. Goat's milk comes in next, around 3 to 3.5 percent, followed by cow's milk, which is about 3 to 4 percent protein.

Fat

Sheep's milk, at 6 percent, also has the highest concentration of fat, followed by cow's milk at 3 to 5 percent, and then goat's milk at 3 to 4 percent. Interestingly, different breeds of sheep, cows, and goats have significantly different levels of fat in their milk. Jersey cows, for instance, have more fat than Holstein cows, and Nubian goats have the most milkfat of all the goats, followed by La Mancha goats. Many cheese makers combine the milks of several breeds for their cheeses to take advantage of the different concentrations of fats.

ALERT!

One cup of whole cow's milk has 8 grams of fat, 2 percent milk has 4.7 grams, 1 percent milk has 2.6 grams, and skim milk has no fat at all. Even if you drink 1 cup of whole milk, you are getting less fat than if you ate an ounce of almonds.

Vitamins

The recommended adult allowance of calcium is 1,000 milligrams per day. Take a look at the calcium provided by 1.5 ounces of the following cheeses: feta, 210 mg; mozzarella, 215 mg; blue, 225 mg; Muenster, 305 mg; provolone, 321 mg; Swiss, 336 mg; and Parmigiano-Reggiano, 450 mg.

As with protein and fat, the highest concentrations of vitamins are found in sheep's-milk cheese, followed by goat's milk, and then cow's milk.

Nutrition and Cheese-Making Methods

Different cheese-making techniques can have such a significant effect on the nutritional composition of cheese that many cheeses are regulated to assure certain percentages of moisture and fat.

USDA-FDA Specifications

In the United States, the Food and Drug Administration (FDA) regulates the manufacture and production of all sorts of foods, thereby ensuring consistency of practices and consumer safety. Under the Code of Federal Regulations 21.2, seventy-two cheeses and cheese products, from Asiago to cheese spread, are regulated according to definition, milk type, ingredients, and labeling. What this means, is that when you buy a block of domestic Asiago, for example, you can be sure it contains no more than 45 percent moisture, that the milkfat is at least 50 percent (of dry matter), that it is made with pasteurized cow's milk, and that the cheese has been cured at least 60 days. The maximum moisture content and minimum milkfat for ten of the most popular cheeses are listed in the table below.

Ten FDA-Regulated Cheeses

Cheese	Maximum Moisture	Minimum Milkfat
Asiago	45 percent	50 percent
Blue	46 percent	50 percent
Cheddar	39 percent	50 percent
Colby	40 percent	50 percent
Edam	45 percent	40 percent
Gorgonzola	42 percent	50 percent
Gouda	45 percent	46 percent
Gruyere	39 percent	45 percent
Limburger	50 percent	50 percent
Monterey jack	44 percent	50 percent

Nutritional Comparisons

If you are watching your calorie, fat, or vitamin intake, you should know that not all domestic and imported cheeses have the same nutritional composition. Say you love Swiss cheese, but want to make the best choice between a domestic brand and an imported brand. By looking at the nutrition information supplied by the manufacturers on the label, you can make these types of comparisons easily.

For example, you might notice that an ounce of Swiss Emmental contains 10 percent more vitamin A, but also has 20 milligrams more sodium, than an ounce of American Emmental. Danish Havarti has 2 percent more vitamin A, and 10 milligrams more sodium, but it is lower by 1 gram in both protein and fat, than an American Havarti. Polly-O Parmesan has the most striking difference in sodium, coming in at 450 milligrams per ounce, compared to 180 milligrams in Parmigiano-Reggiano. It is also 2 percent lower in vitamin A, 1 gram lower in fat, and 1 gram higher in protein. You should also look for the use of emulsifiers, gum, and coloring agents, as these will differ according to the manufacturer of the cheese.

The Truth about Cheese Fat

Just how much fat does cheese have? First, don't forget that the percentages of milkfat (also referred to as butterfat and/or "cream") you see on cheese labels (e.g., 70 percent maitre grasse, or m.g.) refer to the percentage of fat found in the dry matter only. This type of labeling is done throughout the world and serves almost as a code to indicate how much cream has been used in making the cheese. In addition, cheeses are very moist, so you can usually divide the percentage of fat in two to get a sense of the overall fat content. That means a label of 45 percent m.g. is about 22.5 percent fat.

In a diet-conscious world, it's easy to think of fat only in terms of calories, and to assume that all fat will contribute to unwanted weight gain. However, the truth is hardly that simple, and though you are wise to avoid unhelpful fats—trans fats for example—the fats in cheese are saturated, and made up of chains of fatty acids. In moderation, saturated fats turn out to be pretty important to your health. Saturated fats provide energy, carry fat-soluble vitamins (like vitamins A, D, and E, and riboflavin in cheese) throughout the body, assist in the building of membranes, and help in the regulation of bodily functions.

ALERT!

If you've been avoiding cheese because of its fat, you should take a look at how it compares to a few other well-loved foods. An ounce of almonds has almost 10 grams of fat. Avocados have 5 grams of fat per ounce, as does sirloin steak. One ounce of coconut has 0 grams of fat, and an ounce of potato chips has 15 grams of fat.

So, as you get to know your cheeses you'll also want to learn about their relative percentages of fat. In general, though they vary according to how they were made, the ratios of moisture to dry matter, the type of milk used, and the amount of cream included, this is how they stack up: Per ounce, ricotta and fresh goat's milk generally contain 4 and 5 grams of fat, respectively. Next, coming in at 6 grams of fat per ounce, are Brie and mozzarella. Next is Parmigiano-Reggiano at 7 grams, then Emmental at 8 grams, and then Cheddar at 9 grams. Somehow, when you put together all the health benefits of cheese along with the delicious tastes, at 4 to 9 grams of fat per ounce, cheese doesn't seem as fat anymore.

What about Lactose?

Many lactose-intolerant people assume they will have trouble digesting cheese, and because of this they avoid cheese as much as they avoid other milk products. Certainly some people with difficulty digesting milk also have difficulty digesting cheese. However, this is not always the fault of lactose.

Lactose, Lactase, and Lactic Acid

The Oxford Companion to Food defines lactose as "the main and almost the sole sugar in milk . . . composed of the simple sugars dextrose and galactose." *The Oxford Companion* goes on to describe how lactose is digested:

"Splitting lactose into these two sugars is the first stage in digesting it, and is done with the aid of the enzyme lactase." Therefore:

- Lactase is an enzyme that occurs naturally in the intestines of mammals (including people), and is also a byproduct of some yeast.
- Lactic acid is what lactose becomes as it ferments. The fermentation occurs naturally in milk and is caused by milk.

Raw milk contains enough natural milk bacteria to produce lactic acid; however the rate of lactic acid production can be unpredictable. Pasteurized milk does not contain these milk bacteria. As a result, most cheese makers rely on starter cultures that contain the necessary bacteria to begin the production of lactic acid in a controlled setting. After most of the lactose has been converted to lactic acid, the process of separating curds from whey begins, and most of the lactic acid remains with the whey.

Lactase, the enzyme that digests lactose, is something your body can produce naturally, and is not a part of cheese. However, not everyone produces lactase. It is generally believed that over several thousand years, people living in areas dependent on milk and cheese (northern, central, and southern Europe; parts of Africa; most of the Americas; Australia and New Zealand) retained or developed the genetic coding needed to produce lactase throughout their lives. In other parts of the world, such as in Asian countries, this genetic coding was not as necessary because few people drank milk or ate milk products beyond infancy. This is not to say that people from Asian countries cannot digest milk or that all people from milk-drinking countries can digest milk. It is simply a way of illustrating the fact that people's bodies have developed tolerances for milk digestion that seems to follow thousand-year patterns of milk consumption. So, your ability to produce enough lactase to digest milk is partly dependent on your genetic coding, which may also be related to the countries of your ancestors.

Now for the really good news for the lactose intolerant. All that lactose in milk? Most of it has been converted into lactic acid or drained away with the sugar and water (the whey), and doesn't make its way into cheese! In fact, unless you're talking about a whey-based fresh cheese, like ricotta, about 95 percent of the lactose is gone, and many people who have experienced intolerance to lactose find they can easily digest cheese.

Lactose in Different Milks

Some people find they can digest goat's milk more easily than cow's milk and believe this has to do with the amount of lactose contained in each. The difference, however, is slight. One cup of cow's milk contains approximately 11 grams of lactose, and 1 cup of goat's milk contains about 9 grams. When made into cheese these differences are so slight as to be immeasurable.

What to Do

Lactose intolerance has garnered a lot of media attention, and an entire folklore has grown up around the term. When people experience bloating, discomfort, or gas after drinking milk or eating cheese, they are tempted to blame it on being either partially or fully lactose intolerant.

QUESTION?

Do people digest cow's, goat's, or sheep's milk differently?
There is no evidence to suggest one animal's milk is easier to digest than another's, but as with any food, different people will tolerate some foods better than others. If you've had any discomfort after eating cheese from one animal's milk, try another type and see what happens.

Lactose intolerance is a real condition. But if you haven't been diagnosed with it and simply suspect you are lactose intolerant, talk to your doctor about it first and see if the condition is truly diagnosable. Or, if the symptoms you've experienced are not severe, think about trying small amounts of cheese to see if you are able to digest them. You may be pleasantly surprised.

Influence of the Terrior

Terrior (pronounced tear-WAHR) is another term becoming more and more popular these days. In terms of cheese, it has become synonymous with cheese made from seasonal ingredients, and is often associated with artisanal or farmstead cheese. People interested in sustainable agriculture often refer to *terrior* as a way to describe farming in concert with local eco-logical and seasonal cycles. Whether *terrior* has any effect on the nutrition of cheese is debatable, and depends on how much influence an animal's diet has on the nutrition of its milk, and the cheese made from the milk.

In terms of overall cheese calories and protein, *terrior* is rather inciden-tal. But milkfat is influenced by a ruminant's reproductive cycle and diet. Because of this, it is possible for the fat in cheese to be influenced by sea-sonal grazing and the animal husbandry practices that go along with a *ter-rior* diet.

If you want to know more about how *terrior* affects the flavor and nutri-tion of your cheese, talk to some artisan and farmstead cheese mak-ers. You can often find them at farmers' markets or when you visit their creamery. They'll be able to tell you what their animals have eaten and how their diets have influenced the cheese.

Another influence that some claim is the effect of seasonal grasses and flowers on the immunity of the people eating the cheese. Again, by grazing, rather than eating a diet of grain and silage, animals are taking in the natu-ral grasses and flowers of the area. Some people believe the resulting nutri-ents transmitted through their milk and into cheese help their immunity to seasonal allergies. So, for those who have found seasonal and local eating practices a way to help alleviate allergies or gain access to the complement of local vitamins and nutrition available through animals and plants, *terrior* can have significant nutritional benefits.

Chapter 10
Cheese at Home

In a perfect world, everyone would live close to a very good cheese shop and daily buy small slivers and delicate chunks of cheese. Unfortunately, not everyone can do that. As such, this chapter will help you keep your cheese alive and fresh, advise you on freezing it, tell you what to do with forgotten cheese, teach you how to tell when cheese goes bad, show you what types of cheese accoutrements are helpful to have on hand, and discuss when and how to slice your cheese.

Keep Your Cheese Alive

The first thing to remember about cheese at home is that it is alive. Not alive in the sense of being conscious, of course, but alive in the sense of being a collection of microorganisms that feed off oxygen, carbon dioxide, and the nutrients of the rind and paste. In Chapter 3, you read about how cheese continues to age gracefully before it has been cut. The aging (up to a point) contributes to enhanced texture, aromas, and flavors. After a cheese is cut, it no longer ages in the same way. Instead, it releases moisture through the cut paste. Therefore, if you are lucky enough to buy whole wheels of cheese at a time, at the proper temperature and humidity, they will keep quite a bit longer than cut pieces of cheese. Practically speaking, however, at home, most of us are dealing with pieces of cheese, cut from larger wheels.

ALERT!

Don't forget that cheese naturally absorbs the flavors of its environment. If you store it with strong-smelling foods, it will absorb the smells and tastes of those foods. So, unless you want your cheese to smell and taste like onions, for example, keep the two apart.

Temperature and Humidity

In the United States, most people are used to keeping blocks of commodity-style (e.g., American, processed Cheddar, domestic provolone, string, and Monterey jack) cheese in the deli drawers of their refrigerators, where temperatures are normally below 40°F, and conditions are low in humidity (the safest conditions to prevent spoilage and the development of unwanted bacteria). These cheeses often contain preservatives, or have been made in a uniform manner and encased in plastic wrap, both of which are methods that contribute to preservation under a variety of conditions. However, for optimal aromas and flavors, cheeses can be kept at higher temperatures for short periods of time. Temperatures of 50°–55°F, and humidity readings of 80–90 percent are the ideal ranges to store soft, semisoft, and semihard cheeses. Within this range, moisture and textures will stay fairly constant. Blue cheeses need to be kept cooler and more humid, and are best kept at 42°–46°F and 85–95 percent humidity, and hard cheeses are best kept a bit warmer, at 55°–60°F and about 80 percent humidity. So, at 40°F and subject to drafts from the door opening and closing, most refrigerators are not ideal homes for cheese.

FACT

Some refrigerators have temperature- and humidity-controlled cheese drawers, much like wine-storage units. If you have one, you can set it to maintain your cheeses according to the previously given temperature and humidity parameters.

If you eat your cheese within a few days, it will not be noticeably distressed by refrigerator conditions. However, if you have a cellar, check the temperature and humidity conditions there. It may be the ideal place to store your cheese (protected from house pets or other animals!). Or you may find a temperate corner of your kitchen for cheese. If you have neither a cellar nor a temperate corner, use your refrigerator to store soft, semisoft, and semihard cheeses, and remember, if the temperature is too cold and the humidity too low, cheese will become dry and prone to cracking. Store hard cheeses in the coolest part of your kitchen, but outside the refrigerator, and remember, if the temperature is too hot and humidity too high, cheese will release butterfat and lose its structure. It will become dry on the inside and oily on the outside. During hot months, the refrigerator will be a better environment for hard cheeses.

Wrapping Cheese

There may be as many opinions in the cheese world about wrapping cheese as there are in the wine world about corks, plastic plugs, and screw tops, and for good reason. Corks, plastic plugs, and screw tops are designed to help, or at least not hinder, wine's aging. Cheese rinds are designed the same way: they help, or do not hinder, aging. Once opened, a bottle of wine can be recorked, and even though the next sip will be different from a sip of a freshly uncorked bottle (uncorking will always degrade some aroma and flavor), this is a fairly accepted method of preserving a bottle of wine. When a cheese is cut, however, you have cut its protective layer, the rind. People who think quite hard about preserving cheese are, in fact, trying to figure out how to re-create a rind. Ideally, wrappings allow cheese to breathe, help maintain the appropriate amount of moisture, and do not introduce any new and unwanted flavors. Cheese mongers often use specially designed cheese paper to wrap cut pieces of cheese. Cheese paper consists of two parts; it's made up of a thin, waxy plastic on one side and a thin, breathable paper on the outside. Many believe this paper preserves cheese for an extended period of time and that it is the ideal cheese wrapping. Here are some tips you can follow at home to preserve your cheese:

- Cut off only the cheese you will use and return the well-wrapped remainder to its storage place.
- When rewrapping cheese, use fresh wrapping to prevent unwanted bacteria from forming.
- Double-wrap your cheese in thin plastic wrap, followed by a layer of parchment paper. The combination won't breathe quite as well as cheese paper, but it will help the cheese remain protected. (Don't forget to mark the name of the wrapped cheese on the outside of the parchment paper.)
- Use plastic wrap for cheeses that won't be stored very long (more than a few days).
- Double-wrap pungent cheeses to protect other foods from their smells.
- Though not always practical, you can order cheese paper from various cheese supply companies listed in Appendix B, and keep a store on hand.
- Damp cheesecloth is also a good way to protect your cut cheese. Unfortunately, though, cheesecloth dries out very quickly, so unless you're able to keep it damp on a daily basis, avoid this technique, as dry cheesecloth will draw moisture from the cheese.

Whenever buying cheese at a counter, ask for an additional sheet of cheese paper to rewrap your cheese at home. Most cheese mongers are happy to give you an extra sheet or two. They are pleased you are that concerned about how to keep your cheese!

Scraping Cheese

When you taste at a cheese counter, the cheese monger will scrape the surface of the cheese, or make a fresh cut before cutting a piece to taste. The cheese looks perfectly fine before it's scraped or cut, so why do they do this? It's done so that you can taste the cheese, not the wrapping or any tastes that have developed on the surface of the cheese. If cheese has been wrapped in plastic, it will take on a hint of a plastic taste, and it has probably developed surface molds. It's a good idea to scrape your cheese at home, too. When you unwrap a cheese, cut off the amount you intend to eat, then hold the flat blade of a knife perpendicular to the cheese surface, and give it a few quick, firm scrapes. You don't want to remove a lot of cheese, only a thin outer layer. If mold has penetrated beyond this layer, then scrape a bit deeper, or use a cheese plane to remove the outer, moldy layer. Now your cheese is ready to enjoy!

Flipping Cheese

Again, the same principles of promoting graceful cheese aging apply equally at home as they do in a retail or cheese-aging facility. To maintain an even distribution of moisture, cheeses need to be flipped regularly so that moisture doesn't pool in any one spot. If you have cheese around the house for more than a day or two, especially a soft or semisoft cheese, turn it regularly so the moisture can redistribute itself. If you find a puddle of moisture or a damp spot, expose that area to the air for a while.

Freezing Do's and Don'ts

Most cheese experts cringe when you talk about freezing cheese. Think about it. All the care that's gone into keeping up the moisture content and developing just the right curd simply cannot be helped through the process of freezing. In fact, freezing draws the moisture out of the cheese, making it crumbly when brought back to room temperature. The first rule of freezing cheese, then, is don't. If you do, be prepared for an entirely different object to come out of your freezer. In other words, it may not resemble that piece of cheese you tasted before it was frozen.

On the other hand, people have been successfully freezing cheese for quite some time, and many chefs advocate keeping a bag of grated cheese in your freezer. And those large packages of grated cheese, sold in warehouse-style grocery stores, are certainly meant to be frozen.

If you must freeze your cheese, do it only for cheeses you intend to use for cooking, and grate the cheese first. Then store the cheese in airtight, plastic bags, and freeze it fast. It may take a bit of experimenting to determine which cheeses freeze well and which don't.

Where does the truth lie? It depends on whether you're using processed, grated, or blocks of cheese. Processed cheeses are cheese products combined, rather than separated milk, and can often withstand freezing without noticeable changes in texture or taste. Grated cheeses are usually meant to start out fairly dry and eventually be melted, so again, it's hard to notice a change in taste or texture when used in cooking. Avoid freezing blocks of cheese because they will lose too much moisture when frozen, and then end up crumbly and tasteless.

When Cheese Goes Bad

With all the talk about the benefits of aging cheese, how the aromas and flavors lengthen and become more complex with age, you may be wondering where (and if) cheese experts draw a line between aged and spoiled cheese. We've already established the smell of gym socks as being a good indicator of spoilage, the state of ooziness as being delightful, and the glory of all sorts of exotic molds. Interestingly, even with some pretty clear signals of cheeses gone bad, there are still cheese aficionados who consider virtually all stages of a cheese's life as different stages of ripeness.

As you come to know different cheeses, you will find yourself enjoying richer, more aged, and ever-more-pungent varieties. But this is different than enjoying cheeses that are truly spoiled. Generally speaking, here are signs of cheeses gone bad: pink or red mold; very salty or bitter tastes; dull gray paste; excessive gooiness; and excessive or very wet mold.

As mentioned previously, milk fermentation occurs when microorganisms change milk into acids, gas, and other compounds. To make cheese, some fermentation has to happen, but the wrong conditions or too much age will allow the acids and gas to take over, causing cheese to spoil.

Forgotten Cheese

Even with the best intentions of eating cheese every day, or most days, other foods occasionally take center stage, and sometimes, days or even weeks will go by and cheese will be forgotten. We've all done it: pulled open that deli drawer and reeled backward from the smell, or reached in and flicked around a couple of things with the hardness of a hockey puck. Most people throw these remnants of cheeses away as quickly as possible and vow restraint the next time they are tempted to buy too much cheese. But this (especially the restraint part) isn't always necessary. Forgotten cheese, in two words, is simply very aged, and it's time to apply your cheese-counter skills to your own cheese drawer.

First, look at the cheese. Most likely it's covered with an intense layer of mold or a thick bit of cheese that looks like a rind, and that's because the cheese has been working hard to protect itself against its environment. It's grown a protective layer that may mean the inside is still good to eat.

Second, feel the cheese. Is it soft and gooey, or firm and hard? Compare the feel to what you bought in the first place. Recall that soft cheeses become softer with age, and hard cheeses become harder with age. Unfortunately, the soft cheeses also develop unwanted bacteria and molds fairly quickly, so a particularly gooey soft cheese may need to be thrown away, but again, feel it for any sense of firmness or retention of its original texture.

Third, smell the cheese. At this stage its doubtful you need to bring it very close to your nose, but this is a crucial step. Strong ammonia, barnyard, or rotting vegetation smells are those to avoid, and indicate the cheese should be thrown away. However, if you don't detect any of these smells, you can safely move ahead.

QUESTION?

What is a saggy cheese?
A cheese sags when too much moisture has collected in one spot. The moisture creates a lump, and the cheese bulges out. Unfortunately, this also means that another part of the cheese has lost moisture and is too dry. Keep your cheese from sagging by turning it frequently and keeping the temperature and humidity within the best range for the cheese.

At this point you'll need to scrape, or clean, the cheese of its surface mold or hard, protective rind. Use the flat of a knife blade, or a cheese plane, or a knife if you need to cut large chunks away. When the cheese is clean, then you can taste it. If it's a soft cheese, you'll want to avoid extremely salty or bitter tastes. Other cheeses will most likely taste flat or dull, and the best thing to do with these is combine them with other forgotten cheeses by grating them or melting them, and using them over pasta or eggs, or incorporating them into a recipe that calls for cheese.

Cheese Cutlery

Cheese knives, wires, boards, and domes are designed to enhance and celebrate cheese. They make cheese cutting easier, and help retain a cheese's health when served. When serving a platter of cheese, it's good to provide one knife per cheese to preserve the purity of tastes, but also to make it easier to cut different cheeses. Sets of cheese knives are common in specialty kitchen stores, and are intended for cutting small, individual serving pieces from a platter of larger cheese pieces. Cheese knives fall into several categories:

- Thin, long knife blades work well because the surface of the knife doesn't touch very much of the cheese. Likewise, cheese knives with holes in the blade are designed to cut cleanly while avoiding any binding to the cheese surface. These knives are ideal for soft or semisoft cheese.
- Short paring knives or butter knives are good for cutting small wedges of soft cheese, and have the added advantage of spreading well.
- Knives with prongs or teeth serve as both knife and fork. The prongs are intended for picking up individual pieces of cheese.
- Short, angled knives with knobs on the end are used to cut hard grating cheeses, where often a rough-cut wedge will suffice.

Cheese wires are wonderful tools, as they cut cheese very cleanly and never stick to the cheese's surface. Many kitchen stores sell small wires attached to boards, and they work well on small pieces of cheese. Also look for wires on metal handles that can be dragged through or across cheese, and, if you will be cutting large pieces of cheese regularly, you might want to invest in a large, more industrial-style cheese wire.

Cheese boards should be easy to clean and sturdy enough to withstand the use of cheese knives. Wood is common, and very attractive for showcasing wedges of cheese. Slate and marble boards also make elegant presentations for cheese and have the advantage of staying cool. They can be refrigerated ahead of time and will retain this coolness for quite some time, thereby allowing cheese to gently arrive at room temperature and not become overheated. Many cheese boards come with glass domes, and these also help retain coolness and humidity while cheese is arriving at room temperature. They are also an effective deterrent to flies and pets.

When and How to Cut

How do you know when and how to cut cheese, especially for company? Is it wise to cut lots of small pieces, or better to leave the wedges mostly whole? What are the guidelines for cutting different shapes of cheeses?

First, cheese is best if cut just before it is eaten. This way, no additional moisture has a chance to leach out, and the flavor profile is at its fullest. This would imply you should leave fairly large pieces of cheese on each platter, with few if any precut slices, and many hosts go this route. The problem is that many guests are shy about cutting into a large wedge of cheese, and often these large pieces end as big as they began, with just a few timid slices missing. You are the best judge of your guests, but if you think the crowd will be shy, slice enough of each wedge so that each person can have one or two pieces before having to cut into the wedge. This will also show them how the cheese is meant to be cut, and they will be bolder when they have to cut the cheese themselves.

Many people are startled when they taste a cheese that's cold, and then taste the same cheese when it's come to room temperature. Cold cheese simply doesn't have the fullness of aromas and flavors that a cheese at room temperature does. So, don't forget to bring cheese to room temperature before cutting and serving. This ensures everyone's maximum enjoyment.

Small cheeses are often served whole, and several larger cheeses are often served as rounds like this: Brillat Savarin, a triple-cream, bloomy-rind cheese, is served whole. The top layer of bloomy rind is removed to reveal the buttery paste, and butter knives are provided for each guest. Large, round slices of Stilton are often served this way, with the middle broken up into chunks for easy nibbling. Brie is often wrapped and baked in phyllo dough, then opened from the top to reveal the creamy, warm center.

Here's a quick guide to how to cut different cheeses:

- Rectangular blocks of cheese should be cut and sliced along the narrower and shorter side.
- Triangular blocks of cheese should be cut along the long side, as they most likely were cut this way to begin with.
- Square blocks of cheese should be cut on one side, or cut into two large rectangles or triangles and then cut according to the previous rules.
- Wedges of cheese can be cut as you would a piece of pie.
- Small crottins or Chevrots, or small wheels of cheese, should be cut as you would a piece of cake. Cut a small wedge into one part, then continue cutting along those same lines. Pyramid-shaped cheeses should also be cut this way, with tall wedges notched from each corner.
- When in doubt, follow the shape of the cheese and be sure that each slice represents all the cheese has to offer.

An exception to these rules is Humboldt Fog, a goat's-milk cheese from Cypress Groves in California. This cheese is made as an eight-inch cake, with morning milk on the bottom layer, a vegetable ash layer as the filling, and evening milk on the top. Then the entire wheel is coated in vegetable ash and aged from the outside in as it develops a bloomy rind. The entire wheel looks like a velvety, white birthday cake, and when cut open, you see a thin layer of aged cheese just underneath the rind. A wedge of this type of cheese is best cut like a cake, so that everyone can enjoy the full complexity of morning and evening milk, along with the vegetable ash and bloomy rind.

Chapter 11

Cheese and Wine

"I'm having some people over for wine and cheese." How often have you said this? Pairing cheese and wine is so classic you may never have stopped to consider whether the cheeses and wines you're serving are truly a good match. Or, if you have a good pairing, perhaps you've stuck with it a little too long, and are now looking for something new. Either way, there's a huge world of wine and cheese to explore, and with a few hints, you'll find endless new possibilities.

A Matter of Taste and Balance

Next time you're wine or cheese tasting, take a moment to listen to your fellow tasters. No doubt you'll hear someone describe a cheese as strong that you find almost bland. Or you'll taste a tang where others taste sweet, or a few will talk about a slightly bitter finish, while others have bewildered looks. That's because everyone tastes things differently.

Follow your instincts. Everyone's palate registers flavors with different intensities, enabling them to recognize certain flavors but not others. That's the best argument there is for following your own instincts, because no matter what anyone else says, if you detect flavors that please you, you will like what you eat.

Wine and cheese have enormous ranges of aromas and flavors, some bold and others subtle. The fun thing about pairing wine and cheese is that they can work together to bring subtle flavors to the forefront, thereby opening up an entirely new world of aroma and taste. By focusing on the elements of wine and cheese that work together, the ones that provide each other the right balance, you'll find ways to open up these heady doors. When pairing wine and cheese:

- Match the body.
- Pair the complexity.
- Balance the primary flavors.

When wine and cheese are balanced, they both finish well. That is, you won't detect any bitterness, or too much saltiness, or those strange off tastes at the end.

Match the Body

The body (as opposed to the moisture) of cheese is made up of protein and fat, with fat providing a lot of the texture. This texture translates to mouthfeel. A high-fat cheese coats your mouth with a buttery mouthfeel. It's a little heavy and possibly creamy. A cheese lower in fat is lighter on your palate, coming and going more quickly, and generally has a cleaner, quicker mouthfeel.

The body of wine is largely determined by the amount of alcohol it has. The lower the alcohol content, the thinner the body. The higher the alcohol content, the fuller the body. Sometimes body is referred to as viscosity, which is a nice way to think about it because one way to guess if wine has low, medium, or high alcohol, is to swirl it in your glass and watch how it coats the glass. Viscous wines will leave a swirl of wine around the inside of a glass that then falls slowly. Wines without much viscosity will fall so fast you can't see them.

QUESTION?

What are "legs" in wine?

The term *legs* refers to the number and length of droplets falling inside the glass after wine is swirled. The longer and slower the droplets fall, the longer the legs. You can tell a lot about the level of alcohol in wine by the speed of its legs. Fast legs usually mean low alcohol content, and slow legs usually mean high alcohol.

When matching cheese and wine, one of the first things to think about is matching the fat and alcohol content, which is really just a matter of common sense. Alcohol feels viscous in the mouth and leaves a warm sensation behind, and high alcohol has a way of overpowering food, so high-alcohol wines generally pair better with heavy, robust meals because they don't overpower the food. That's why you often see high alcohol reds like Cabernet Sauvignon and Syrah paired with steak. With cheese it's the same thing. The cheeses best able to stand up to high levels of alcohol are the ones that are heaviest in body, that is, the heaviest in fat. Fat coats your mouth much as alcohol does, and the two, the fat and alcohol, are enough of a contrast to work quite well together. So before you think about aromas, flavors, and gentle nuances, think first about pairing moist, young cheeses (which are generally lower in fat) with low-alcohol wines, and drier, older cheeses (which are generally higher in fat) with higher-alcohol wines.

Pair the Complexity

Not all cheeses are created equal. Some are very simple and straight-forward. Their aroma matches their flavor, you get both immediately, and nothing's left behind. Others are as complicated as directions to your best friend's beach house. In the case of the house, you start out thinking you know the way and what it will be like, but as the road winds through turn after turn you question all your assumptions, and when you get there, hope-fully, it takes your breath away. Complex cheese, complicated directions, or fine wine; it's all the same. They start out one way, transform into some-thing else, and then become something you never expected. And just as you wouldn't want to cut a good journey short, you don't want to cut a cheese or wine short, and that's just what happens if you pair a simple cheese with a complex wine or a complex cheese with a simple wine. The complex taste will be cut short by the simpler taste. Instead, match cheese and wine com-plexities, and together they'll reveal the magic of the unexpected.

Balance the Primary Flavors

Avoid pairing tannin (the bitter chemical compounds found in grape skins and seeds) and salt. Have you ever eaten Brie while drinking a robust red wine? Did it leave you with the taste of rubbery burned mushrooms and the desire to rinse your mouth with clean, cool water? This is because robust red wines are high in tannin, and Brie is high in salt. Together these two collide. The two will never balance each other out.

Different wines have different levels of alcohol. The lowest you'll see is around 7 percent, and the highest in table wines (as opposed to dessert wines) is about 15 percent. Alcohol levels have to be printed on wine labels, but the actual alcohol content can be off by 1.5 percent either way. So, a wine label showing 11.5 percent alcohol can range from 10 to 13 percent.

Pair cheese with high-acid wine. Wine's sweetness comes from the natural sugar of grapes. However, when the grapes are fermented, yeast converts a lot of this sugar into alcohol, making the wine less sweet. That means sweet wines are lower in alcohol, and high-alcohol wines are more acidic. In wine terms this translates from acidic to sweet as follows: bone dry, dry, medium dry, medium sweet, sweet, or very sweet. Different types of wines need different balances between acidic and sweet to achieve their best flavors. Bone-dry wines are often crisp and refreshing, and very sweet wines almost fall away from the concept of wine. In wine terms, a wine with too little acid is called flabby.

Acidity is tasted just inside the outer edges of your tongue, and acidity makes your mouth water. The salt and sweet of cheese almost always partner well with acidic flavors in wine. The acidity will open your palate and make sweet and salty flavors rounder and fuller. So when you have a wine high in acidity, bring out the cheese.

What to do with a bitter wine: As far as salt and bitterness go, these two flavors, with a few notable exceptions, are rarely found in wine. Sherry is salty, making it an interesting cheese partner (more on that later). And some Italian wines (Brunello di Montalcino, Barolo, and Barbaresco) are made more interesting by a hint of bitterness at the end. When pairing these wines you simply have to be careful to avoid cheeses with any bitterness; otherwise the two tip the scale of bitterness from interesting to unappealing.

Pairing with the Whites

In general, white wines are easier to pair with cheese because they rarely contain any tannin. Because the grape skins and seeds are removed before the grapes are fermented, there is little material from which tannin will be drawn.

Chardonnay

Chardonnay grapes grow well in both cool and dry climates, and Chardonnay is aged both in oak barrels and in stainless steel vats. Each of these different climates and aging techniques imparts different levels of acid, alcohol, and flavors to the wine. Cool-climate Chardonnays are generally dry, giving them a certain crispness combined with clean fruit tones. Warm-climate Chardonnays are sweeter and rounder, often containing tones of honey and butterscotch. Oak-aged Chardonnays often have more character, meaning they contain complex tastes and aromas contributed by the oak and aging process, but because of the oak, they also have some tannin. Chardonnays make the cheese lover's job both difficult and intriguing, because what you learn with one Chardonnay and cheese won't necessarily apply to another set.

FACT

Some white wines are made by extracting the juice from the grapes before the skins and seeds are removed. This is called "rough cutting." The skins and seeds are removed before the juice is fermented into wine, but they leave behind some astringency, similar to that found with tannic wine. Your mouth gets a little dried out and puckered by the wine, and for this reason you should look for less salty cheeses to pair with rough cut white wines.

Dry, acidic, high-alcohol Chardonnays pair well with high fat, granular, and fruity cheeses such as Piave, aged Asiago, and Grana Padano. Sweet, low-alcohol Chardonnays pair well with Monterey jack, Emmental, and Camembert. Be sure to choose creamy, rather than salty, cheeses to balance the tannin in oak-aged Chardonnays.

The Blancs

Chenin Blanc grapes are sturdy, tough-skinned grapes naturally high in acidity. They produce crisp, dry, and sparkling wines, and generally have less than 12 percent alcohol. These wines are often aged in stainless steel vats, which gives them a bit of a steely quality. Chenin Blanc pairs well with Alpine cheeses such as Cantal and Comte, with young Goudas, and with some of the milder washed-rind cheeses such as Pont l'Eveque and Taleggio. Sauvignon Blanc grapes are high in acid making them crisp and tart. They often have distinctive grassy or herbaceous, aromas, and are generally low in alcohol.

Try playing off the herbal aromas and flavors with Sauvignon Blanc by pairing it with complementary herbal cheeses, such as a fresh goat cheese Fleur Verte, or the sheep's milk Brin D'Amour. You'll create some heady bouquets!

Pinot Gris

The Pinot Gris grape is almost mottled in color, ranging from grayish blue to brownish pink. The wine is relatively sweet, low in alcohol, and often has citrus tones. Light Pinot Grises are usually thin and pale, with herbal aromas. Robust Pinot Grises are fuller and rounder, with slightly more body and headier aromas.

The sweet fruitiness of Pinot Gris is a great match for natural-rind chèvres. Try pairing a Pinot Gris with a medium-aged Chevrot. Or try toning down the pepper of a robust, fruity blue cheese like Rogue River Blue with a full-body Pinot Gris.

QUESTION?

Why do wines sometimes taste hard or flinty?
When wine is aged in stainless steel vats, sometimes it picks up a steely sort of quality. It isn't a metallic taste; instead it's more of a mouthfeel, the sense that something steely or flinty has passed through your mouth. Sauvignon Blancs seem to be particularly prone to this mouthfeel.

Viognier

Viognier grapes are just as versatile as Chardonnays. They ripen in different climates, but where a Chardonnay has an almost bland taste, a Viognier bursts with vibrancy. You'll smell hints of jasmine, honeysuckle, cinnamon, and cloves, and you'll taste apricot, peach, lychee, and mango. Although they vary with climate, in general Viogniers have a mouth-coating viscosity mixed with a certain amount of sweetness.

The mouthfeel of a Viognier calls for rich, creamy, and salty cheeses. The fruitiness calls for pungency with a hint of smokiness, so pair some of your boldest and most complex cheese loves with this complex wine: Vacherin Mont d'Or, Gubbeen, or even Epoisse.

Riesling

Riesling grapes range from bone dry and crisp to ultrasweet, primarily because these grapes can be converted into successful wines at different stages of ripeness. In general, Rieslings are fairly acidic. When picked early, they produce lighter and drier wines. When picked a bit later, they produce sweeter wines, and when picked late they produce sweet and dense wines. In addition, Rieslings age fairly well, and when aged, their flavor profiles will change. Alcohol levels range from 7.4 to 12 percent.

When pairing Riesling with cheese pay attention to the dryness and acidity of the wine, then to the alcohol content. The higher in alcohol, the creamier the cheese you should use; the lower in alcohol, the thinner the cheese. Cheeses with hints of fruit and nuts often pair well. Try Piave, Grana Padano, aged Asiago, Cheshire, antique Gruyere, and medium-aged Goudas.

Gewurztraminer

Some people think of Gewurztraminer as a dessert wine because it is often sweet and spicy. The aroma of flowers is strong, and the flavors are heady, ranging from the delicate lychee to dense and ripe mangoes. The Gewurztraminer grape is a mutated form of the Traminer grape. Alsacian varieties are dry or sweet, but all are high in acidity, making them a good match for many cheeses. Their high alcohol content (around 13 percent) also makes them a good candidate for triple-cream cheese. Pair Gewurztraminers with relatively complex cheeses like medium-aged Asiago to washed-rind reblechon to medium-aged Goudas.

Pairing with the Reds

Red wines get most of their color during fermentation, when the natural heat generated by the fermenting process extracts the color from the grape skin. As a result, red wines almost always have some degree of tannin in them, which makes them a harder match for cheese. When aged in oak barrels, red wines will have rounder, more subtle tastes. When aged in stainless steel vats, the flavors will be steelier, more fruity and simpler.

FACT

The main difference between a red and a rose is the length of time the skins ferment with the juice. For roses, that time is very short, resulting in lower tannin, less fruitiness, and a brisker mouthfeel. Pair roses with lighter cheeses that don't have much fruitiness, like Jarlsberg or fresh Asiago, or a young Gouda such as Vlaskaas.

Merlot

The name Merlot, rolls off your tongue almost like the word *mellow*, and that's exactly what it is: a mellow, friendly sort of wine. The grapes are dark blue and relatively thin skinned, which means they contain low levels of tannin, and ripen early. Merlots are low in acidity and have tones of plum, black cherry, currant, violet, and rose (some say Merlot smells like fruitcake). Merlots have a soft, almost velvety mouthfeel, and usually have medium-high levels of alcohol.

Sheep's-milk cheeses, with their high fat and mellow nutty flavors, work well with Merlots. Try Ossau Iraty, Manchego, or Roncal. A particularly fruity Merlot pairs well with a mild Cheddar such as Lancashire, or Cheshire.

Pinot Noir

The Pinot Noir grape is thin skinned and delicate, requiring a long, cool growing season to ripen. The payoff is in the texture, which is full and light at the same time, almost like liquid silk. High in alcohol, without being too acidic or tannic, Pinots can be wonderful matches for many different types of cheese.

Play off the Pinot Noir's aromas of raspberries, cherries, and subtle bits of smoke when pairing Pinot Noirs with cheese. Go for medium levels of complexity to full complexity, and lean slightly to the sweet end of things. Antique Gruyere, Redwood Hill Bucheret, Piave, and Alsacian Muenster are all worth a try.

Syrah

Syrahs come from black, thick-skinned grapes that thrive both in cool climates and on sunny slopes. Young Syrahs are deeply colored, tannic, and have a distinct spiciness. Aged Syrahs are fruitier than they are spicy, with blackberry and plum tones, and often have a bit of smokiness about them. They tend to have medium acidity and high alcohol, which leaves a clean but round feel in your mouth. Pair Syrahs with flavorful, fruity, and creamy cheese, such as Beaufort, Comte, and aged Goudas.

Sangiovese

If you're looking for tannin and acidity look no further than Sangiovese, but know that good vintners working with this grape balance its tannic acidity by bringing out whole orchards of fruit. You'll find deep cherry tones, raspberries, blackberries, and blueberries in this wine. Sangioveses have medium to high alcohol, and are relatively dry. This is a traditional wine of Italy. Try pairing it with some of Italy's favorite cheeses: Taleggio, Pecorino Renero, and Piave.

ALERT!

Wine tannin makes your mouth pucker and feel stripped of all its moisture. Salt accentuates this effect, which is why cheese (most of which is high in salt) rarely pairs well with high-tannin wines. Grape skins and seeds ferment with red wine (and are later skimmed off), giving red wine its color and tannin.

Cabernet Sauvignon

Cabernet grapes are small, black, and very tough skinned, and they produce some of the most tannic wine. They are rarely intended to be drunk as young wines; instead, the best Cabernet Sauvignons are aged until their tannin mellows out, which allows deeper flavors to emerge. In youth, a Cabernet Sauvignon will have tones of black currants, bell peppers, chocolate, and spice, and be very acidic and tannic. As it ages, hints of tobacco, blackberries, and other, deeper flavors emerge.

The high tannin of a Cabernet makes pairing cheese difficult, and a matter of individual taste and experimentation. But the complexity of this wine means you can pair it with some of your favorite, most complex cheeses. Try robust, sweet, glossy sorts of cheese like Black Foil Appenzeller, a medium-aged Epoisse (too aged, and the salt will clash with the tannin), Roquefort, or Zamorano.

Zinfandel

Zinfandel comes from the Primitivo grape and varies considerably depending on the objectives of the winemaker. The results can be light and almost simple in taste, with high acids and tannins, or complex, fruity, and spicy. Most Zinfandels are high in both acid and alcohol.

Zinfandels are big wines that need to be paired with flavorful, robust cheeses. Try antique Gruyere, Ossau Iraty, Roncal, Montgomery's Cheddar, and Garrotxa.

Pairing with Dessert Wines

What sets dessert wines apart from others is their concentrated sweetness. Some sweet wines are the result of fermented late-harvest grapes (which are very sweet), and others are the result of a fungus. Brandy is added to wine in Portugal, which turns it into Port, and Sherry is made from yeast cultures.

FACT

Dessert wines are much higher in alcohol than other wines. This is mostly due to the fact that other alcohols are added. Generally speaking, dessert wines have anywhere from 17 to 20 percent alcohol, but like other wines, what's listed on the label has to be only within 1.5 percent of the real alcohol content.

Madeira

Madeira is made in Portugal, usually from white wine. It came about when winemakers began shipping over long distances and found that between the motions of the ship and variations in climate during the journey, the wines would not last. They added distilled cane sugar to the wine, and then learned that if the wine was heated it tasted even better. Soon Madeira, a decidedly sweet Portuguese wine, was developed.

Don't hold back when you pair cheese with Madeira. All that sweetness just loves good cream and salt. Try Roquefort, triple-cream Brillat Savarin, or a rich and a creamy sheep's milk, such as Zamorano.

Port

Port, like Madeira, originated in Portugal. More than eighty different grape varieties are used in making port. However, instead of stabilizing the wine with distilled cane sugar, brandy is added during fermentation, which results in a sweet, high-alcohol wine. There are many different types of port, but all can benefit from a piece of cheese.

You'll never go wrong pairing the creamy, salty, piquant Stilton blue with port. It's an age-old tradition. Then try branching out a bit with other creamy blue cheeses like Point Reyes Farmstead Blue or Saint Agur. Triple-cream Brillat Savarin or St. Andre will be lovely, as will some Buratta.

Sauternes

Sauternes are made from grapes that have developed an edible fungus. The fungus shrivels the grape, leaving the sweetest part behind, almost like a raisin, and from this partially fermented grape, great Sauternes are made.

Treat a Sauterne as you would a round Gewurztraminer. Try it with pungent washed-rind cheeses, bodacious blues, and four-year-old Goudas. Epoisse, Roquefort, and Saenkaenter will all work.

Sherry

Sherry is another alcohol-fortified wine. However, the fermentation is achieved through two different strains of mold. Fino sherry is made in open casks that develop a thin film of yeast and a salty, briny, nutty sort of high-alcohol wine. Then brandy is added to the mix. Fino sherry is normally bone dry and crisp, and has an almost salty tang.

Oloroso sherries oxidize as they age. That is, they don't develop the yeast layer on top. The oxidation gives the sherry a nutty, smoky, and almost earthy sort of taste. With the added brandy, this is a full-flavored brew.

Pair fino sherries with nutty, buttery sorts of cheese: medium-aged sheep's-milk pecorinos or Zamorano, and aged goat cheeses like Majorero and Garrotxa. Pair Oloroso sherries with rich, creamy, or smoked cheese of any milk type: triple-cream Brillat Savarin, smoky Idiazabal, or Midnight Moon goat Gouda.

Pairing with Champagne and Sparkling Wines

Pair a wonderful, ripe, triple-cream cheese with Extra Brut Champagne, and you'll never again want one without the other. The effervescence of Champagne and sparkling wines is refreshing and palate cleansing, a perfect match for the buttery, almost whipped-cream nuances of the most decadent triple creams.

Champagne

For the most part, Champagnes are made from Chardonnay, Pinot Noir, or Pinot Meunier grapes, and sometimes mixes of two or three. Almost all Champagnes are high in acidity, and the sweetness of Champagne comes mostly from added sugar instead of the ripeness of the grapes. Sugar combined with effervescence and relatively low alcohol change the way you pair cheeses with Champagne (as opposed to wine). The cleansing effect of Champagne bubbles changes everything. Creamy, full-fat cheeses are refreshed by Champagne, and the added sweetness in Champagne creates a wonderful balance for rich, creamy blues.

Go for the gusto when pairing Champagne and cheese. Rich, creamy, triple-cream Explorateur is spectacular with an Extra Brut, and try a Stilton with Demi-Sec or Doux.

When pairing cheese with Champagne, pay attention to the sweetness level of the Champagne. Extra Brut is the driest and least sweet, followed by Brut, then Extra Dry, then Sec, Demi-Sec, and, finally, Doux, which is very sweet.

Sparkling Wines

In France, real Champagne is name protected and can only be made from Chardonnay, Pinot Noir, or Pino Meunier grapes, or some combination of those grapes. Any other effervescent wine is a sparkling wine. This is a little confusing in the United States because, for a long time, several large American Champagne makers have used the name Champagne more loosely, and many people have come to regard all effervescent wines as a form of Champagne. The good news is that sparkling wines are as complex and varied as Champagne and easy to understand once you understand the grapes they're from. Here are a few you should know about for cheese:

Sparkling Brut Roses are made from the grapes of France's Loire Valley. They are refreshing, with hints of strawberry and some minerality. The lemony tang of a light goat's-milk cheese pairs beautifully with this sparkling wine. Try pairing it with a Chevrot or a goat's-milk Brie.

Moscato d'Asti is sparkling wine made from the grapes of Italy's Piedmont region. It is lightly sweet and very refreshing, making it a good match for pecorinos of all ages, fruity table cheese, such as Piave or Taleggio, and creamy Bries.

American sparkling wines are plentiful, delicious, and far reaching. You will rarely find a mismatch between Chardonnay- or Pinot Noir–based sparkling wines and creamy cheese. If you're pairing cheese with a Blanc-based grape, remember to take into account the crispness and citrus tones of the wine, and avoid cheeses with strong salt, pungency, or marked sharpness.

Pairing with Old World Wines

Many rich, intriguing, and heady flavors emerge when you pair wine and cheese by region. The elements of *terrior* come into their own as the same climate, similar soils, minerals, natural vegetation, temperatures, humidity, and water all contribute in unique ways to the cheeses and wines of each region. Together, cheese and wine accentuate each other's fruit, floral and herbal aromas, minerality, and depth.

France

The Bordeaux region is one of France's most prolific wine-producing regions. The whites are blends of Sauvignon Blanc and Semillon, and the reds are blends of Cabernet Sauvignon, Merlot, Cabernet Franc, Malbec, and Petit Verdot. Pair the whites with light cow's- and sheep's-milk cheeses of the Aquitaine, and the reds with some of the washed-rind cheeses of the Aquitane and lower Pyrenees, like Saint Nectaire and Bethmal.

You can often tell a New World wine from an Old World wine by the name. New World wines are usually named after individual grapes, like Chardonnay, Riesling, Pinot Noir, and Cabernet Sauvignon. In most Old World wine countries, like France, Italy, and Spain, wines are named after regions or districts, and often contain blends of several different grapes.

A delightful range of white and red wines come from France's Burgundy region, which is east of the Jura and slightly south of the Loire. Whites are generally from Chardonnay grapes, and reds are Pinot Noirs or Beaujolais, a light and fruity red from the Gamay grape, which is low in tannin. The Beaujolais is almost light enough to treat as a white wine, so your pairing choices are many and varied. Pair these wines with cheeses from the Bourgogne and Jura such as Beaufort, Comte, and Eppoise.

Look for earthy, bold whites and reds from the Rhone region. Whites are often made from Viognier grapes, and reds from Syrah and Grenache grapes. Pair with some of the boldest cheeses from the Jura like aged Comte and antique Gruyere.

Loire Valley wines are usually white, coming from Chenin Blanc and Sauvignon Blanc grapes. They pair beautifully with young natural-rind chèvres.

Alsacian wines are fruity, high in alcohol, and full bodied. They are made from Riesling, Gewurztraminer, and Pinot Gris grapes, and often can stand up to some of the most pungent and salty cheeses from the region, like Alsacian Muenster.

Italy

In Italy there are twenty wine regions. As you start to pair Italian wines and cheeses, start with three regions: the Piedmont, Tuscany, and the Veneto.

In Piedmont, as mentioned previously, don't miss Barolo and Barbaresco, two robust and bone-dry reds with a hint of bitterness on the end. Match these up against Dolce Latte Gorgonzola for a zippy Italian dessert.

In Tuscany, look for Brunello di Montalcino, another big, fruity, tannic wine with lots of alcohol. Italian table cheese like Piave pairs well with this wine, as does a medium-aged pecorino.

Spain

Spain's Rioja wines are renowned for both whites and reds made from Tempranillo, Garnacha, and Cabernet Sauvignon grapes. Only when you get to the Cabernet Sauvignon–based Riojas do you need to worry about tannin. Rioja wines pair well with Garrotxa, Ibores, and Zamorano.

Spanish Albarinos are a little harder to find, but you might have more luck finding wines from the La Mancha region, which are based on grapes that survive windy and sometimes dry climates. They have thick skins and minimal amounts of juice, but often produce creamy mouthfeels, and complex apricot, peach, and citrus flavors. High acidity makes them clean and vibrant, and better in their youth. Pair with Majorero and Manchego, and don't forget the *membrillo* (fruit paste made from quince).

Chapter 12

Cheese, Beer, and Spirits

Ever try a sharp Cheddar with a pale ale? How about green olives stuffed with piquant blue cheese in a martini? Cognac and aged Gouda? Don't be fooled into thinking wine is the only beverage for cheese. In fact, it's generally harder to pair wine with cheese than with beer. And when it comes to high-alcohol spirits and cheese, with attention to just a few things, you'll find they complement each other perfectly.

Beer and Cheese Harmonize and Contrast

The story of beer and cheese is another testament to the wisdom of ancient people and their discoveries of food. No one knows when beer was discovered, but as with cheese, evidence of beer making is found in ancient Egypt, right around the same time people were figuring out all the things a person could do with grain. At the same time they were making cheese and wine, they were making bread, cereal, and beer, and though no one can say these ancient brewmasters, chefs, and cheese makers were purposely looking for foods and beverages that complemented each other, they certainly had a knack for finding them.

FACT

Pairing cheese and beer is a balancing act. Balance high-fat cheese with high-alcohol beer, and low-fat cheese with low-alcohol beer. Balance salty cheese with nutty beer, and pungent cheese with hoppy beer. Sweet cheeses balance delightfully with acidic beer, and fruity cheeses often go well with fruity beers.

Fast-forward to isolated farmhouses in Europe and America, where people grew acres upon acres of grain and kept cows for milk, butter, and cheese, and you'll find several centuries of people dedicated to perfecting the subtle and complex flavors and properties of brews and cheese alike. From them, the world's gained harmonious combinations of nutty, roasted, and sweet beers that round out and finish nutty, buttery, and sweet cheese flavors. Effervescent, dry, and fruity beers balance a triple-cream cheese just right. And washed-rind cheeses? The strident ones chock-full of pungency? Line them up with a hoppy stout to accentuate the hidden tones of fruit. With a little information on what makes beer sweet, bitter, acidic, effervescent, and alcoholic, you'll easily find your way to enjoying cheese and beer with all the gusto of your wise ancestors.

Beer Ingredients

Beer is made up of four ingredients: water, grain, hops, and yeast. The mineral content, acidity, and alkaline properties of water all contribute to a beer's flavor. Barley, corn, rice, wheat and rye are the principal grains used, and each imparts different flavors. There are many different varieties of hops, and again, different growing conditions impart different degrees of flavor. And though specific strains of yeast are used for beer (brewer's yeast), each tastes different, affects the tastes of the other ingredients differently, and when wild yeast is used, you get a little wildness in the brew.

QUESTION?

Is it really the water that makes a beer unique?
Beer is 90 percent water, and in different places water has different flavor profiles. For example, brewmasters generally avoid highly chlorinated water or water with distinct metallic tones, and when they find a source of clean, sweet water, the kind that doesn't introduce unwanted tastes, they use it.

What Makes Beer Sweet

The sweetness in beer comes from the grain. Whether the grain used is barley, corn, rice, wheat, or rye, the grain is all crushed, mashed, or processed to release the carbohydrates and convert them into sugars. Barley is the most common grain used to make beer, and most barley is malted before being mashed. Malting involves steeping barley kernels in water until they sprout, then drying them. During malting, sugars and starches begin to differentiate from the whole grain. The following types of unmalted and malted barley are used to make different types of beer:

- Roasted barley is unmalted barley roasted at high temperatures. It tastes a little like bitter coffee.
- Malted barley is barley grain sprouted in water and then dried.

- Black malt (also called Black Patent) is roasted malted barley, and is primarily used in small amounts to produce dark, almost black beer colors.
- Chocolate malt (no, it's not *really* chocolate) is malted barley roasted less time than black malt. It is lighter in color (dark brown), aromatic, and sweeter than black malt.
- Crystal malt (or caramel malt) is malted barley dried in two stages that cause the sugar to crystallize. Later, during fermentation, these sugar crystals remain intact. Therefore, small additions of crystal malt add caramel, toffee, and almost baked-cookie tones to beer.

By itself, barley produces dense, almost heavy beers. That's why brewmasters often look to other grains when making lighter beers, or beers with special flavor components such as fruit flavors or particular flavors of spice.

Other grains are most frequently used in small amounts and added to unmalted or malted barley to contribute lightness and introduce other flavors:

- Corn, by itself, is basically a neutral beer flavor, but it acts to lighten other flavors and the body of beer. It can contribute to a smooth beer finish.
- Rice is often used by commercial breweries because it is neutral in flavor, ferments cleanly, and also contributes to a beer's lightness.
- Wheat is used in malted and unmalted forms, and both will contribute bread flavors. Wheat also acts to lighten beer.
- Rye contributes dryness and crispness to beer, so it tones down the sweetness of barley.

Lots of other grains are used from time to time, and each imparts the essence of its flavors and properties. Heavy, gelatinous grains will make beer heavier and more viscous, and lighter grains will do the opposite.

Bitter Balances Sweet

Have you ever tasted a bland apple? The kind you eat because you should be eating an apple? How about a really tasty, crunchy apple? Chances are the apples you really like are sweet and tangy all at the same time. That's because the tang balances the sweetness, and the two work in tandem to open your taste buds and satisfy them. So it is with hops and grain. By itself, fermented grain would be almost sickeningly sweet, but when paired with the bitterness of hops, a little bit of magic takes place. Hops add just the amount of bitterness needed to tame the grain, and they help keep beer from spoiling.

There are hundreds of different varieties of hops, and each thrives in different soils, climates, and terrain. For example, Mt. Hood hops, grown in Washington, make excellent lagers with full, good flavors. Mittelfrueh hops, grown in different parts of the United States and Germany, are herbal, spicy, and earthy in flavor, and are often used to give German lagers their unique tastes.

Fermentation and Flavor

If you were looking for all the historical connections between cheese, wine, bread, and beer, you wouldn't fail to come across the work of Louis Pasteur again. The same Frenchman who discovered pasteurization, the process of heating wine and milk to kill bacteria, also discovered the properties of yeast that cause fermentation. Coming slightly before Pasteur was Emil Hansen, a Danish man who identified and isolated yeasts that worked best for fermenting beer.

Up until that time, uncovered kegs of wort were set out to ferment, and were often stirred with the same wooden paddle that had stirred unfermented beer for hundreds of years. Most likely, yeast strains beneficial to fermenting grew on the paddles, and unbeknownst to the brewmaster, magically hastened the process. Even without magic paddles, however, yeast naturally forms on fruit- or grain-based liquid, and is responsible for fermenting your juice when it's been left out too long. Yeast converts sugar to alcohol, introduces carbon dioxide that carbonates beer, and adds a whole range of flavor. For today's beer making, three types of yeast prevail: ale, lager, and wild yeast.

- Ale yeast ferments in relatively warm temperatures (55–75°F), and is used to make ale beer.
- Lager yeast ferments at cooler temperatures (32–55°F), and usually produces a smoother beer. The need to keep lager yeast cool requires refrigerated vats and more complex procedures than are needed for ales.
- Wild yeast ferments at any temperature and forms on the surface of uncovered kegs. Commercial brewmasters in Belgium make Lambic beer with wild yeasts that usually produce very complex fruit flavors.

FACT

Once the mixture of barley, corn, rice, wheat, rye, or a combination of some of these ingredients is mixed with hops, it is called a wort. *Wort* is a term referring to this mixture before the yeast is added, when it is still unfermented and nonalcoholic.

More Flavors

The particular properties of fermented wort are an ideal base for all sorts of flavors, allowing brewmasters and home brewers all sorts of room to experiment. Here are some of the other flavors you'll often find in beer:

- **Sugars:** Sugars of all types can be added at various stages. To add sweetness and lighten beer, corn sugar is added, and to get toffee and buttery sweetness, molasses is good.
- **Honey:** Honey will contribute the flavors of its origins. A robust honey, such as sage honey, will contribute sweet and savory hints of sage. Clover and alfalfa honeys, which aren't strong in floral or herbal tones, contribute mostly sweetness.
- **Fruits:** Peaches, mangoes, cherries, you name it, all sorts of fruits contribute their unique flavors to beer.
- **Vegetables:** You might find flavors from chili peppers, peas, parsnips, or pumpkins in the occasional beer.

Also look for herbs and spices: cinnamon, coriander, ginger, heather, juniper berries, Kaffir lime leaf, licorice, orange peel, spruce tips, yarrow, cardamom, cloves, allspice, nutmeg, and peppercorns can all flavor beer. You're sure to find others as well. Really, there are few limits to the flavors you'll find in beer. And yes, on occasion, you'll find chocolate- or coffee-flavored beer too.

Texture, Alcohol, and Complexity

When it comes to pairing beer and cheese, you'll want complementary mouthfeels and degrees of complexity. That is, if you have a creamy, rich Brie, you'll want to pair it with a particularly effervescent beer, because the bubbles of an effervescent beer will cleanse the buttery mouthfeel of a creamy Brie, making your palate ready and eager for another bite.

When pairing cheese with beer, be sure to match up the titans: high-fat cheeses with high-alcohol beer, and complex cheeses with complex beer. A lowfat cheese or a cheese short on flavor will taste bland in the presence of a complex, high-alcohol beer, and a high-fat, complex cheese will overpower a mild, low-alcohol beer.

Beers vary considerably in carbonation, depending on the type of grain, yeast, and methods of brewing used. As you experiment with beer and cheese pairings, pay attention to the levels of carbonation, and soon you'll be able to associate ales, lagers, and Lambic beers with the amount of fizz or pop they carry in each mouthful.

Pairing with Ales

Ales are top fermenting, meaning the yeast works in temperate climates and doesn't need to be chilled. Ales are quite common, and home brewers are able to experiment easily with making them. Ales originated in England and

Belgium, and now there are thousands of ale brewers throughout the world. If you love ales, you'll swoon when you pair them with the cheeses suggested in the following sections. Then take it further with all sorts of specialty ales and yummy cheeses!

Three British Ales

Mild ales are low in hops and alcohol, making them low in bitterness and good companions to light food. Mild ales pair well with mild cheeses that are also very eatable. Try mild ales with Wensleydale, Chantal, or Bellwether Carmody.

Bitter ales vary greatly, but as named, they are known for their bitter hop tones. They can also be quite sweet, sour, and even salty, and are generally low in alcohol. Bitter-ale pairing with cheese will take some experimenting. Pay attention to low alcohol by pairing it with cheeses lower in fat. Then take into account bitter ale's sweet, bitter, and salty characteristics. Contrasts are best here, so choose cheeses low in fat, perhaps a little tangy, and with mild saltiness, something along the lines of Vella Dry Jack.

Pale ales are named to distinguish their amber-colored brew from the dark, almost black stouts and porters. They are robust in taste, with hoppy (sometimes bitter tones), yeasty, herbaceous, and savory flavors. They are dry, and therefore not too sweet, and often you'll find them listed as Burton Ale (named after the English town ale originated in), or India Pale Ale (this was the brew most frequently shipped to India). Pale ales harmonize well with sharp Cheddars. Try Cabot Cheddar, Black Diamond Cheddar, or Beecher's Flagship Cheddar with them.

American Ales

All types of ales are made in the United States, and all reflect the region where the hops are grown, the water used, and the distinct characteristics of the grains added. Your best bet is to pay attention to the type of ale (mild, bitter, or pale); then pay attention to fruit, floral, and grain tones that come through on the nose. Pair with cheeses according to harmonizing or contrasting tastes. For example, an American cherry ale, made along the lines of a mild ale, harmonizes beautifully with a goat's-milk Brie. Or if you're looking for contrast, try fruity ale with sweet mascarpone. Like bread and Swiss cheese? Pair wheat ale with Emmental.

Porters

Porters are characterized by the use of roasted or toasted malted barley. They are very dark in color, some almost black, and often possess coffee, cocoa, or roasted tones. The reaction of yeast with roasted or toasted barley adds fruit flavors. Porters have a fairly low alcohol content.

Porters pair according to their roasted, nut, and fruit tones. Antique Gruyere, which is nutty and fruity, complements Porter beautifully, as do the fruity tones of an aged Comte, or the somewhat lighter tones of a Beaufort.

ALERT!

Don't be surprised to hear people from other countries describe American beer in much the same terms as they describe Americans: brash, hoppy, assertive, and perhaps a bit fresh.

Stouts

Stout beer is known for its bitterness and roasted flavors and, like Porter, is almost black in color. This intense brew often brings forward flavors of chocolate, caramel, and yeast, and is thick and creamy. Look for dry stouts reminiscent of amontillado sherry, and sweet stouts with milky, fruitcake flavors. Dry stouts are mellowed a bit by a semihard cow's-milk cheese like Montgomery's Cheddar. Sweet stouts make a divine and unusual afternoon treat when paired with a creamy blue cheese.

Pairing with Lagers

Lagers are much more uniform in flavor profile than ales, partly because lager yeasts produce cleaner and rounder flavors that do not lend themselves to widely ranging complexity. When partnering with cheese, you'll pay less attention to the range of flavors and more attention to other elements, like alcohol content.

Dark Lagers

These are made with Black Patent and chocolate malted barleys. Lager yeasts have a mellowing affect on malted barleys, and usually tone the roast, chocolaty flavors to mellow spiciness. Alcohol content ranges from 3 to 4 percent by weight. Dark lagers lend themselves to contrast. Try pairing with slices of fresh buffalo mozzarella, Ossau Iraty, Petit Basque, or Breibou.

Pilsners

These beers are characterized by a clear golden color, with well-developed malts, solid hop tones, and some floral aromas. They are usually light and dry, with good effervescence. Alcohol contents can run higher in Pilsners as compared to other beers. They pair well with a creamy Brie de Meaux, young to medium-aged Goudas, and nutty Cheddars.

Bocks

Bocks are usually strong lager beers smooth in texture, strong in malts, and occasionally sweet. Alcohol content is usually fairly high. Bock beer has enough malt and sweetness to stand up to a flavorful smoked Gouda, or toasted Scarmoza on wheat bread.

Pairing with Specialty Beers

Though many Europeans would argue against putting Lambic and wheat beers in a category together, in the United States, where many people are most familiar with the light and crisp flavors of Coors and Budweiser, Lambic and wheat beers have an almost cult following. Steam beers appeared in Europe and America during the industrial revolution, prompting some to believe they were made with steam-engine power. However, their steam comes from using uncooled lager yeasts.

Belgian Lambic Beer

Belgian Lambic beer is distinguished by the use of wild yeasts. Spontaneous fermentation occurs as the result of leaving the beer in uncovered vats and allowing wild yeasts to develop of their own accord. In addition, the grain is 30 percent wheat and malted barley, and some describe the taste of Lambic beer as reminiscent of a fino sherry or a hard cider. Flavors are all over the place, but often fruity. Cherries and raspberries are often added as flavoring, and combined with earthy aromas and tartness, Lambic beer is in a class of its own. Lambics pair well with sharp cheeses like Cheddar and aged Gouda, and with fruitier Lambics, try full-flavored Brie de Meaux and Camembert.

FACT

The name *steam beer* comes from the way this beer hisses while it ferments. With steam beer, lager yeasts are fermented in shallow tanks that allow cooler temperatures, and as the fermentation takes place, the mixture hisses and sighs, as if powered by a large, gentle locomotive machine.

Wheat Beers

Wheat beers are made by adding substantial amounts of wheat to the barley mash. The results are particularly thirst quenching, low in alcohol, and sharply acidic from lactic fermentation. Wheat beers pair well with semihard cheeses like Cantal, Laguiole, medium-aged sheep's milk, and young Goudas.

Steam Beers

Steam beers often vary in flavor more than traditional lager beers, often have distinct malt flavors, and take on unique fruity characteristics. Pair steam beers with robust nutty cheese like Gruyere or a hard, fruity table cheese like Piave.

Pairing with Spirits

Some people blanch at the idea of pairing high-alcohol drinks with food because they claim the alcohol wipes out their taste buds, making the food impossible to taste. To some extent this is true. For example, if you wanted to fully enjoy the complexity of a goat's-milk crottin or the subtly long flavors of a raw sheep's-milk cheese from the Pyrenees, it would be a mistake to blot the flavors with an extra-dry martini. However, think for a moment of fondue. That dash of Kirsch, the exquisite and very dry distillation from cherries, adds the needed alcohol to lighten up the density of the cheese and bring the flavors to life. And the goat's milk in a Banon is drenched in cognac before being wrapped in chestnut leaves. On occasion, spirits are just the right touch. The trick is to use them with care, to think of spirits as a way to make cheese sparkle.

The color of a beer is a clue to the type of beer. Brewers use a Standard Reference Method (SRM) to measure color intensity: Pilsners are straw and golden in color. Pale ales are amber colored, dark beers are brown, and stout is black. Interestingly, beers with 50 percent wheat are almost white in color.

Martinis and Blues

Whether you make your martinis with gin or vodka, both liquors have the effect of taking your breath away. One sip, and the heat of the gin or vodka travels immediately to the back of your throat, its volatile vapors escaping upward to your olfactory nerves, the heat of the liquid tracing a path on the way down. What kind of cheese stands up to something like this? Certainly not a mild little square of Monterey jack. You'd hardly taste it at all. Gin and vodka are both made from distilled grains (or sometimes potatoes in the case of vodka and juniper berries in the case of gin), and again, the elements of pairings, boldness to boldness, high alcohol to high fat, come into play. Think of cheeses that immediately fill your senses with their own essence, and ones with enough fat to challenge that amount of alcohol, such as Brin d'Amour, Idiazabal, or Pepato.

Scotch and Whiskey

Thinking about the ingredients of Scotch and whiskey brings you right back to beer. These spirits originate the same way as beer, with barley, malted barley, rye, malted rye, wheat, and corn. However, instead of being fermented, they are distilled. The alcohol is drawn out of the mash in a much purer form. Nevertheless, these spirits are influenced by their original choice of grain, and often they are aged in oak barrels. Their nutty, caramel, thick, oaken, aromatic, and smoky tones are all prime candidates for delicious pairings with cheese. Again, match robust flavors, and high fat to high alcohol content. One of the classic pairings of all time is perfectly ripe Stilton and whiskey.

Rum

Rum is in a class of its own. Distilled from sugarcane and aged in oak casks, it has distinctly sweet, fruity, rich, and almost smoky tastes. The key here is to play off the sweetness of this liquor and treat it like a dessert. Rum drizzled over mascarpone is truly decadent, and with a fruity blue, like Roaring Forties Blue, you have a virtual fruit cocktail.

FACT

Gin and vodka pair well with sharp, creamy, piquant blue cheese. Try this with your next martini. Take a large, crisp martini olive, stuff it with a healthy dollop of piquant blue, and put it in a martini. Voila! Have your breath spirited away on the blues.

Cognac

Cognac is distilled wine, made from grapes. It has the breathiness and heat of vodka, the sweetness of sherry, and the subtle hints of caramel and nuts. Pair a special cognac with Epoisse, or a four-year-old aged Gouda, something along the lines of Saenkaenter, and you won't look back.

Kirsch

As mentioned previously, Kirsch is the distilled juice of the small black cherry. It originated near the Black Forest of Germany. It is breathless and sweet, refreshing, and phenomenally crisp. It's a classic ingredient of fondue, but try it as an aperitif with a piquant blue, or with a dessert of figs topped with a Gariotin.

Epoisse is washed in a mixture of brine and Cognac as it drains and ages. As it ages, the cheese is gently washed in Cognac and develops its distinct orange- and rust-colored rind. Next time you're about to taste Epoisse, smell it first and see if you can detect the Cognac notes.

Kahlua

Kahlua is a coffee liquor, rich, creamy, and sweet. It has a fairly low alcohol content, making it a good match for the cheeses made with partially skimmed milk. Antique Gruyere, which pairs so well with coffee, is an excellent choice as a pairing for Kahlua, and paired with Saenkeanter, Kahlua will knock your socks off.

Cheese and Menus

13

Ricotta Spread

Serves 4

1 cup fresh ricotta

¼ cup dates, finely chopped

¼ teaspoon cinnamon

¼ teaspoon freshly ground nutmeg

1 vanilla bean, scraped

Ricotta spreads are terrific and healthy toppings for toast. Substitute dried apricots, dried pears, or raisins for the dates, and try it on different types of toast: sourdough, whole wheat, or walnut levain.

Combine all ingredients in a food processor or blender and process until smooth.

Goat Cheese and Tomato Frittata

Serves 4

1 tablespoon extra-virgin olive oil

¼ cup white onion, finely chopped

1 large, ripe tomato, cut into small chunks

8 large eggs, lightly beaten

½ cup fresh goat cheese, crumbled

1 teaspoon fresh lemon thyme, finely chopped

½ teaspoon kosher salt

¼ teaspoon freshly ground pepper

The zing of goat cheese, ripe tomatoes, and lemon thyme are sure to get your Sunday brunch off to a delicious start. Or, serve this frittata as a refreshing summer dinner on a hot day.

1. Heat the olive oil in a 10-inch non-stick skillet over medium heat. Add the onions and sauté until almost transparent, then add the tomatoes and heat until the juices are almost absorbed.

2. Meanwhile, in a large bowl combine the lightly beaten eggs with the crumbled goat cheese, lemon thyme, kosher salt, and pepper.

3. Pour the egg mixture into the skillet over the onions and tomatoes, and then turn the heat to medium low, and cook until the bottom is set and lightly browned. Turn by gently lifting with two spatulas, and cook on the other side until set and lightly browned. Serve immediately.

Blanc Blintzes

Note: You can try all sorts of fresh cheeses for blintz fillings. Substitute fromage blanc, cottage cheese, or cow's-milk ricotta for sheep's-milk ricotta. They'll all be delicious.

1. Combine the blintz ingredients in a blender or food processor, then process until smooth, and let stand at room temperature for 30 minutes.

2. Combine filling ingredients in a blender or food processor, process until smooth, and then set aside.

3. Place an 8-inch nonstick or seasoned pan over medium heat. Coat with a little unsalted butter. Pour about 3 tablespoons of blintz batter into the pan, then tilt and rotate the pan until the batter forms an even layer. The blintz is done when the top is dry and the underside is lightly toasted. Continue cooking blintzes until the batter is finished, and stack them between sheets of parchment paper.

4. Spoon about 2 tablespoons of filling into the center of each cooked blintz, and fold the sides of each blintz around the filling to form a rectangular package. Melt 2 tablespoons of butter in a large, nonstick skillet over medium heat, and then cook the filled blintzes until they are lightly toasted on both sides.

5. Melt 1 tablespoon butter into ¼ cup honey. Top blintzes with fresh blueberries and a drizzle of the butter and honey mixture. Serve immediately.

Blintzes Are Great for a Crowd
If you have guests for the weekend, prepare blintz batter ahead of time. The batter can be made up to two days beforehand. Cover and refrigerate it, then give the batter a little whir in the food processor or blender just before you begin to cook.

Serves 8

FOR THE BLINTZES:
1 cup unbleached, white flour

1 cup milk

3 large eggs, lightly beaten

2 tablespoons melted, unsalted butter

2 teaspoons sugar

Pinch of salt

FOR THE FILLING:
1 cup fresh sheep's-milk ricotta

4 ounces cream cheese

1 large egg

1 tablespoon sugar

¼ teaspoon ground cinnamon

¼ teaspoon freshly ground nutmeg

1 vanilla bean, scraped

¼ teaspoon salt

FOR COOKING AND TOPPING:
3 tablespoons unsalted butter

¼ cup honey

1 pint fresh blueberries

Cream Cheese Spread

Serves 4

1 cup cream cheese

1 tablespoon fresh chives, finely chopped

1 clove garlic, finely chopped

Pinch of sea salt

Pinch of freshly ground pepper

A savory cream cheese spread on whole-wheat toast is a spectacular way to start your day. Try it on different types of toast—sourdough, whole wheat—or on an English muffin.

Combine all ingredients in a food processor or blender and process until smooth.

Classic Omelet with Sharp Cheddar

Serves 1

1 teaspoon extra-virgin olive oil

2 large eggs, lightly beaten

⅛ teaspoon kosher salt

Pinch of freshly ground black pepper

¼ cup sharp Cheddar, coarsely grated

¼ teaspoon scallions, finely chopped

This is a variation on the classic French omelet, served with sharp Cheddar and lightly flavored with scallions. Use an aged white Cheddar, like Cabot Cheddar, Canadian Black Diamond Cheddar, or New Zealand White Cheddar.

1. Warm the olive oil in an 8-inch nonstick or seasoned skillet over medium heat. Pour in the eggs, then tilt the pan to spread the eggs evenly over the pan bottom. Sprinkle with salt and pepper.

2. When the bottom has set and a thin coating of egg is uncooked on the top, add the grated cheese in the omelet's center.

3. Using the back side of a fork, fold ⅓ of the omelet over its center with the cheese, then fold the other side over that. Cook until egg is set, 1–2 minutes.

4. Slide the omelet onto a plate, top with chopped scallions, and serve immediately.

Spinach Poached Eggs with Pancetta and Grana

There's no hollandaise sauce here, but there's loads of good cheese and nutrition.
This is also a delicious breakfast with Grana Padano, Piave, or a medium-aged Gouda.

1. In a small skillet, gently heat the pancetta until warm. Meanwhile, prepare poached eggs and toast the sourdough bread. Wash and pat dry the spinach leaves.

2. Brush each piece of toast with olive oil, then layer as follows: 4–5 spinach leaves, half of the shaved Parmigiano-Reggiano, a slice of pancetta, one egg, a sprinkling of chives, and salt and pepper to taste. Serve immediately.

Zippy Cheese Straws

These giant cheese straws are so buttery and rich you could serve them as bread
for a light dinner. Lots of different cheeses work well, but melting ones are best.
Try this with Gruyere and Cheddar, or aged Asiago and Grana Padano.

1. Heat oven to 425°F.

2. Lightly flour a flat, rolling surface, and a rolling pin. Separate the pastry dough into two pieces, and roll each out into rectangles about 9" × 12". Brush one side of each pastry rectangle with the beaten egg.

3. Combine grated cheeses, cayenne, salt, and pepper, and then sprinkle evenly over one pastry rectangle. Cover with remaining pastry rectangle (egg side down), and then lightly roll with a rolling pin to meld the two layers and the cheese. Brush the top with the beaten egg.

4. With a sharp paring knife, cut the pastry with layered cheese into strips about 1 inch wide. Twist each strip lightly at either end to create a loose spiral, and then put the strips on a buttered cookie sheet.

5. Bake for 10 to 12 minutes, and serve immediately.

4 ounces cream cheese

2 to 4 tablespoons crème fraiche

½ teaspoon garlic powder

1 tablespoon chives, chopped

1 tablespoon French thyme, finely chopped

1 tablespoon Italian parsley, finely chopped

½ teaspoon kosher salt

¼ teaspoon freshly ground black pepper

1 cup Parmigiano-Reggiano, finely grated

Parmigiano Cups with Herbed Cheese Dip

These elegant appetizers are deceptively easy to make and guaranteed to please. The Parmigiano-Reggiano cups can be filled with seasoned fish, caviar, and any number of savory spreads.

1. Preheat oven to 325°F.

2. Combine cream cheese, crème fraiche, garlic powder, chives, thyme, parsley, salt, and pepper in food processor and process until just blended.

3. On two nonstick baking sheets or baking sheets lined with a Silpat, spoon 1 tablespoon of grated Parmigiano-Reggiano into 2-inch ring molds, and even out the cheese with your finger. You should have 16 rounds when you are finished. Bake for 8 to 10 minutes until golden brown.

4. Remove rounds from oven, cool for 30 seconds, then press each round into the hollow of an egg carton to form a cup. Remove immediately and set on a serving dish. Repeat to make seven more rounds.

5. Fill each Parmigiano-Reggiano cup with about 2 tablespoons of the filling and serve.

Silpat Sheets

Silpat sheets are thin, pliable silicon mats that can be used to line cookie sheets and prevent foods from sticking. They do not affect the taste of food and almost guarantee good baking results. Cleanup is simple; you simply rinse Silpats in warm, sudsy water, then clear water, and dry. You can find them at most good kitchen stores.

Crostinis with Roasted Garlic, Sun-Dried Tomatoes, and Chèvre

These crostinis are a perfect appetizer to get everyone's taste buds ready for a hearty meal. They're a wonderful complement to a hearty red wine, such as Syrah, Sangiovese, or Zinfandel.

1. Preheat oven to 350°F.

2. Cut the top off each head of garlic to expose the meat of the cloves. Drizzle 1 tablespoon of olive oil on each head of garlic, and then place in a small roasting pan. Bake for 45 minutes to an hour; they are done when the cloves are tender and lightly browned.

3. Slice the baguette in ¼ inch pieces, across the grain. Brush each piece with olive oil, then place them olive-oil-side-up on a baking sheet. Toast at 350°F for 8 to 10 minutes until lightly browned. Cool.

4. Layer crostinis with a small slice of sun-dried tomato, 1 clove roasted garlic, and 1 teaspoon of fresh chèvre. Serve immediately.

Serves 12

2 heads garlic

¼ cup plus 2 tablespoons good-quality extra-virgin olive oil

1 sourdough baguette

1 cup sun-dried tomatoes

1 cup fresh goat cheese (chèvre)

Eggs and Butter

Cuisines from all over the world include some version of eggs cooked in frothy butter. The French word *omelette* dates back to the sixteenth century and is derived from the Latin *lamella*, which means "small, thin plate." In Persia, a *kookoo* involves beating and frying eggs mixed with herbs in butter. Middle Eastern cuisine includes the *eggah*, a thick egg cake filled with vegetables, meats, and even noodles. Spanish tortillas and Italian frittatas are near cousins of the omelette, too.

Parmigiano Artichoke Dip

Serves 6 to 8

1 can artichoke hearts
packed in water, drained

1 cup good-quality
mayonnaise

¼ cup Parmigiano-Reggiano,
finely grated

*This warm dip is the perfect beginning to a dinner of roasted chicken
or a party with lots of different hors d'ouevres. Serve it with seeded
flatbread, crispy corn chips, or sliced sourdough baguettes.*

1. Preheat oven to 375°F.

2. In the bowl of a food processor combine artichoke hearts, mayonnaise, and grated Parmigiano-Reggiano. Blend until smooth, and then put in an oven-proof serving dish.

3. Bake for 20 minutes, or until golden brown and bubbling. Let cool 10 minutes or more, and then serve.

Melted Brie in French Bread

Serves 12 to 24

1 round or long loaf of
sourdough French bread

2 cloves garlic, minced

⅓ cup extra-virgin olive oil

1½ pound wheel of Brie

*Many people think this has to be made with a round wheel of Brie that fits
exactly into a round loaf of French bread. Not so. The Brie can be cut into chunks
and fit into any size loaf. You can also use a good Camembert for this recipe.*

1. Preheat oven to 350°F.

2. With a serrated knife, cut the top off the loaf of bread, leaving ½ inch on all edges. Cut downward to within ½ inch of bottom of bread, then gently, with your fingers, pull the bread away from the bottom and remove in one piece, leaving a shell for baking the Brie. Cut the bread you removed into chunks for dipping.

3. Rub the inside of the hollowed-out loaf with garlic, then with oil. Add Brie to the shell, and place on a cookie sheet. Place this in an oven at 350°F for 20 minutes, until lightly browned and bubbling.

4. Toast the cut-up bread chunks for about 10 minutes, until lightly browned.

5. Serve Brie loaf with the bread chunks immediately.

Gruyere Boats

Try these as a side dish to French onion soup for a party of six. Or if you're making minestrone soup, fill the rolls with 1 small chunk each of fresh and aged Asiago.

Serves 6

6 sourdough rolls

2 cloves garlic, minced

⅓ cup extra-virgin olive oil

1½ pounds antique Gruyere, cut into 6 chunks

1. Preheat oven to 350°F.

2. With a small, serrated paring knife, cut the top off each roll, leaving ¼ inch on all edges. Cut downward to within ¼ inch of the bottom of each roll, then gently, with your fingers, pull the middle away from the bottom and remove in one piece, leaving shells for baking the Gruyere. Cut the bread you removed into chunks for dipping.

3. Rub the inside of each hollowed roll with garlic, then with oil. Add 1 chunk of Gruyere to each hollow roll, and place them on a cookie sheet in an oven at 350°F for 10 minutes. Check, and continue cooking until each boat is lightly browned and bubbling.

4. Toast the cut-up bread chunks for about 10 minutes, until lightly browned.

5. Serve with French onion soup.

Classic Panini

Serves 4

1 sourdough baguette, cut into four even lengths

4 tablespoons extra-virgin olive oil

¼ pound prosciutto, thinly sliced

½ pound Pecorino Fresco, thinly sliced

1 medium tomato, thinly sliced

Butter lettuce

Kosher salt

Nothing satisfies a weary traveler quite like panini. Next time you spend a day shopping or sightseeing, take a panini with you and see how it gives you an instant boost of energy.

1. Slice each length of baguette in half, lengthwise, and brush insides with olive oil.

2. Layer proscuitto, Pecorino Fresco, tomato, and lettuce evenly on half of each baguette. Sprinkle with salt, top with other baguette half, and serve.

Cheese Focaccia

Yields 2 loaves

1¼ cup ice water

2 teaspoons fast-acting dry yeast (1 package)

2 teaspoons kosher salt

3 cups plus 2–3 tablespoons unbleached white flour

4 tablespoons olive oil

¾ cup sharp Cheddar, coarsely grated

A classic cheese focaccia bread can make your sandwiches sing! Or, toast a piece for an instant, grilled cheese treat. Use a mixer with a dough hook to make preparing this bread easy.

1. In the bowl of a sturdy mixer, add water, yeast, salt, and 3 cups flour. Mix on low for about 2 minutes, until ingredients begin to form a ball. Attach the dough hook to the mixer, then add 2 tablespoons olive oil and ½ cup of cheese and mix for about 5 minutes, until smooth but not elastic. Add additional 2–3 tablespoons of flour if needed to produce smooth dough. Remove dough from mixer, place in a bowl, and drizzle with remaining 2 tablespoons olive oil, turning until it is lightly coated. Cover with warm towel and let rise for an hour.

2. Remove dough from bowl and put on a floured surface. Divide dough in two. Press dough with your hands until each piece is about 15 inches long and 8 inches wide, then transfer to separate greased baking sheets. With a spray bottle, mist each the dough lightly with water. Sprinkle both loaves evenly with remaining ¼ cup of grated cheese.

3. Bake each loaf 15 to 20 minutes, until golden brown.

Cheese and Chutney Focaccia Sandwich

To make these sandwiches sweet, substitute cream cheese for the Cheddar cheese, and to make them more savory, try something bold and fruity like Uplands Pleasant Ridge Reserve cheese.

Slice each square of focaccia in half lengthwise, making a top and bottom layer for the sandwich. Spread 1 tablespoon of chutney on each side, then layer ham and Cheddar on the bottom, and top with the other focaccia layer. Enjoy!

Roasted Vegetables and Cheese Focaccia Sandwich

Let your imagination go with this sandwich. Use fresh summer vegetables, winter root vegetables, or spring greens. It's always a winner.

1. Preheat oven to 400°F.

2. Place sliced vegetables and onions on a cookie sheet. Drizzle 2 tablespoons of olive oil over vegetables and sprinkle with salt and pepper. Roast for 20 minutes, until they soften and begin to crisp around the edges.

3. Slice focaccia into a top and bottom piece, and then into sandwich-size pieces about 3 inches square. Brush the insides of each square with olive oil, then layer bottom piece with roasted vegetables and chèvre. Drizzle with balsamic and crushed thyme, top with foccacia, and serve.

Serves 4

1 red bell pepper, cored and quartered lengthwise

1 yellow zucchini squash, sliced lengthwise

¼ red onion, sliced in thin rounds

2 tablespoons plus 4 tablespoons extra-virgin olive oil

Kosher salt

Freshly ground black pepper

Cheese Focaccia (page 158)

¾ cup fresh chèvre, crumbled

2 tablespoons good balsamic vinegar

½ teaspoon lemon thyme, crushed

Serves 4

2 skinless chicken breasts, roasted

8 slices of good rye bread

2 tablespoons good-quality mayonnaise

½ cup sharp, creamy blue cheese, crumbled

¼ red onion, thinly sliced

Arugula

Pressed Blue Cheese and Chicken Sandwich

Try this with Shropshire Blue cheese and roast beef, or smoked turkey with Roaring Forties Blue cheese.

1. Preheat a panini sandwich press.

2. Slice the roasted chicken breasts in thin strips.

3. Spread mayonnaise on inside of four slices of rye bread. Top with chicken slices, crumbled blue cheese, sliced red onion, arugula, and remaining slices of bread. Carefully slide the sandwiches onto the hot press and toast for 2 to 5 minutes until golden brown and gooey. Serve immediately.

Serves 4

Fresh spring greens and curly endive (enough for 4 salads)

1 tablespoon unsalted butter

1 tablespoon good-quality olive oil

2 large egg whites, lightly beaten

1 tablespoon water

½ cup fresh, white breadcrumbs

8 ounce log of fresh goat cheese

FOR THE DRESSING:

2 teaspoons sherry vinegar

2 teaspoons Dijon-style mustard

¼ teaspoons kosher salt

⅓ cup extra virgin olive oil

Sautéed Goat's-Milk Cheese with Spring Greens

If goats needed a reason to be, this would be it. Make sure the cheese has a chance to soften before removing it from the pan.

1. Combine dressing ingredients in a small bowl and whisk until well blended. Set aside.

2. Wash and spin-dry the greens, toss with dressing, then arrange on four serving plates.

3. Heat butter and olive oil in a medium-sized skillet on medium heat. Combine egg whites and water in a shallow bowl and beat lightly. Put breadcrumbs on a small plate. Slice the goat cheese into eight ½-inch-thick slices (see page 179 for a handy dental-floss trick).

4. Dredge the goat cheese rounds in the egg whites, coat with breadcrumbs, and place in skillet. Sauté until golden brown and the cheese is slightly oozing.

5. Top each salad with 2 warm rounds of goat cheese and serve.

Fennel and Cheese Salad

This recipe is inspired by Linda Hughes of The Pasta Shop, in Oakland. Don't let the simplicity of this recipe fool you into thinking this salad has simple tastes. It's the perfect balance between sweet, tart, nuts, butter, and salt. Make it for your next potluck. It keeps well, and people adore it.

Wash and slice fennel and apple into very thin slivers, all about the same size. Shave the Pecorino Stagianato, and then combine all of the ingredients in a serving bowl. Let sit for 30 minutes, so flavors all combine, and serve.

Serves 6

3 fresh fennel bulbs

1 crisp red apple

½ pound Pecorino Stagianato

¼ cup walnut oil

Pinch of sea salt

Freshly ground pepper

Easy Roasted Beets with Fresh Chèvre

In the heart of winter this refreshing salad will feel like a breath of sweet spring. Try it with feta or a sharp blue cheese instead of goat cheese if you want some extra tang.

1. Preheat oven to 375°F.

2. Wash beets and put them in a shallow baking pan with ¼ cup water. Cover tightly with foil, and bake for 30 to 45 minutes, until soft, but not mushy. Cool and peel beets, cutting off the tops and roots while you work. Chop into ½-inch to ¾-inch pieces.

3. Place dressing ingredients in a blender and puree until smooth. Pour over warm beets, toss, and let cool.

4. Add crumbled cheese, walnuts, and sliced blood orange, and serve.

Serves 6

1½ pounds fresh red and orange beets

¼ pound fresh goat cheese, crumbled

¼ cup walnuts, coarsely chopped

1 blood orange, peeled and sliced

FOR THE DRESSING:

⅓ cup olive oil

1 tablespoon lime juice

1 tablespoon orange juice

1 tablespoon lemon juice

Zest of ½ orange

¼ teaspoon fresh jalapeño, finely diced

1 teaspoon fresh ginger, grated

Serves 6

1 bunch fresh asparagus

⅓ cup extra-virgin olive oil

2 tablespoons balsamic vinegar

¼ teaspoon sea salt

⅛ teaspoon freshly ground black pepper

½ cup Mimolette, coarsely grated

Asparagus with Shaved Mimolette

Talk about simple: steamed vegetables tossed in a vinaigrette with grated cheese. Try this with broccoli and Piave, cauliflower and an aged Gouda, or Brussels sprouts and an aged Gouda.

1. Wash and steam the asparagus, and then arrange on a serving platter.

2. Combine olive oil, balsamic vinegar, sea salt, and black pepper, taste and adjust seasonings, then drizzle over the warm asparagus. Top with grated Mimolette and serve immediately.

Taming the Tannin

Asparagus has a tendency toward the metallic or tannic tastes. By adding a bit of sweet balsamic vinegar and sweet cheese, the tannin relaxes and the true flavors of the asparagus are brought to life. Try this trick with Brussels sprouts or older cauliflower. You'll get the same results.

Easy Chiliquiles

This classic Mexican casserole is sure to please those with a spicy cheese palate.

1. Preheat oven to 350°F.

2. Warm 2 tablespoons olive oil in a large sauté pan over medium-high heat, and then add the onions and sauté until transparent. Add garlic, and cook until aromas are blended, about 3 minutes. Then add tomatoes, salt, jalapeños, and cilantro and sauté until the flavors have combined, about five minutes. Set aside.

3. Heat lard in heavy skillet. Dip tortilla quarters in the hot lard, remove immediately, and drain on a paper towel. They should be soft.

4. In a 2-quart baking dish, layer the tortillas, tomato mixture, black beans, and queso fresco until all ingredients are used, finishing with queso fresco. Top with grated chipotle Cheddar, then bake at 350°F for 15 to 20 minutes or until heated through.

5. Top with sour cream and sprigs of cilantro, and serve.

Serves 6

FOR THE FILLING:
2 tablespoons extra-virgin olive oil

2 medium white onions, chopped

1 clove garlic, minced

4 cups fresh, skinned tomatoes, chopped

Pinch of sea salt

¼ cup jalapeños, finely chopped

¼ cup fresh cilantro, minced

FOR THE TORTILLAS:
½ cup lard

1 dozen corn tortillas, cut in fourths

FOR LAYERING:
1 cup black beans, cooked

2 pounds queso fresco cheese, crumbled

½ cup chipotle Cheddar, coarsely grated

1 pint sour cream

A few sprigs of cilantro

4 skinless, boneless chicken
breasts

¼ teaspoon kosher salt

⅛ teaspoon freshly ground
black pepper

8 thin slices of pancetta

⅓ pound Morbier cheese,
sliced

8 slices of fresh tomato

4 large arugula leaves

1 tablespoon fresh Italian
parsley, chopped

2 tablespoons extra virgin
olive oil

¼ cup aged Asiago, finely
grated

Morbier, Pancetta, Arugula Chicken Breasts

If you can't find Morbier, try this recipe with fontina,
Saint Nectaire, or another mildly pungent washed-rind cheese.

1. Preheat oven to 400°F, and grease a roasting pan with olive oil.

2. Slice horizontally through the chicken breasts without cutting all the way through. Open each chicken breast like a book, pound with a meat mallet, and season with salt and pepper.

3. Place 1 slice of pancetta on each open half of each chicken breast (2 per breast), then on one half, place 1 Morbier slice, 1 tomato slice, and 1 arugula leaf. Fold together and secure with toothpicks or cooking string. Place in baking dish, top each folded breast with 1 tomato slice, sprinkle with chopped Italian parsley, and drizzle with olive oil. Sprinkle with salt and pepper and cover dish with foil. Bake at 400°F for 15 minutes or until chicken is no longer pink.

4. Remove from oven, discard foil, and top chicken with grated aged Asiago. Broil until chicken browns slightly and cheese melts, then serve immediately.

Keep Your Cutting Surfaces Clean

When working with raw chicken, always clean utensils and cutting surfaces with warm, sudsy water. This will prevent bacteria from developing on the surface and tainting other foods. It's a good practice to keep in mind for fish and meat. If you're working with blue cheese or a cheese with a luscious bloomy rind, do the same.

Caprese Salad with Kalamata Olives and Tuna

*This makes a fantastic summer dinner. Serve it with a baguette and a
bottle of Chianti or rose, and you'll be transported to the Italian countryside.*

1. Break lettuce leaves into large pieces and arrange on individual plates.

2. Combine remaining ingredients in a medium bowl and stir to evenly coat
   with olive oil and balsamic vinegar. Divide evenly on lettuce-lined plates
   and serve.

*4 large romaine lettuce
   leaves*

*4 medium, fresh ripe
   tomatoes, chopped*

*4 balls of fresh mozzarella
   (about ¼ pound each),
   chopped*

*4 ounces tuna packed in
   olive oil*

*¼ cup kalamata olives,
   pitted and chopped*

*8 tablespoons fresh basil,
   chopped*

*6 tablespoons good-quality
   virgin olive oil*

*3 tablespoons good-quality
   balsamic vinegar*

1 teaspoon sea salt

*¼ teaspoon ground black
   pepper*

Chard and Feta Soufflé

The possibilities for cheese in soufflé are delightfully unending. Play around with this one by replacing the feta with fresh goat cheese, or Camembert, or some aged Asiago.

1. Position a rack in the middle of the oven, and preheat oven to 300°F.

2. Rinse and chop the chard into large pieces, then steam in a medium-size saucepan until it is limp. Remove, cool, and chop finely.

3. In a medium-size saucepan, melt butter, and then add the flour slowly, forming a roux. Slowly add the milk, mixing or whisking continuously to prevent lumps from forming. Add the crème fraiche, salt, and pepper, and allow sauce to thicken, stirring continuously. Stir in the crumbled feta and continue stirring until it melts. Remove pan from heat, add the Swiss chard and chopped kalamatas, and allow to cool while you prepare the eggs.

4. Lightly beat the egg yolks in a small bowl. Using an electric mixer, beat the egg whites in a separate bowl until stiff peaks form. Add a small amount of the cooled milk sauce to the egg yolks, stir, then slowly add egg yolks into larger pot of milk sauce. Slowly fold in the egg whites until all ingredients are blended, but do not overstir.

5. Pour into a greased 1½ quart straight-sided soufflé dish and bake at 300°F for 35 to 40 minutes until doubled in size and lightly browned. Serve immediately.

Can You Open the Oven?

Some people think you should whisper in the kitchen and never open the oven when baking a soufflé. It's true that soufflés are delicate and prone to imploding when jarred, but that doesn't mean they will respond to loud noise. It's okay to open the oven gently, just a little, to see how it's doing, but don't hold the door open or bang it shut.

Halibut Fillets in Cheese Sauce

*A hint of pungent cheese mixed with savory leeks and dill form
a delicious sauce for halibut. Try this sauce with any white fish, or replace
the fontina with mild Havarti, some fresh Asiago, or Monterey jack.*

1. Preheat oven to 350°F.

2. Clean and slice the leeks on the diagonal, then in a medium frying pan, sauté with the garlic until lightly browned.

3. Prepare cheese sauce by melting butter in a medium saucepan over medium heat. Add the flour and form a roux, then slowly add the milk, stirring continuously to prevent lumps forming. Add the wine, the mustard, pepper, and dill, then remove from heat and stir in the grated cheese.

4. Place halibut filets in an ovenproof baking dish, top with leeks, garlic, and sauce, then bake for 15 minutes, until the halibut flakes lightly.

Serves 4

2 medium leeks without tops

1 clove garlic, minced

2 tablespoons unsalted butter

2 tablespoons flour

1 cup milk

½ cup full-bodied white wine

1 teaspoon dry mustard

¼ teaspoon ground white pepper

⅓ cup fresh dill, chopped

1 cup fontina, grated

1½ to 2 pounds halibut fillets

Serves 4

1½ to 2 pound flank steak

1 tablespoon extra-virgin olive oil

A dozen or more arugula leaves, washed and dried

4 slices roasted red bell pepper

¼ cup Greek feta, crumbled

Cooking string

Rolled Flank Steak with Feta

This makes such an elegant presentation, and it is so easy to make. Everyone will think you worked for hours on this dish.

1. Preheat oven to 425°F.

2. Rinse and pat dry the flank steak, and then cut it in four pieces, about 8 inches long and 2½ inches wide.

3. Brush each strip of flank steak with olive oil, then arrange arugula leaves, roasted red bell pepper, and crumbles of feta in a line down the center of the meat.

4. Cut string into 8 pieces, about a foot long each. Then roll each strip of flank steak up around the other ingredients and secure the bundle with two pieces of string. Knot the string and clip the ends.

5. Roast at 425°F for 20 to 30 minutes until meat is cooked medium. Let rest for a few minutes, then serve.

Roasting Red Bell Peppers

If you have a gas stove, red bell peppers are easy to roast. Light one burner and place the pepper directly on the burner, where the flames will reach it. Allow the pepper to char, and turn it often so that all sides are cooked. Remove it from the stove and let it cool, then peel away the skin, rinse, and slice into pieces to fit your recipe.

Classic Cheese Dessert Plate

These are generous amounts for four people, but you never know when someone will fall in love with a cheese and devour most of it. With ⅓ of a pound each, everyone stands a chance of enjoying several luscious morsels.

Arrange cheese wedges on a platter with individual knives for each cheese. Scatter candied walnuts and dried apricots on the platter, and serve.

Serves 4

⅓ pound Fromage D'Affinois

⅓ pound Bucheron

⅓ pound Cantal

⅓ pound reblechon

⅓ pound Fourme d'Ambert

¼ cup candied walnuts

Half a dozen dried apricots

Easy Biscotti with Mascarpone, Saba, and Berries

If you can't find biscotti use any firm tea-style cookie with nuts. The biscotti serves as a spoon, and substitutes should not crumble too quickly under moisture.

Divide the mascarpone evenly into four small bowls, top with fresh boysenberries, and drizzle with 1 teaspoon of Saba in each bowl. Arrange two biscotti in each bowl and serve.

Serves 4

8 almond biscotti

½ pint mascarpone

½ cup fresh boysenberries

4 teaspoons Saba

More Platter Ideas

Cheese platters are so fun to put together. Take a look at the platter suggestions in Chapter 17 for ideas on putting together creamy and regional cheese platters. The cheese pairings in Chapter 14 will give you all sorts of ideas for nut, jam, and fruit garnishes, and the dessert wine pairings in Chapter 11 will guide you through the drinks.

Parmigiano-Reggiano with Saba and Ice Cream

The perfect finish to a romantic dinner.

Serves 2

1 pint French vanilla ice cream

¼ pound Parmigiano-Reggiano cheese

1–2 tablespoons Saba

Divide ice cream into two bowls. Break Parmigiano-Reggiano into chunks with a sharp knife and arrange on a plate to share. Drizzle Parmigiano-Reggiano with Saba, and nibble on the cheese between spoons of ice cream.

What Is Saba?

Saba is balsamic vinegar before balsamic vinegar becomes vinegar. A rich and sweet syrup, it's commonly drizzled over Parmigiano-Reggiano, added to spaghetti sauce, and used to counter acidic foods. It can be found in specialty food stores wherever real balsamic vinegars from Italy are sold.

Crostata Crust

This is one of those all-time simple and tasty crust recipes. It's supposed to be rustic, so don't worry if it cracks while you're rolling it out. Just smoosh it back together and keep going.

Yields 2 crusts

2 cups unbleached white flour

¼ cup sugar

½ teaspoon kosher salt

½ pound unsalted butter, diced

¼ cup ice water

1. Use cold butter straight from the refrigerator, dice, and return to the refrigerator while you work with remaining ingredients.

2. In a food processor combine flour, sugar, and salt and pulse with metal blade until ingredients are combined. Add the butter a little at a time and pulse until ingredients have formed into small balls, about the size of peas. With motor running, pour ice water (without ice) through feed tube, then pulse until dough is just combined.

3. Remove dough, form into 2 balls, wrap and refrigerate for an hour. This dough can be made ahead of time and frozen. Simply defrost for an hour, then roll out and use.

Shropshire Cheese and Pear Crostata

Most people think of apples and peaches when they think of crostatas. But this combination of pears and Shropshire cheese is a lovely sweet and sharp surprise.

1. Combine peeled and chopped pears in a bowl with lemon zest, lemon juice, and fig jam. Toss and set aside.

2. In a food processor combine sugar, flour, and ground walnuts, and blend until well mixed. Add cold, diced butter and pulse until ingredients are well combined and dough begins to form into small pellets.

3. On a well-floured surface, roll crostata dough out to about 10 inches around, then place on a parchment-paper lined baking sheet.

4. Preheat oven to 450°F.

5. Leaving about 2 inches of dough all around, place pears in the middle of the crostata dough. Sprinkle with sugar, flour, walnut, and butter mixture, then fold the edges of the dough up and around the fruit and flour mixture so it forms a folded edge all around. Crimp loose edges with your fingers. Bake at 450°F for 20 minutes, remove, sprinkle crumbled Shropshire cheese over the top, and return to the oven for 5–10 minutes until cheese is just melted and crust is a golden brown. Cool and serve.

Serves 6 to 8

1 Crostata Crust (page 170)

3 Bosc pears, peeled and chopped into medium-size pieces

1 teaspoon lemon zest

1 tablespoon fresh lemon juice

¼ cup fig jam

¼ cup sugar

2 tablespoon unbleached white flour

2 tablespoons walnuts, finely ground

4 tablespoons cold unsalted butter, diced

2 ounces Shropshire cheese, crumbled

Chapter 14
Cheese with Sweet and Savory Foods

14

⅓ pound wedge of Manchego cheese, sliced into triangles, about ⅛ of an inch thick

¼ pound membrillo, sliced into small strips

Red grapes for garnish

Classic Manchego and *Membrillo*

Membrillo is a fruit paste, made from quince, and Manchego and membrillo together are a traditional Spanish appetizer. The nuttiness of Manchego pairs well with the sweet tartness of membrillo.

Place Manchego slices on a serving tray. Top with membrillo slivers, garnish serving tray with red grapes, and serve.

The Quince

The quince's yellow color and rather lumpy half-pear, half-apple shape make some people think it is a hybrid of a pear and an apple. But quince is a unique and ancient fruit. Because it must be caooked before being eaten, it is not terribly common in today's supermarkets.

Yields 2 cups

¼ pound wedge of Parmigiano-Reggiano cheese

¼ pound sweetened, dried cranberries

¼ pound roasted, salted almonds

⅛ pound roasted pumpkin seeds

¼ pound golden raisins

Italy's Energy Mix

In Italy, children are given wedges of Parmigiano-Reggiano to snack on for quick energy. This mix of sharp and salty cheese, fruits, and nuts is also wonderful for hiking, a quick snack, or for your family's lunchboxes.

Crumble or cut the Parmigiano-Reggiano into small pieces or cubes (about ¼ to ½ inch in size). Mix all ingredients and package for the trail.

Parmigiano-Reggiano Nutrition

One ounce of Parmigiano-Reggiano has the same amount of protein, fat, and most of the vitamins and minerals of 12 ounces of milk; in other words, just a small amount of Parmigiano-Reggiano is packed with nutrition. Because this cheese does not need to be refrigerated, it is a handy source of daily nutrition. Next time you're tempted to pack an energy bar, reach for some Parmigiano-Reggiano instead.

Raisin Biscotti and Sharp Blue Cheese

*Excellent biscotti can be found in most supermarket cookie sections,
or at good bakeries. If you can't find raisin biscotti, substitute hazelnut, date,
or other sweet and nutty biscotti to balance the sharpness of a good blue cheese.*

1. Arrange the biscotti on a dessert serving platter.

2. Blend the blue cheese with a fork until somewhat creamy.

3. Spread 1–2 teaspoons of blue cheese on each biscotti, decorate with nasturtium blossoms, and serve.

Serves 12

12 raisin biscotti

8 ounces good-quality sharp blue cheese, crumbled

6 nasturtium flowers (or other edible flower)

Strawberries Topped with Goat Brie

*Serve this appetizer at a luncheon, or before a light summer meal. Your guests
will delight in the brightness of these flavors. If you're pressed for time, serve whole
strawberries with a wedge of brie, and let your guests do the combining.*

Place each strawberry half on a serving tray. Spoon a generous ½ teaspoon of Brie on top of each halved strawberry. Taste. If the strawberries are not fully ripe, this may be too tart. Drizzle with balsamic vinegar and taste again. Everything should blend well now.

Goat's-Milk Brie

Most of the Brie sold in the United States is made from cow's milk. But both commercial and artisan cheese makers are making excellent goat's-milk Brie as well. It is lighter in flavor than cow's-milk Brie, and has a delightful tang that pairs well with acidic fruit.

Serves 24

1 dozen fresh, ripe strawberries, tops off, sliced in half

⅓ pound goat's-milk Brie cheese

1 tablespoon good balsamic vinegar (optional)

Peluso's Teleme with Fresh Blackberries

Serves 4

2 tablespoons blackberry jam

¼ loaf of sweet French bread

⅓ pound of Peluso's teleme cheese

½ cup fresh blackberries, washed

Ripe teleme has a kick of sharpness toward the end. The blackberries and jam combine to make this kick a sweet one. Enjoy this delicious treat for breakfast or serve it on a thinly sliced, sweet baguette as a light dessert.

1. Warm the blackberry jam in small saucepan until it is syrupy (don't boil).

2. Slice the bread across the grain into ¼ to ½ inch slices.

3. Spoon 3–4 tablespoons of teleme on each slice, top with fresh blackberries, and drizzle with blackberry jam. Serve immediately.

The Oldest California Cheese

Peluso's teleme is the oldest cheese made in California. Reminiscent of Stracchino-style cheese (a soft, milky, pungent Italian cheese), it has a strong following among people familiar with traditional Italian cheeses. It is a soft cheese, treated with rice flour. At its peak it oozes gently when cut.

Brebiou with Fresh Apricots

Serves 4

1 tablespoon apricot jam

⅓ pound of Brebiou cheese, cut into small wedges

¼ loaf of sweet French bread, sliced ¼ inch thick

2 fresh ripe apricots, pitted and cubed

Brebiou is a mild, creamy, and almost sweet sheep's-milk Brie from France. Combined with the tartness of apricots and a bit of jam, it makes a delicious treat for breakfast, or can be served on a thinly sliced, sweet baguette as a light dessert.

1. Warm the apricot jam in small saucepan until it is syrupy (don't boil).

2. Place one wedge of Brebiou on each slice of bread. Top with fresh apricots, and drizzle with warm apricot jam. Serve immediately.

Walnuts over St. Andre

St. Andre is a triple-cream Brie, well known for its buttery flavor. Combine with walnuts to accentuate the butter and nut flavors. Serve as a creamy dessert or a decadent appetizer.

1. Place wedge of St. Andre on a serving plate, sprinkle with crushed walnuts, and decorate with walnut halves.

2. Drizzle with walnut oil and serve.

Serves 6 to 8

½ pound St. Andre cheese

1 to 2 walnut halves

¼ cup walnuts, crushed

Drizzle of walnut oil

Nut Oils

Nut oils are becoming increasingly popular. Look for pure walnut, hazelnut, and pistachio oils to liven up your recipes. They are not inexpensive, but you only need small amounts, so don't buy nut oils in quantity. Once open, keep them in the refrigerator to prevent these delicate oils from becoming rancid.

Pistachios over Fresh Pecorino

In Italy Pecorino Primosale is fresh pecorino—a nutty, smooth sheep's-milk cheese—dotted with pistachios. This recipe will let you make your own when you can't find Pecorino Primosale in the stores.

Place the wedge of fresh pecorino on a serving plate. Sprinkle with crushed pistachios (leaving a few pistachios whole for decoration), then drizzle with pistachio oil and serve.

Serves 6 to 8

½ pound fresh pecorino cheese

½ dozen pistachios, roasted, salted, and peeled

¼ cup roasted, salted pistachios, crushed

Drizzle of pistachio oil

A South Seas Pair

Serves 6 to 8

½ pound Lighthouse Blue Brie cheese

¼ cup New Zealand Tawari honey

Light crackers or sweet baguette

Cheeses from Tasmania are growing in popularity. Lighthouse Blue Brie is an exceptionally creamy and flavorful Brie. When combined with honey from New Zealand, the flavors pop.

Place the wedge of Lighthouse Blue Brie on a serving plate, then drizzle with New Zealand Tawari honey. Serve with light crackers or a thinly sliced sweet baguette.

New Zealand Honey
Honeys from New Zealand carry flavors of the island's flowers. The Tawari tree is found in the north, where the island is more forested. The Tawari tree's flower is waxy and white. The aroma of honey made by bees frequenting Tawari tree flowers is reminiscent of butterscotch.

White Truffle Honey and Tomme Affine

Serves 6 to 8

½ pound of Tomme Affine cheese

1 teaspoon hazelnuts, roasted and crushed

1 tablespoon of white truffle honey

This combination is an excellent dessert to finish a meal of roasted chicken or fresh fish. The flavors are heady, tart, and surprising. Tomme Affine is a natural-rind, large goat cheese, similar to a large Chevrot. If you can't find Tomme Affine, look for a natural-rind goat cheese like a Chevrot or a crottin.

Place Tomme Affine wedge on a serving plate, top with crushed hazelnuts, and drizzle with white truffle honey.

White Truffle Honey
White truffle honey combines the headiness of white truffles with honey to create an intoxicating treat. The truffles are added to the honey after it is collected from the hives. At its most elegant, white truffle honey is made from fresh truffles instead of truffle oil.

Fresh Goat's-Milk Cheese and Lavender Honey

This is another wonderful way to combine the tang of goat's milk with other flavors. The heady scent of lavender infuses the goat's-milk cheese with almost roasted earthiness and depth. Serve this to start a romantic meal, or a very special summer meal.

Arrange fresh goat's-milk cheese in a small mound on a serving plate. Drizzle with lavender honey, decorate with lavender sprigs, and serve with light crackers.

Dental Floss in the Kitchen?

Keep a roll of unwaxed, unflavored dental floss in your spice cupboard for cutting goat cheese. Wrap a piece between two fingers on opposite hands, and then use it to cut a log of goat cheese into neat rounds.

Serves 6 to 8

½ pound fresh goat's-milk cheese

2 tablespoons lavender honey

3 sprigs of fresh lavender

A dozen light crackers

English Chutney and Montgomery Cheddar

This recipe is a classic pairing of long Cheddar flavors mixed with spicy and fruity chutney. This is sure to delight on a cool autumn day. Serve for tea, appetizers, or dessert. If you can't find Montgomery's Cheddar, substitute with Keen's Cheddar, or an excellent, nutty, but not overly sharp Cheddar.

Place Montgomery's Cheddar wedge on a plate next to a bowl of chutney. Give each guest a small spoon for the chutney and a paring knife for the cheese.

Serves 6 to 8

½ pound wedge of Montgomery Cheddar cheese

¼ cup good-quality English chutney

Stilton and Fig Jam

The creaminess of Stilton blends beautifully with the sugars of fig jam.
Look for fig jam that doesn't contain extra sugar or additives.

Place Stilton wedge on a plate next to a bowl of fig jam. Give each guest a small spoon for the jam, and a paring knife for the cheese.

Serves 6 to 8

½ *pound wedge of Stilton cheese*

¼ *cup fig jam*

Italian Table Cheese with Pear Preserves

Italian table cheeses are a fruit-lover's gift. Piave is available young- and medium-aged, and both, combined with pears, create complex fruity flavors you'll remember for days.

Place Piave wedge on a plate next to a bowl of pear preserves. Give each guest a small spoon for the pear preserves, and a paring knife for the cheese.

Serves 6 to 8

½ *pound Piave or hard Italian table cheese*

¼ *cup pear preserves*

What Are Some Other Fruity Italian Table Cheeses?

Grana Padano, often mistaken for Parmigiano-Reggiano, is a wonderfully fruity table cheese. Grana Padano is made in the Poe River Valley, and Piave in the Veneto region. Look for other hard cheeses from these areas, like Montasio cheese, to find similar hints of fruit.

Crudite and American Cheese Picnic

This combination is always welcome at a picnic.
Fresh vegetables and semi-hard cheeses make for good eating!

Arrange all ingredients on a platter, with a bowl of mustard in the middle, and a knife for each wedge of unsliced cheese.

Vella Dry Jack's Rind

Most Monterey jack cheese is made from curds washed in water or whey. Vella Dry Jack curds are not washed in whey. Instead, the drained wheels are rubbed with a mixture of vegetable oil, unsweetened cocoa, and black pepper. This preserves the cheese without penetrating the paste, and creates a flaky, chocolate-colored rind and a rich, creamy mouthfeel.

Serves 4 to 6

2 carrots, peeled, and sliced

2 celery stalks, sliced

1 medium English cucumber, peeled and sliced

1 small bunch fresh radishes

1 dozen cracked green olives

4 tablespoons Dijon mustard

¼ pound Tillamook sharp Cheddar cheese, partially sliced

¼ pound Vella Dry Jack cheese, partially sliced

¼ pound piquant blue cheese, partially sliced

Radishes and Triple Cream, Bloomy Cheese

The combination of radishes, unsalted butter, and sea salt is a traditional afternoon snack in France. Try this variation out on adults and kids alike.

Arrange a platter with radishes and ¼ pound Brillat Savarin for dipping.

About Radishes

There are many different radish varieties. Almost all have a bit of peppery heat to them, but some are almost sweet. You'll find black radishes, daikon radishes, French Breakfast radishes, Korean radishes, red globes, watermelon radishes, and white icicle radishes. French Breakfast radishes are small and carrot shaped. When fresh in spring, they are surprisingly sweet.

Serves 4

12 fresh French Breakfast radishes

¼ pound Brillat Savarin, or any other triple-cream, bloomy cheese

Sautéed Chard with Shaved Prima Donna

*Try this easy recipe as a side dish to grilled chicken, steak, or fish.
It's a little bit of Italy and Holland, combined.*

1. Warm the olive oil in a large sauté pan over medium-high heat, then sauté the sliced garlic until it is lightly browned. Add the chopped chard, toss with the garlic and oil, and continue tossing lightly until the leaves wilt. Let simmer a minute longer, then remove the pan from the heat.

2. Slide chard and garlic onto a serving platter, drizzle with balsamic vinegar, and add salt and pepper to taste. Top with Prima Donna shavings, and serve immediately.

Chard and Spinach Goat Cheese Puff

*This is a wonderful blend of cow's- and goat's-milk cheeses, chard,
and spinach. Try it with other combinations of cheese and vegetables.*

1. Heat oven to 350°F.

2. In a small saucepan and steamer, steam Swiss chard and spinach until just wilted.

3. In a medium-size bowl, combine goat cheese, aged Asiago, and eggs, and gently stir. Add dill, salt, steamed Swiss chard, and spinach. Pour contents of bowl into a 1½ quart oiled baking dish. Bake in a 350°F oven for 15 minutes.

4. Meanwhile, melt butter in a small saucepan on low heat, add breadcrumbs, and toss. Remove from heat. Sprinkle breadcrumbs over casserole, then bake 15 minutes longer. Serve immediately.

Summer Tuscan Quiche

A perfect lunch entrée on a hot summer day.
Please note that this recipe calls for a prepared pie crust.

Serves 6 to 8

3 tablespoons olive oil

½ white onion, chopped

1 large clove garlic, minced

3 medium zucchini, sliced into ¼ inch rounds

2 large Roma tomatoes, peeled and chopped

3 eggs, lightly beaten

1 cup milk

1 tablespoon fresh basil, chopped

½ tablespoon fresh parsley, chopped

2 tablespoons good balsamic vinegar

1 10" uncooked pie crust

1 cup aged Asiago, grated

¼ cup Pecorino Romano, grated

1. Heat oven to 350°F.

2. In a large saucepan, heat olive oil over medium heat, add onions, and cook until almost transparent. Add garlic and continue cooking for 2 minutes. Add zucchini and tomatoes to sauté pan and continue cooking for about 8 minutes, until the flavors have blended. Remove from stove.

3. Meanwhile, in a mixing bowl combine eggs, milk, basil, parsley, and balsamic vinegar.

4. Line a 10" pie plate with the pie crust, crimp the edges, and prick the bottom with a fork a few times.

5. Spread Asiago evenly on top of pie crust. Top with warm zucchini and tomatoes, then pour egg and milk mixture over the top. Sprinkle with grated Pecorino Romano. Cook for 40–45 minutes, until center is set. Remove and let cool for 10 minutes, and then serve.

Dutch Goudas with Italian Names

Many Dutch Gouda makers name their cheeses with Italian names. It adds a bit of whimsy, and certainly lends a greater international presence. True to their names, these fantastic Goudas are up to the task of world emissaries. Once you've tasted Prima Donna, you'll agree!

⅔ cup kalamata olives,
  pitted

½ teaspoon anchovy paste

1 tablespoon capers

2 tablespoons extra-virgin
  olive oil

¼ cup fresh chèvre

¼ teaspoon lemon juice

Fresh Chèvre Tapenade

*This is a perfect topping for crostinis, a sliced baguette,
or fresh tomatoes. Or use it as a sandwich spread.*

1. Combine olives, anchovy paste, and capers in food processor or blender, and blend at low speed until the mixture becomes a coarse paste. Drizzle in olive oil and continue processing until just blended.

2. Place fresh chèvre in a small bowl, then add contents of blender and lemon juice. Fold together until just blended.

Have You Ever Seen a Caperberry?

A caper is the flowering bud of the *Cappardaceae* shrub, native to Mediterranean climates. A caperberry is the hip of the flower, which swells after the flower has bloomed and fallen off, much like a rose hip. Caperberries are very similar in taste to capers, and make an excellent addition to a martini.

Serves 4

¼ cup fresh chèvre

½ cup French dry-cured
  olives, pitted

¼ teaspoon chopped fresh
  lemon thyme

¼ teaspoon lemon zest

½ teaspoon extra-virgin
  olive oil

Seeded crackers

French Olives with Chèvre

*Dry-cured olives are cured in the air, instead of in oil or brine. They often
have a hint of smokiness and many are herb flavored. Good quality
black olives or nicoise olives can be substituted for dry-cured olives.*

1. Arrange the fresh chèvre on a small serving plate and surround with olives.

2. Sprinkle chopped lemon thyme and zest of lemon on chèvre, then drizzle with olive oil. Serve with seeded crackers and a knife suitable for spreading.

Marinated Olives with Bocconcini

When you're doing lots of entertaining, this is an easy recipe to keep on hand in the refrigerator.

Mix all ingredients together in a medium bowl and refrigerate for thirty minutes to an hour before serving.

Ovilinis, Bocconcinis, and Cillicinis

Fresh mozzarella balls are made in several sizes. The large, ovilini, weigh about a quarter of a pound. Medium-sized bocconcinis weigh just a few ounces and are about one inch in size. Cillicinis are the smallest, and resemble a garbanzo bean. They can be mixed for a fun salad combination.

Serves 6

½ cup good-quality green olives, pitted

½ cup good-quality black olives, pitted

¼ cup nicoise olives, pitted

1 cup mozzarella bocconcinis

¼ cup extra-virgin olive oil

¼ teaspoon fresh thyme

¼ teaspoon fresh oregano

¼ teaspoon fresh marjoram

Zest of one lemon

Cerignolas with Three Pecorinos

Serve this as an appetizer to a hearty Italian meal. The three pecorinos are sheep's-milk cheeses of varying ages. Their textures range from semisoft to hard, and your guests will need a sharp knife to cut the aged pecorino.

Arrange on a medium size serving dish along with knives for each guest.

Serves 6 to 8

½ cup Italian Cerignola olives

¼ pound fresh pecorino

¼ pound medium-age pecorino

¼ pound aged pecorino

Olive Focaccia (page 186)

1¼ cups ice water

2 teaspoons fast-acting dry yeast (1 package)

2 teaspoons kosher salt

3 cups plus 2–3 tablespoons unbleached white flour

4 tablespoons olive oil

1 cup green olives, pitted and sliced into rounds

Olive Focaccia

Focaccia is a classic background for any number of wonderful cheeses. With olives, it's the perfect accompaniment.

1. In the bowl of a sturdy mixer, add water, yeast, salt, and 3 cups of flour. Mix on low for about 2 minutes, until ingredients begin to form a ball.

2. Attach the dough hook to the mixer, then add 2 tablespoons olive oil and olives, and mix for about 5 minutes, until smooth but not elastic. Add additional 2–3 tablespoons of flour if needed to produce smooth dough. Remove dough from mixer, place in a bowl, and drizzle with remaining 2 tablespoons olive oil, turning until it is lightly coated. Cover with warm towel and let rise for an hour.

3. Preheat oven to 475°F.

4. Remove dough from bowl and put on a floured surface. Divide dough in two. Press dough with your hands until each piece is about 15 inches long and 8 inches wide, then transfer to separate greased baking sheets. With a spray bottle, mist each the dough lightly with water.

5. Bake each loaf 15 to 20 minutes, until golden brown.

Focaccia and Pizza Dough

Though there are many types of bread and pizza doughs, focaccia dough is almost identical to basic pizza dough. So, if you get a craving for pizza while you're making focaccia, simply pat the dough into a large round and follow the pizza recipes in Chapter 16.

Olive Focaccia with Grilled Cheese

Grill this open-face sandwich under the broiler for an afternoon snack.

1. Heat broiler and position rack within 3 inches of the top heating element.

2. Cut a square of focaccia bread, then slice in half, lengthwise. Spread 1 teaspoon of tarragon mustard on each slice of bread, and top with grated cheese.

3. Place open-face sandwich under broiler and heat until cheese is bubbly and warm.Remove, let cool a minute or two, and then enjoy!

Serves 2 to 4

4 slices Olive Focaccia (page 186)

½ cup Asiago, Monterey jack, or sharp Cheddar, grated

4 teaspoons tarragon mustard

Crecenza and Lemon Olive Oil

Crecenza is a fresh, soft cheese made from cow's or sheep's milk. After minimal curd cutting, it is formed into small, flat squares that ripen within a week. The lemon olive oil makes this already bright cheese luminescent.

Put Crecenza on a small serving plate or in a shallow bowl. Drizzle with olive oil and serve with sliced baguette.

Taste Your Olive Oil
Always taste your olive oil before combining it with other ingredients. Olive oil is made from freshly harvested olives and is heavily influenced by climate and geography. You want to match light cheeses with light oils, and heavy cheeses with more robust oils.

Serves 6

4–6 ounces fresh Crecenza cheese

¼ cup lemon olive oil

1 sweet baguette

Marinated Crecenza

Another way to bring out the fresh lemon brightness of Crecenza.

Place Crecenza in a shallow bowl and cover with olive oil. Crumble the fresh lemon thyme over the Crecenza and olive oil, them cover and refrigerate for 1 hour or overnight. Serve with crackers, sliced baguette, or as a topping on a green salad.

Serves 6

4–6 ounces fresh Crecenza cheese

½ cup extra-virgin olive oil

2 teaspoons fresh lemon thyme

Marinated Chèvre

Picandous are small, firm discs of goat cheese, about 1¼ inches across and ⅜ of an inch high. Their firm texture allows them to hold their shape in a marinade. Other firm goat cheeses can be substituted in this recipe. If you use other cheese, slice or chop it into sizes that can be immersed in the marinade.

Place Picandous in a shallow bowl and cover with olive oil. Crumble Herbs de Provence over Picandous and olive oil, then add zest of ½ lemon. Cover and refrigerate. Picandous can stay in marinade for up to a week and should be kept refrigerated. Bring them to room temperature before serving.

Forgotten Chèvre
Marinating is a terrific way to use forgotten chèvre. Left unattended and with access to air, chèvre will age in your refrigerator and develop a natural rind. If the rind is moldy, scrape off the mold before marinating.

Serves 6

6 Picandou or firm rounds of fresh goat cheese

1 cup extra-virgin olive oil

1 teaspoon Herbes de Provence

Zest of ½ lemon

Marinated Feta

Feta marinates beautifully and can be kept for several weeks in the refrigerator. Crumble marinated feta over salad, put it on warm toast, or sprinkle it on scrambled eggs.

Place all ingredients in a shallow bowl, cover, and refrigerate.

Serves 6

⅓ pound firm feta

½ cup extra-virgin olive oil

½ teaspoon dry oregano

½ teaspoon black peppercorns

Marinated Mozzarella

These can be served as an appetizer, a side dish, or eaten as a snack. They keep for a week or two in the refrigerator. Make a batch during the holidays and bring them out when unexpected company arrive.

Place all ingredients in a small bowl, cover, and refrigerate.

Serves 6 to 8

1 pint bocconcini size fresh mozzarella balls

½ cup extra-virgin olive oil

¼ teaspoon red pepper flakes

1 teaspoon chopped fresh basil

¼ teaspoon black peppercorns

Serves 4 to 6

¼ to ½ cup very good
balsamic vinegar

¼ to ½ pound piece of
Parmigiano-Reggiano
cheese

Parmigiano-Reggiano Cheese Dipped in Balsamic Vinegar

Serve this as an appetizer to a hearty meal or even for dessert.
It makes a delightful and surprising combination.

1. Pour balsamic vinegar into a dipping bowl, or separate dipping bowls for each guest.

2. Arrange Parmigiano-Reggiano on a plate with small paring knives or Parmigiano knives.

3. Dip small pieces of Parmigiano-Reggiano in vinegar and eat.

Chapter 15

Melt and Grill Your Cheese

15

How Cheese Melts

Recall from Chapter 3 the discussion of how curds separate from whey. The introduction of rennet causes protein molecules to release water molecules and bond with fat molecules. Once the curd is cut, formed, and aged, the protein and fat link stays intact until the cheese is heated, and then the two separate. This is why cheese left in the sun develops an oily slick on the outside, or why cheese left too long in high temperatures begins to sweat with oil. Similarly, if you melt cheese quickly or cook it too long, the fats and proteins separate, which is why grilled-cheese sandwiches become so oily.

Four Tips for Melting Cheese: (1) Use cheeses made from cooked curd: Appenzeller, Aged Gouda, Cantal, Comte, Emmental, Grana Padano, Gruyere, Parmigiano-Reggiano, Pecorino Romano, and Piave. (2) Add a starch to your dish (potatoes, pasta, rice, cornstarch, etc.). (3) Add a dash of liquor. And (4) Grate cheese before you melt it.

When you're cooking with cheese, however, you want the tastes of fat and protein to work together and the moisture to stay intact. In other words, you want to prevent heat from separating fat and protein molecules. Fortunately, there are a few things that help.

First, cook cheeses made with cooked curd. These cheeses melt at higher temperatures for longer periods of time than uncooked-curd cheeses. Cooked-curd cheese fats and proteins take longer to separate. This is because cooking the curds binds the fats and proteins together, before they are pressed and aged, and they retain their link for a longer period of time under higher stress. This is primarily why Swiss, Gruyere, and Appenzeller cheeses are often used in recipes that call for melted cheese; their curds are all cooked.

Second, introduce starch to your recipe. The starch of potatoes or pasta helps fats and proteins remain connected, which helps when melting Cheddar cheese, for example, or a Monterey jack, both cheeses with uncooked curds.

Third, introduce a bit of liquor to your recipe, which is why most fondue recipes call for a bit of Kirsch, wine, or cognac. The alcohol in liquor helps the fats and proteins stay together and prevents melted cheese from recurdling. Try it. Melt your fondue cheeses before adding the liquor and look at the granularity of the cheeses. They almost look like curds and whey. Then introduce the liquor and see how the texture becomes smooth again.

The fourth thing you can do is grate your cheese so that it melts quickly and doesn't need to be heated for very long. This way, the fats and proteins don't have time to separate.

Grating Cheeses

Most people think of grated Parmesan or shredded mozzarella when they think of grated cheese, and in the deli section you'll most commonly find those two, along with packages of grated or shredded Cheddar and Monterey jack. But as you expand your cheese knowledge and begin experimenting with recipes, you'll find an extensive range of cheeses that easily lend themselves to grating. Italian cheeses like Pecorino Romano, Grana Padano, and Piave are all excellent grated toppings for pastas. Gruyeres, Comte, Appenzeller, Emmental, Laguiole, and Cantal share regional proximity and make excellent additions to dishes calling for grated and melted cheese. Mimolette and medium-aged Goudas are also good choices.

1 tablespoon extra-virgin
  olive oil

2 shallots, thinly sliced

¾ cup chicken broth

1½ cups Gruyere cheese,
  grated

2 cloves garlic, minced

2 pounds Yukon gold
  potatoes, cut into ¼-inch-
  thick slices

½ teaspoon salt

¼ teaspoon pepper

1 tablespoon unsalted butter

Classic Potato and Gruyere Gratin

Potatoes are the perfect stage for melted Gruyere.
Use an aged Gruyere to intensify all the flavors of this dish.

1. Preheat oven to 375°F.

2. Heat olive oil in a medium frying pan over medium heat, and then sauté the shallots until they are softened.

3. Put chicken broth on the stove or in the microwave and heat to just under the boiling point. Turn to low and keep warm.

4. Meanwhile, coarsely grate the Gruyere, mince the garlic, and mix the two in a bowl. Layer half the potatoes on the bottom of the prepared dish. Spread shallots evenly over the potatoes, sprinkle with half the salt and pepper, and then layer with remaining potatoes. Sprinkle with remaining salt and pepper. Pour warm broth over the top, then sprinkle the Gruyere and garlic mixture evenly over the top.

5. Cut butter into small cubes and dot the surface of the gratin with butter. Butter a piece of aluminum foil and cover the baking dish with buttered foil, buttered side down. Bake for 30 minutes, uncover, and continue baking until the potatoes are tender, about 30 minutes longer. Serve immediately.

Keep Potatoes from Turning Brown

When you slice potatoes, the oxygen in the air causes them to turn brown. A good way to prevent this is to immerse them in cool water after you slice them. They can stay in the water while you do the rest of your preparation. Then simply drain the water and add the potatoes to your dish.

Smokey Red Potato Gratin

Try this smoky variation as a side dish to baked chicken or your favorite soup. Bacon can be substituted for pancetta.

1. Preheat oven to 375°F.

2. Heat olive oil in a medium frying pan over medium heat, and then sauté the shallots until soft. Add pancetta and heat until softened, about 3 minutes. (If using bacon, cook separately, drain, and then add to shallots.) Add mustard and stir until combined.

3. Put chicken broth on the stove or in the microwave and heat to just under the boiling point. Turn to low and keep warm.

4. Layer half the potatoes in an oiled 9" × 13" baking dish or 10" gratin dish. Spread shallots, pancetta, and mustard evenly over the potatoes, sprinkle with half the salt and pepper, and then layer with remaining potatoes. Sprinkle with remaining salt and pepper. Pour warm broth over the top, then mix the Gruyere with the garlic and sprinkle mixture evenly over the top.

5. Cut butter into small cubes and dot the surface of the gratin with butter. Butter a piece of aluminum foil and cover baking dish with buttered foil, buttered side down. Bake for 30 minutes, uncover, and continue baking until the potatoes are tender, about 30 minutes longer. Serve immediately.

Serves 6 to 8

- 1 tablespoon extra-virgin olive oil
- 2 shallots, thinly sliced
- ⅛ pound pancetta, sliced into ½-inch squares
- 4 teaspoons grainy French mustard
- ¾ cup chicken broth
- 2 pounds red potatoes, cut into ¼-inch-thick slices
- ½ teaspoon salt
- ¼ teaspoon pepper
- 1½ cups Gruyere cheese, coarsely grated
- 2 cloves garlic, minced
- 1 tablespoon unsalted butter

1 tablespoon extra-virgin
olive oil

2 shallots, thinly sliced

1 cup chicken broth

2 pounds Yukon gold
potatoes, cut into ¼-inch-
thick slices

1 black truffle, shaved

½ teaspoon salt

¼ teaspoon pepper

1½ cups aged Asiago cheese,
coarsely grated

2 cloves garlic, minced

1 tablespoon unsalted butter

½ cup Pecorino Tartufo
cheese, grated

Pecorino Truffle Gratin

The truffles add richness and depth to this special dish.
Serve it in winter, with filet mignon and a fresh green salad.

1. Preheat oven to 375°F.

2. Heat olive oil in a medium frying pan over medium heat, and then sauté the shallots until they are softened.

3. Put chicken broth on the stove or in the microwave and heat to just under the boiling point. Turn to low and keep warm.

4. Layer half the potatoes on the bottom of an oiled 9" × 13" baking dish or 10" gratin dish. Spread shallots evenly over the potatoes, and then layer with shaved truffles. Layer with remaining potatoes. Sprinkle with salt and pepper. Combine Asiago and garlic until well mixed, then set aside. Pour warm broth over the top of the layered potatoes, then sprinkle Asiago and garlic mixture evenly over the top.

5. Cut butter into small cubes and dot the surface of the gratin with butter. Butter a piece of aluminum foil and cover baking dish with buttered foil, buttered side down. Bake for 40 minutes, uncover, and continue baking until the potatoes are almost tender, about 10 minutes longer. Top with grated Pecorino Tartufo, return to oven, and bake for 10 minutes more. Serve immediately.

Pecorino Tartufo

If you want to get a hint of how this dish will taste, buy some Pecorino Tartufo, slice it, and hold it to your nose. You'll smell earthy, roasted, and full-flavored aromas. *Tartufo* means *with truffles*, so Pecorino Tartufo is an unpressed Italian sheep's-milk cheese studded with shaved, black truffles. It is medium-aged and lends itself to grating and quick melting.

Zucchini Gratin

*Make this in summer, when zucchini are plentiful. It's a great way
to cook with large zucchini. Serve as a vegetable main course or side dish.*

1. Preheat oven to 375°F.

2. Heat olive oil in a medium frying pan over medium heat, and then sauté the shallots until they are softened.

3. Put vegetable broth on the stove or in the microwave and heat to just under the boiling point. Turn to low and keep warm.

4. Layer half the zucchini slices on the bottom of an oiled 9" × 13" baking dish or 10" gratin dish. Spread shallots evenly over the zucchini, sprinkle with half the salt and pepper, and then layer with remaining zucchini. Sprinkle with remaining salt and pepper. Combine Gruyere and garlic until well mixed, then set aside. Pour warm broth over the top of the layered zucchini, then sprinkle Gruyere and garlic mixture evenly over all.

5. Cut butter into small cubes and dot the surface of the gratin with butter. Butter a piece of aluminum foil, and cover baking dish with buttered foil, buttered side down. Bake for 20 minutes, uncover, and continue baking until the zucchini are tender, about 20 minutes longer. Serve immediately.

Serves 6 to 8

1 tablespoon extra-virgin olive oil

2 shallots, thinly sliced

½ cup vegetable broth

2 pounds zucchini, cut into 3/8-inch-thick slices

½ teaspoon salt

¼ teaspoon pepper

1½ cup Gruyere cheese, coarsely grated

2 cloves garlic, minced

1 tablespoon unsalted butter

2 cups elbow macaroni

½ medium white onion, minced

2 tablespoons unbleached white flour

1 cup whole milk

1 cup heavy cream

1 cup sharp white Cheddar, coarsely grated

1 cup Monterey Jack, coarsely grated

Salt and pepper to taste

4 tablespoons butter, divided use

½ cup fresh white breadcrumbs

¼ cup Parmigiano-Reggiano cheese, finely grated

Creamy Mac and Cheese

A combination of sharp and creamy cheeses mixed with heavy cream makes this a delicious treat.

1. Preheat the oven to 350°F.

2. Bring 2 quarts of water to boil in large pot, then add elbow macaroni, stir, bring to boil again, and then boil about 11 minutes, until tender. Drain macaroni and put in a large bowl.

3. Meanwhile, melt 1 tablespoon butter in a medium-size sauté pan over medium heat, then add minced onions and sauté until transparent. Set aside.

4. Melt 2 tablespoons butter in a medium saucepan over medium-low heat. Add 2 tablespoons flour and whisk gently until butter and flour form a roux (about 3 minutes). Gradually whisk in the milk and heavy cream. Stir frequently until thickened, about 15 minutes. Combine grated Cheddar and Monterey Jack and mix until well blended. Add 1½ cups of the blended Cheddar and Monterey Jack and sautéed onion to the cream sauce.

5. Add milk, cheese, and onion mixture to hot macaroni noodles and stir gently until the noodles are evenly coated. Put this mixture into an oiled 1½-quart-deep baking dish.

6. Combine grated Parmigiano-Reggiano with remaining ½ cup of grated Cheddar and Monterey jack, and set aside. Melt 1 tablespoon butter in a saucepan over medium heat. Add breadcrumbs to melted butter, toss until evenly coated, and then sprinkle breadcrumbs and grated Parmigiano-Reggiano, Cheddar, and Monterey Jack cheese over macaroni. Bake at 350°F for 30 minutes, let stand for 5 minutes, then serve.

What's a Roux?

A roux is melted butter or fat combined with flour to thicken a sauce. It is ready when the bubbles become glassy, and the stirring spoon leaves a path.

Scarmoza and Caramelized Onion Mac and Cheese

*The smoky, elegant flavors of Scarmoza (also called
smoked mozzarella) are brought out by heat.*

Serves 6 to 8

3 tablespoons, plus one
teaspoon unsalted butter,
divided use

1 teaspoon extra-virgin olive
oil

½ cup yellow onion sliced
into ¼-inch-thick slices

2 cups elbow macaroni

2 tablespoons unbleached
white flour

1 cup whole milk

1 cup heavy cream

2 cups grated Scarmoza
cheese

Salt and pepper to taste

½ cup fresh white
breadcrumbs

1. In a medium sauté pan over low heat, melt 1 teaspoon butter. Add olive oil and then sliced onions. Cook for about 1 hour until onions are tender and lightly browned.

2. Preheat oven to 350°F.

3. Bring 2 quarts of water to boil in large pot, then add elbow macaroni, stir, bring to boil again, and boil about 11 minutes, until tender. Drain macaroni and put in a large bowl.

4. Melt 2 tablespoons butter in a medium saucepan over medium-low heat. Add 2 tablespoons flour and whisk gently until butter and flour form a roux (about 3 minutes). Gradually whisk in the milk and heavy cream, Stir frequently until thickened, about 15 minutes. Add 1½ cups of the grated cheese and sautéed onion. Add salt and pepper to taste.

5. Add milk, cheese, and onion mixture to hot macaroni noodles and stir gently until the macaroni noodles are evenly coated. Put mixture into an oiled 1½-quart-deep baking dish.

6. Melt 1 tablespoon butter in a saucepan over medium heat. Add breadcrumbs, toss until evenly coated with butter, and then sprinkle breadcrumbs and remaining grated cheese over macaroni. Bake at 350°F for 30 minutes, let stand for 5 minutes, then serve.

2 cups penne

1 tablespoon unsalted butter

½ medium white onion, minced

3 tablespoons butter, divided use

2 tablespoons unbleached white flour

1 cup whole milk

1 cup heavy cream

2 cloves garlic, minced

2 cups aged Asiago cheese, coarsely grated

1 shaved black truffle

Salt and pepper to taste

½ cup fresh white breadcrumbs

Asiago Truffle Baked Penne

A rich and elegant side dish blends the piquancy of aged Asiago with the headiness of truffles.

1. Preheat the oven to 350°F.

2. Bring 2 quarts of water to boil in large pot, then add the penne, stir, bring to a boil again, and then boil about 11 minutes, until tender. Drain penne and put in a large bowl.

3. Meanwhile, melt butter in a medium-size sauté pan over medium heat, then add minced onions and sauté until transparent. Add minced garlic and sauté for 1 minute, and then set aside.

4. Melt 2 tablespoons butter in a medium saucepan over medium-low heat. Add 2 tablespoons flour and whisk gently until butter and flour form a roux (about 3 minutes). Gradually whisk in the milk and heavy cream, Stir frequently until thickened, about 15 minutes. Add 1½ cups of the grated cheese, sautéed onion and garlic mixture, and shaved truffle. Taste, then season lightly with salt and pepper to taste.

5. Add milk, cheese, and onion, garlic, and truffle mixture to hot penne and stir gently until the penne are evenly coated. Put penne mixture into an oiled 1½-quart-deep baking dish.

6. Melt 1 tablespoon butter in a saucepan over medium heat. Add breadcrumbs, toss until evenly coated with butter, and then sprinkle breadcrumbs and remaining grated cheese over penne. Bake at 350°F for 30 minutes, let stand for 5 minutes, and then serve.

Ramekins Are Great

Ramekins are small, straight-sided bowls. They come in different sizes and hold anywhere from ¼ of a cup to 2 cups, and are ovenproof. They are designed to bake individual portions of custards, pastas, gratins, and desserts, like crème brulee. If you can't find ramekins, use small, oven-proof Pyrex bowls.

Orecchiette Pancetta Bake

The shape of orecchiette (which translates to little ears*) pasta makes it ideal for baked pasta dishes. Its shape easily holds small pools of liquids and flavors.*

1. Preheat oven to 350°F.

2. Bring 2 quarts of water to boil in large pot, then add orecchette, stir, bring to boil again, and then boil about 11 minutes, until tender. Drain orichette and put in a large bowl.

3. Heat olive oil in medium-size sauté pan over medium heat, then add minced onions and sauté until transparent. Add garlic and pancetta and warm until softened, about 3 minutes.

4. Melt 2 tablespoons butter in a medium saucepan over medium-low heat. Add 2 tablespoons flour and whisk gently until butter and flour form a roux (about 3 minutes). Gradually whisk in the milk and heavy cream, Stir frequently until thickened, about 15 minutes. Add salt and pepper to taste. Add 1½ cups of the grated Asiago and sautéed onion with pancetta and garlic.

5. Add milk, cheese, and onion mixture to hot orecchiette and stir gently until the orechiette are evenly coated. Put orecchiette mixture into an oiled 1½-quart-deep baking dish.

6. Melt 1 tablespoon butter in a saucepan over medium heat. Add breadcrumbs, toss until evenly coated with butter, and then sprinkle breadcrumbs and remaining grated Asiago and Parmigiano-Reggiano over orechiette. Bake at 350°F for 30 minutes, let stand for 5 minutes, and then serve.

2 cups orecchiette

1 tablespoon extra-virgin olive oil

½ medium white onion, minced

2 cloves garlic, minced

⅛ pound pancetta, cut into ½ inch cubes

3 tablespoons unsalted butter, divided use

2 tablespoons unbleached white flour

1 cup whole milk

1 cup heavy cream

2 cups aged Asiago cheese, coarsely grated

salt and pepper to taste

½ cup fresh breadcrumbs

¼ cup Parmigiano-Reggiano cheese, finely grated

Classic Raclette

Raclette can be found at most specialty cheese counters. Swiss raclette is more robust in flavor than French raclette. French raclette is made in two forms: one is cow's milk, and the other is goat's milk. All are fabulous.

1 pound raclette cheese, cut into 1½-inch-square and ¼-inch-thick slices

2 pounds small new red potatoes

½ pint cornichons, sliced into rounds

1. Steam or roast the potatoes, then put them on top of the heated raclette grill. (Most raclette grills have heating elements for melting the cheese underneath a grill on top.)

2. Put squares of raclette cheese into trays and melt according to grill instructions. When the cheese is melted, put some potatoes on a plate, pour melted cheese over the potatoes, and top with sliced cornichons. Serve immediately, but be careful; the cheese will be hot.

Three-Cheese Raclette

Vacherin Fribourgeois and fontina add pungency, and aged Gruyere adds a hint of toasted nuts to this traditional raclette recipe.

Serves 6

2 pounds small new red potatoes

½ pound Vacherin Fribourgeois, cut into 1-inch square and ¼-inch-thick slices

½ pound fontina cut into 1-inch-square and ¼-inch-thick slices

½ pound aged Gruyere cut into 1-inch-square and ¼-inch-thick slices

½ pint cornichons

1. Steam or roast the potatoes, then put them on top of the heated raclette grill. (Most raclette grills have heating elements for melting the cheese underneath a grill on top.)

2. Put one square of each cheese into trays and melt according to grill instructions. When melted, put some potatoes on a plate, pour melted cheese over the potatoes, and top with sliced cornichons. Serve immediately, but be careful; the cheese will be hot.

Raclette the Old-fashioned Way

Traditionally, raclette cheese is melted in front of a fire, and whole wheels, which weigh approximately eighteen pounds, are cut in half for melting. Each half wheel is held in place by a metal holder next to the fire, and the cheese is scraped onto plates of potatoes as it melts.

Classic Cheese Fondue

No discussion of cheese is complete without fondue. Have your cheese-loving friends over, and share your cheese discoveries over this classic dish.

1. Add 1¼ cups of the wine to the top of a double boiler; set over simmering water, and, bring to a simmer. Add grated Gruyere and stir frequently, until cheese is melted.

2. In a small bowl, mix cornstarch and Kirsch thoroughly, then stir into wine and cheese mixture. If cheese mixture is too thick, add some of the reserved wine.

3. To serve, transfer cheese mixture to a fondue or chafing dish and set over a flame. Spear bread pieces with fondue forks, dip into the cheese, and eat!

Serves 4 to 6

1½ cup dry white wine

1 pound Gruyere cheese, grated

1 tablespoon cornstarch

2 tablespoons Kirsch

1 loaf good French bread, cut into pieces about 1 inch square

Sweet Cheese Fondue

This makes a truly elegant and decadent dessert. If you want to, substitute angel food cake or biscotti for pound cake, and fresh peaches or nectarines for strawberries.

1. Add cream to the top of a double boiler; set over simmering water, and, bring to a simmer. Add cream cheese and mascarpone, stirring, until cheese is melted and ingredients are incorporated.

2. In a small bowl, mix cornstarch and cognac thoroughly, then stir into cheese mixture. Then add powdered sugar and a pinch of salt. If cheese mixture is too thick, add some whole milk, one tablespoon at a time.

3. To serve, transfer cheese mixture to a fondue or chafing dish, and set over a flame. Spear pound cake pieces with fondue forks, dip into the cheese, and eat! Hold the strawberries by their tops to dip.

Serves 6 to 8

1 cup heavy cream

8 ounces cream cheese

8 ounces mascarpone

1 tablespoon cornstarch

2 tablespoons Cognac

½ cup powdered sugar

Pinch of salt

¼ cup whole milk (if needed)

1 pound cake, cut into pieces about 1-inch square

2 pints fresh strawberries with tops on

4 slices good-quality French
bread

Unsalted butter

French-style grain mustard

4 slices good-quality ham

¼ cup Gruyere cheese,
coarsely grated

4 cornichons, sliced

2 eggs, beaten

2 tablespoons Gruyere
cheese, coarsely grated

Croque Monsieur with Cornichons

*Almost any sidewalk café in Paris serves this sandwich. Make it at
home to celebrate the cheeses of Switzerland and the French Alps.*

1. Butter both sides of each slice of bread. Spread generous amount of mustard on one side of two slices of bread, and top with sliced ham, ¼ cup grated cheese, sliced cornichons, and remaining slices of bread.

2. Grill sandwich under a broiler, or in a sandwich grill, or in a heavy frying pan until both sides are golden brown and toasted.

3. Dip toasted sandwich in beaten eggs and fry both sides in a heavy frying pan over medium heat, until egg is cooked. Top with one tablespoon grated Gruyere on each sandwich, and serve immediately.

Serves 2

4 slices good-quality French
bread

1 garlic clove, sliced in half

3 tablespoons extra-virgin
olive oil

6 to 8 leaves arugula

4 thin slices of prosciutto

8 small slices of fresh
pecorino

Salt and pepper

Grilled Panini

*This is a very simple panini recipe. Experiment with other sliced meats and different cheeses:
ham, turkey, chicken, Cheddar, fresh Asiago, provolone, Gruyere, and fontina.*

1. Rub one side of each piece of bread with the sliced garlic.

2. Brush a generous amount of olive oil on one side of each slice of bread. Top two slices of bread with arugula leaves, slices of prosciutto, and slices of fresh pecorino. Sprinkle with salt and pepper to taste, and top with remaining slice of bread. Brush the outside of the sandwich lightly with olive oil.

3. Grill in a sandwich grill, a panini press, or a heavy skillet (if using a skillet, weigh the sandwiches down with a heavy pot) until golden brown. Serve immediately.

Panini

Panini is Italian for *little roll*. But ask for a panini in any Italian town, and you'll likely receive a whole sandwich. The word has become synonymous with any number of small sandwiches served on rolls. Grilled or fresh, they are as common in Italy as hot dogs are in America.

Grilled Fontina with Chutney

This is a very easy grilled sandwich with lots of flavor from the fontina cheese and chutney. Taste the cheese and chutney together before cooking to see if you can use this combination as an appetizer without the bread.

1. Butter one side of each slice of bread. Top one slice each with two slices of fontina and the chutney. Sprinkle with salt and pepper to taste, and top with remaining slice of bread. Lightly butter the outside of each sandwich.

2. Grill in a sandwich grill, a panini press, or a heavy skillet (if using a skillet, weigh the sandwiches down with a heavy pot) until golden brown. Serve immediately.

Chipotle Chicken Quesadilla

This easy recipe is a great way to use leftover chicken. But if you need to cook some chicken for this recipe, use boneless, skinless chicken breasts sliced into small pieces, and quickly fried over medium heat in a sauté pan or heavy skillet.

1. On a griddle or the flat of a large skillet, heat tortillas until they are piping hot.

2. Add ¼ cup chipotle Cheddar cheese, ¼ cup cooked chicken, and 1 teaspoon chopped jalapeños to one half of each tortilla. Fold tortilla in half, over the cheese, chicken, and jalapeños, and then cook on griddle or in skillet until the cheese is melted and the tortilla is slightly browned.

3. Top with chopped tomatoes, sour cream, cilantro, and a squeeze of lime. Serve immediately.

Haloumi with Oregano

Serve this as a hot side dish to barbecued chicken, steak, or fish.

Serves 6 to 8

1 tablespoon dry oregano

8 to 10 ounce package Haloumi cheese, sliced into ¼-inch strips

Good-quality extra-virgin olive oil (preferably Greek)

Lemon wedges

1. Rub dry oregano in your fingers and lightly sprinkle on each slice of Haloumi. Drizzle olive oil over each slice.

2. Grill over a barbecue or fry in a skillet until cheese is slightly toasted. Squeeze lemon juice over the top and serve immediately.

Haloumi

Haloumi is from Cyprus and is usually made from a combination of sheep's and goat's milk. The curd is boiled and folded, and often some mint is incorporated at the same time. Because it won't melt and fall apart, it's the ideal cheese for the grill.

Grilled Grape Leaves with Figs and Chèvre

Make this in early summer, when grape leaves are still tender and haven't developed a woody stem. Or substitute preserved grape leaves for fresh ones.

Serves 6

6 wooden skewers

3 fresh figs, chopped

1½ cups fresh chèvre

6 medium grape leaves

Extra-virgin olive oil

1. Soak wooden skewers in water for 30 minutes (this keeps them from igniting on the grill).

2. Mince figs and combine with fresh chèvre in a small bowl. Stir to combine.

3. Brush one side of grape leaves with olive oil, and put 3 to 4 tablespoons of chèvre and fig mixture in the center of each leaf. Fold leaf around mixture and secure with wooden skewer.

4. Brush each leaf package with olive oil and set on edges of grill, away from direct heat. Grill until leaf is slightly crackly and package has softened. Serve immediately.

Feta on the Barbecue

Like Haloumi, feta blocks hold their shape on the grill.
This is so quick and easy you will hardly believe the results.

Serves 6 to 8

8- to 10- ounce block of Greek feta

Extra-virgin olive oil

Slice feta into ½-inch slices and brush with olive oil. Set on edges of grill, away from direct heat. Grill until the cheese begins to soften (just a few minutes) and serve.

Fetas Are Different

Fetas are generally made from sheep's or goat's milk, or a combination of the two, in many different places and countries. Each country seems to have a style of its own in terms of making this cheese. Next time you're at a cheese counter, ask to taste their fetas. You'll be surprised at the difference in creaminess, sharpness, and complexity of different samples.

Grilled Figs Stuffed with Aged Goat Cheese

As they age, some natural-rind goat cheeses begin to melt from the outside in, and positively burst with complexity and flavor. Ask your cheese monger for a natural-rind goat cheese that becomes more pungent and soft as it ages, and you'll find the perfect cheese for this easy recipe.

Serves 6

12 large, ripe figs

8 ounces of natural-rind aged goat cheeses

Wash the figs and slice in half, lengthwise. Cut the goat cheese into pieces about ½ inch in size and put one piece on each halved fig. Set on the outside of the grill and cook until the cheese puddles and the figs have warmed. Serve immediately.

Chapter 16

Cheese as an Ingredient

Serves 6

4 medium, fresh tomatoes,
 thinly sliced

1 pound fresh mozzarella,
 thinly sliced

1 teaspoon sea salt

¼ teaspoon ground black
 pepper

8 tablespoons fresh basil,
 chopped

6 tablespoons good-quality
 virgin olive oil

3 tablespoons good quality
 balsamic vinegar

Caprese Salad

*When the tomatoes are fresh and abundant, no one can resist
a fresh caprese salad! Extra zip can be added with crushed garlic.*

On a medium-size serving platter, arrange sliced tomatoes and sliced mozzarella in alternate layers. Sprinkle with salt, pepper, and chopped basil. Drizzle with olive oil and balsamic vinegar. Serve immediately or within an hour to preserve the freshness of these flavors.

Yields about ½ cup

½ pound triple-cream Brie-
 style cheese

¼ teaspoon kosher salt

½ teaspoon garlic powder

1 tablespoon Italian parsley,
 minced

¼ teaspoon freshly cracked
 black pepper

Homemade Boursin

*Boursin is the brand name of a French triple-cream cheese
flavored with herbs and spices. It's fun to make a little of your own with a
bit of Pierre Robert, Brillat Savarin, or Explorateur triple-cream cheese.*

Remove the rind from the triple-cream cheese and put the cheese in a small bowl. Add remaining ingredients and mix thoroughly. Chill for 1 hour, then bring to room temperature before serving.

Fresh Chèvre with Smoked Salmon

Smoked salmon tastes richer and more flavorful when accompanied by a bright and tangy fresh chèvre. Sweet tarragon enhances the smokiness, making this a perfect hors d'oeuvre. Serve with a sliced sweet baguette.

Arrange smoked salmon on a platter around a mound of fresh chèvre. Sprinkle tarragon on the fresh chèvre, then serve with a freshly sliced sweet baguette, and garnish with quartered lemon.

Serves 6

½ pound good-quality
 smoked salmon

½ cup fresh chèvre

1 tablespoon dry tarragon,
 crushed

1 sweet baguette

Quartered lemon for garnish

Fresh Ricotta over Peaches

*What a fantastic breakfast this makes on a warm summer morning.
Use the freshest summer peaches you can find, and sheep's-milk ricotta if available.*

Place each peach half on a small plate and top with ¼ cup fresh ricotta. Sprinkle with chopped hazelnuts, then drizzle with one tablespoon of honey.

Wait for Sheep's-Milk Ricotta

In the heart of the Italian countryside, fresh ricotta is available every day there's milk. Italians are used to eating ricotta made that morning or the day before. In the spring and fall, after lambing, the ewes are milked for ricotta, but between those times it's hard to come by. Several cheese makers in America make outstanding sheep's-milk ricotta. Check with your local cheese monger and find out when it's normally available. Then be sure not to miss it. This stuff is really a treat!

Serves 4

2 ripe peaches, peeled and
 halved

1 cup fresh ricotta

¼ cup roasted hazelnuts,
 finely chopped

4 tablespoons clover or
 alfalfa honey

Herbed Ricotta Cherry Tomatoes

Yields 24

24 ripe cherry tomatoes

¾ cup fresh ricotta

1 tablespoon fresh basil, minced

1 tablespoon Italian parsley, minced

Pinch of sea salt

Pinch of freshly cracked black pepper

4 tablespoons extra-virgin olive oil

48 pine nuts

Fresh ricotta has enough buttery warmth in it to create easy and dazzling appetizers. You can use this spread as a dip for crudites, or spread it on crostinis.

1. Slice enough off the tops of the cherry tomatoes to be able to hollow them out with a small knife, then scrape the insides to remove seeds, and place the tomatoes on a serving platter.

2. In a small bowl, blend ricotta, basil, parsley, salt, and pepper until smooth. Add enough (1–2 teaspoons each) of the ricotta mixture to each hollowed-out tomato so that it creates a small mound above the tomato top. Drizzle scant amounts of olive oil on each tomato, then top with a pine nut or two. Serve immediately or refrigerate for several hours before serving.

Classic Cheese Sauce

Yields 1 cup

2 tablespoons unsalted butter

2 tablespoons unbleached white flour

1 cup milk

¼ cup grated or crumbled cheese

¼ teaspoon kosher salt

⅛ teaspoon ground white pepper

1–2 tablespoons wine or liquor (optional)

Every cheese cook needs a good cheese sauce in their repertoire. The cheese can be almost any kind. Sharp Cheddar, Gruyere, fontina, crumbled blue, Gorgonzola, and fresh chèvre all make superb cheese sauces.

1. Melt butter in a medium, heavy saucepan over low heat.

2. Slowly sprinkle in flour and stir continuously over medium heat until butter and flour form a roux. Add the milk slowly, stirring after each addition to prevent lumps from forming. Then turn heat back to low and stir frequently until the mixture is as thick as cream.

3. Meanwhile, grate the cheese, then remove sauce from heat and stir in grated cheese. Season with salt and pepper and if desired, wine or liquor.

Triple-Cream Cheese Sauce

Using triple-cream Brie-style cheese turns this into an elegant dessert sauce.

1. Melt butter in a medium, heavy saucepan over low heat.

2. Slowly sprinkle in flour and stir continuously over medium heat until butter and flour form a roux. Add the milk slowly, stirring after each addition to prevent lumps from forming. Then turn heat back to low and stir frequently until the mixture is as thick as cream.

3. Remove sauce from heat and stir in cheese. Season with salt, nutmeg, and Kirsch.

Yields 1 cup

2 tablespoons unsalted butter

2 tablespoons unbleached white flour

1 cup milk

¼ cup chopped-up triple-cream Brie, with rind removed

¼ teaspoon kosher salt

⅛ teaspoon freshly ground nutmeg

1–2 tablespoons Kirsch

Gorgonzola Cream Sauce

Pt. Reyes Original Blue, Buttermilk Blue, Maytag Blue, or a crumbly Roquefort will all deliver delicious results.

1. Melt butter in a medium, heavy saucepan over low heat.

2. Slowly sprinkle in flour and stir continuously over medium heat until butter and flour form a roux. Add the milk slowly, stirring after each addition to prevent lumps from forming. Then turn heat back to low and stir frequently until the mixture is as thick as cream.

3. Remove sauce from heat and stir in cheese. Season with salt.

Yields 3 cups

2 tablespoons unsalted butter

2 tablespoons unbleached white flour

1 cup milk

¼ cup Gorgonzola, crumbled

¼ teaspoon kosher salt

Basil Parmigiano-Reggiano Pesto

The key to great pesto is to use fresh ingredients. This is so simple and delicious. Keep pine nuts in your freezer to use whenever you have fresh basil and real Parmigano-Reggiano around.

Put all ingredients except olive oil in a blender and finely chop. With motor running, drizzle olive oil in until the pesto is smooth. Refrigerate or use immediately.

Summer Basil

When summer basil is going strong, harvest it and make as much of this pesto recipe as you can. Then freeze it in an ice-cube tray. All winter, you'll have wonderful memories of your summer garden every time you defrost a cube. It's fabulous over a plate of pasta.

Arugula Pecorino Romano Pesto

Salt and pepper, what could be more versatile? The pepper of the arugula is matched by the salt of the Pecorino Romano, making this the perfect topping for piping-hot pasta.

Put all ingredients except olive oil in a blender and finely chop. With motor running, drizzle olive oil in until the pesto is smooth. Refrigerate or use immediately.

Yields ½ cup

1 cup fresh basil leaves, loosely packed

¼ cup pine nuts

¼ cup Parmigano-Reggiano, finely grated

¼ teaspoon kosher salt

⅛ teaspoon freshly ground black pepper

4–6 tablespoons extra-virgin olive oil

Yields ½ cup

1 cup fresh arugula leaves, loosely packed

¼ cup pine nuts

¼ cup Pecorino Romano, finely grated

¼ teaspoon kosher salt

⅛ teaspoon freshly ground black pepper

4–6 tablespoons extra-virgin olive oil

Parmigiano Vinaigrette

Try this over freshly washed, crisp romaine with a few shaves of Parmigiano-Reggiano.

Place all ingredients except olive oil in a blender and puree until smooth. With the motor still running, slowly add the olive oil until just blended. Use immediately, or cover and refrigerate.

Have a Favorite Bottled Vinaigrette?
If you have a favorite bottled vinaigrette, try adding about 3–4 tablespoons of finely grated Parmigiano-Reggiano to it. Shake well, and pour over your salad. The cheese will make the vinaigrette richer and creamier, and you may never go back to serving it alone.

Yields 1½ cups

1 cup very good, extra-virgin olive oil

⅓ cup Champagne vinegar

3 tablespoons Parmigiano-Reggiano, finely grated

1 teaspoon salted capers

1 shallot, minced

1 clove garlic

¼ teaspoon sea salt

¼ teaspoon freshly cracked black pepper

Blue Cheese Dressing

Blue cheese dressing is so thick and rich you can use it on salad or as a dip for crudites. Some people enjoy dipping crackers or potato chips, too.

Place all ingredients except blue cheese in a blender or food processor and mix until smooth. Add blue cheese and mix lightly, until most of the lumps are gone. Serve immediately, or cover and refrigerate.

Yields about 2 cups

1 cup crème fraiche

½ cup sour cream

¼ cup Italian parsley, finely chopped

1 to 2 tablespoons fresh lemon juice

1 teaspoon garlic, minced

1½ teaspoons Worcestershire sauce

Pinch of sea salt

Pinch of freshly cracked black pepper

4 ounces sharp blue cheese, crumbled

⅓ cup red wine vinegar

1 teaspoon dried green peppercorns, cracked

1 shallot, minced

1 clove garlic, minced

1 teaspoon Dijon mustard

⅛ teaspoon sea salt

1 cup very good, extra-virgin olive oil

4 ounces fresh chèvre, crumbled

Chèvre and Green Peppercorn Dressing

If you can't find dried green peppercorns, you can use 2 teaspoons of fresh green peppercorns, but mince them first.

Place all ingredients except olive oil and chèvre in a blender, and puree until smooth. With the motor still running, slowly add the olive oil until just blended. Add the chèvre and blend quickly, leaving some lumps. Use immediately, or cover and refrigerate.

Yields 1 cup

1 cup fresh ricotta cheese

4 tablespoons mascarpone

2 tablespoons milk

2 tablespoons fresh basil, minced

1 tablespoon pine nuts, crushed

Warm Ricotta and Basil Dressing

Use this dressing over barbecued steak, chicken, fish, or vegetables.

Put all ingredients in a small saucepan, and stir until combined. Heat gently over medium-low heat until warmed through, then pour immediately over steak, chicken, fish, or vegetables, and serve.

Parmigiano Rinds and Soup

Italians have known for centuries that a Parmigiano rind added to a pot of soup adds piquant flavor and creaminess. Most cheese shops that sell real Parmigiano-Reggiano also grate it for customers who don't have the time. From this, they save the rinds and sell them to their soup makers.

Chicken Stock with Parmigiano-Reggiano Rinds

You can use any chicken part to make broth, but the less meaty parts provide better flavor. Ask your butcher for wings, backs, and necks, or use these parts from a cut-up fryer (you'll need more than one cut-up fryer, though).

1. Combine chicken parts, parsley, thyme, bay leaf, and water in a large stockpot over high heat. Bring to a boil, reduce heat, and then simmer gently. Add chopped onions, carrots, and celery stalks, and continue simmering, uncovered for 3 hours. Add Parmigiano-Reggiano rinds, and simmer for 30 minutes.

2. Strain stock into a clean pot, and discard all but the broth. Stock may be used right away, frozen, or covered and refrigerated.

Yields 8 cups

5 pounds chicken backs, necks, and wings

Small bunch of parsley

8 sprigs fresh thyme, or 1 teaspoon dried

1 bay leaf

4 quarts cold water

1 onion, coarsely chopped

1 carrot, coarsely chopped

1 celery stalk, coarsely chopped

3–4 pieces of Parmigiano-Reggiano rind, about 3" × 3" each

Roasted Vegetable Stock with Parmigiano Rinds

Use this stock as a base for all your vegetable soups. They will taste creamier and lighter than if you use chicken stock, and the added Parmigiano-Reggiano rind provides just the right amount of cheese.

1. Preheat oven to 400°F.

2. Lightly oil a roasting pan, then add onions, mushrooms, carrots, garlic, and turnip. Roast for an hour, until well browned.

3. Put roasted vegetables in large stockpot, and then deglaze the roasting pan with 1 cup of cold water. Add the scraped-up bits and the water to the stockpot. Add parsley, thyme, bay leaf, Parmigiano-Reggiano rinds, and 2 quarts of water, bring to a boil, and then reduce heat and simmer for 45 minutes. Stock may be used right away, frozen, or covered and refrigerated.

Yields 4 cups

1 onion, coarsely chopped

½ pound button mushrooms, chopped

2 carrots, coarsely chopped

8 cloves garlic, minced

1 small turnip, peeled and coarsely chopped

1 cup cold water

Small bunch of parsley

8 sprigs fresh or 1 teaspoon dried thyme

1 bay leaf

3–4 pieces of Parmigiano-Reggiano rind, about 3" × 3" each

2 quarts cold water

6 cups chicken stock

2 tablespoons extra-virgin olive oil

½ medium white onion, chopped

2 cloves garlic, minced

3 stalks Swiss chard, chopped

1 zucchini, chopped

1 carrot, chopped

1 tomato, peeled and chopped

10 ounces canned cannellini beans

1½ tablespoons fresh basil, finely chopped

1½ tablespoons fresh Italian parsley, finely chopped

½ teaspoon kosher salt

¼ teaspoon freshly ground black pepper

1 3" × 3" Parmigiano-Reggiano rind

Classic Minestrone

If you use the Chicken Stock with Parmigiano-Reggiano Rinds recipe previously listed, you don't need to add the Parmigiano-Reggiano rind to this recipe. Either way, this is a deliciously creamy soup.

1. In a large saucepan, heat chicken stock to boiling, then reduce heat and simmer.

2. Meanwhile, heat olive oil in a heavy stockpot, and then add onions and sauté until translucent. Add the garlic, simmer for a minute or two until just beginning to brown, then add chopped Swiss chard, zucchini, carrot, and tomato, and then sauté until vegetables begin to wilt. Add to this the hot chicken stock, cannellini beans, basil, Italian parsley, salt, pepper, and Parmigiano-Reggiano rind. Bring all to a boil, then reduce heat and simmer for 30 minutes.

3. Taste and adjust seasoning, then serve, or cool and refrigerate.

Acid Brightens Flavors

If a soup tastes a little bland, add a bit of vinegar, lemon, or tomato. All of these foods are high in acids, which bring other flavors to life. Try a few experiments. For example, make this soup without the tomatoes, then add ¼–⅓ cup of red wine vinegar and taste the difference.

Cheesy Broccoli Soup

Make this soup in January, when lots of fresh broccoli is available.
It's delicious for lunch or dinner, or pour it over baked potatoes for a midday snack.

1. Melt butter in a large saucepan over medium-low heat. Add the diced onion, celery, and broccoli, and sauté about 5 minutes.

2. Blend in flour, then slowly stir in the wine and chicken stock, stirring frequently to avoid lumps. Bring to a boil, then reduce heat and simmer until vegetables are tender. Season with salt, pepper, and herbs.

3. Add light cream and warm until cream is heated, then remove from heat and add grated sharp Cheddar cheese. Serve immediately.

What Makes Cheddar Cheese Sharp?

Cheddar gets its sharpness from acidity, which comes from the starter culture and aging process. Different cheese makers use different starter cultures to achieve the level of sharpness they want, and then generally, the more aged the Cheddar is, the sharper it becomes.

Serves 8

3 tablespoons unsalted butter

½ white onion, diced

1 celery stalk, diced

1 cup broccoli, chopped

3 tablespoons flour

½ cup dry white wine

3 cups Chicken Stock with Parmigiano-Reggiano Rinds (page 217)

Pinch of sea salt

A twist of freshly ground pepper

¼–½ teaspoon fine herbs

1 cup light cream

½ cup sharp Cheddar cheese, grated

8 slices (8 ounces) bacon, chopped

1 onion, chopped

1 large leek, thinly sliced

2 celery stalks, chopped

2 medium carrots, chopped

2 potatoes, peeled and cubed

2 cups chicken broth

2 cups whole milk

½–⅔ cup Pt. Reyes Original Blue cheese

Freshly ground pepper

Sourdough French bread

Potato Soup with Original Blue and Bacon

This recipe is borrowed from the Giacomini family, who make Pt. Reyes Original Farmstead Blue.

1. In a heavy saucepan, cook bacon over medium heat until crisp. Remove bacon and drain on a paper towel–lined plate.

2. Spoon off all but 2 tablespoons bacon drippings from the saucepan, then add chopped onion, leek, celery, and carrots. Sauté over medium heat until vegetables soften. Add potatoes and chicken broth, then simmer until potatoes are tender. Add milk and cheese, cook for a few minutes until milk and cheese are heated, then taste and adjust seasonings. Serve immediately with thick slices of crusty sourdough French bread.

Yields 1

1 purchased pizza dough

½ cup crushed, peeled tomatoes

¼ teaspoon dry basil, crushed

¼ teaspoon dry oregano, crushed

¼ teaspoon garlic powder

1 teaspoon freshly squeezed lemon juice

¼ teaspoon kosher salt

Pinch of freshly ground black pepper

One handful basil leaves

¼ pound fresh mozzarella di bufala, thinly sliced

2–4 tablespoons Grana Padano, finely grated

Classic Margherita Pizza

This is such an all-time satisfying pizza, loved by adults and kids alike. Mozzarella di bufala is creamier than cow's-milk mozzarella, but it works just as well. It will simply be a bit creamier and lighter.

1. Preheat baking stone in oven or on the barbecue at the highest heat.

2. Mix crushed tomatoes, dry basil, dry oregano, garlic powder, lemon juice, salt, and black pepper together, then spread on rolled, prepared pizza dough.

3. Arrange sliced mozzarella and basil leaves in a pattern (this is just for looks), and sprinkle with grated Grana Padano.

4. Bake for 8–10 minutes until the crust is brown and tomato sauce is bubbly.

Pizza Cream Sauce

This sauce makes a wonderful base for all sorts of pizzas. It changes the balance from sweet and bright to creamy and flavorful. Have fun experimenting with this one.

1. In a small sauté pan, heat olive oil over low heat, then add minced onion and sauté until onions have softened and become translucent. Set aside.

2. Melt butter in a medium, heavy saucepan over low heat.

3. Slowly sprinkle in flour and stir continuously over medium heat until butter and flour form a roux. Add the milk slowly, stirring after each addition to prevent lumps from forming. Add heavy cream, turn heat back to low, and stir frequently until the mixture has thickened. Add sautéed onions and then season with salt, pepper, and thyme.

Yields 1 cup

1 teaspoon olive oil

¼ cup yellow onion, minced

2 tablespoons unsalted butter

2 tablespoons unbleached white flour

½ cup milk

½ cup heavy cream

½ teaspoon kosher salt

⅛ teaspoon ground white pepper

1 teaspoon fresh thyme, minced

Gorgonzola, Pear, and Pine Nut Pizza

This is such a heady and rich pizza, you might just think about serving it for dessert!

1. Preheat baking stone in oven or on the barbecue at the highest heat.

2. Spread Pizza Cream sauce on rolled, prepared pizza dough.

3. Arrange pear slices, Gorgonzola, and pine nuts loosely but evenly on the dough. Shake one squeeze of lemon juice over the top of the pizza.

4. Bake for 8–10 minutes, until the crust is brown and the sauce is bubbly.

Yields 1

1 purchased pizza dough

1 cup Pizza Cream Sauce (above)

1 Bosc pear, peeled and thinly sliced

⅓ cup Italian Gorgonzola, crumbled

2 tablespoons pine nuts

1 squeeze of lemon juice

1 teaspoon unsalted butter

1 teaspoon extra-virgin olive oil

1 medium yellow onion, thinly sliced

1 purchased pizza dough

1 cup Pizza Cream Sauce (page 221)

1 roasted chicken breast, skin off, and shredded

½ cup sharp blue cheese, crumbled

Caramelized Onions, Blue Cheese, and Roasted Chicken Pizza

The sweetness of caramelized onions calls for a sharp and flavorful blue cheese. If you can't find Pt. Reyes Original Blue, try Buttermilk Blue or Maytag Blue.

1. In a medium sauté pan over low heat, melt the butter. Add olive oil and then the sliced onions. Cook for an hour, until the onions are tender and lightly browned.

2. Preheat baking stone in oven or on the barbecue at the highest heat.

3. Spread Pizza Cream sauce on rolled, prepared pizza dough.

4. Top with shredded chicken, caramelized onions, and crumbled blue cheese.

5. Bake for 8–10 minutes until the crust is brown, and cream sauce is bubbly.

Beware of Unbrowned Pizza Cheese!

Not all cheese melts alike. Whole-milk or part-skim mozzarella brown when cooked, but fresh mozzarella and blue cheeses, for example, don't brown when they melt. If you wait for these cheeses to brown you will scorch both the cheese and the pizza, and you'll have to wait quite awhile to eat your pizza so it won't burn your mouth.

Easy Fresh Tomato Sauce

Make use of summer's abundant tomatoes with this easy sauce. Use with fresh pasta, lasagna, or any other dish that calls for tomato sauce. This sauce can also be frozen or canned, then used during the long winter months.

Yields about 2 cups

6 large, ripe tomatoes

4 tablespoons good-quality, extra-virgin olive oil

1 medium white onion, chopped into small pieces

4 cloves garlic, minced

¼ cup red wine

¼ cup fresh basil, chopped

1 teaspoon kosher salt

½ teaspoon freshly ground black pepper

¼ cup water (if necessary)

1. Bring a large pot of water to boil on the stove. De-stem tomatoes, but leave the tomatoes whole; in other words, do not core them. Put whole tomatoes in the boiling water. When their skins begin to burst, retrieve them with tongs and discard the water. Peel tomatoes by pulling skin from burst areas first. The skin should slip off easily. If part of the flesh remains attached to the skin, scrape the flesh into the bowl you'll place the peeled tomatoes in. Discard skins. Chop peeled tomatoes into 1- to 1½-inch chunks. Retain all the tomato juices and put chopped tomatoes, juices, and scrapings in a bowl.

2. Add olive oil to a large sauté pan over medium-high. Add the onions and sauté until transparent, then add the garlic and sauté a minute or two until aromas have blended. Add chopped tomatoes and all the tomato juices to the onions and garlic. Turn the heat up a bit and stir briskly while ingredients blend and heat together. When the tomatoes start to bubble, turn the heat down to medium-low. Add wine, basil, salt, and pepper, and let simmer for 8–10 minutes. Watch carefully; you don't want all the juices to evaporate. Add water if necessary, or additional wine. Taste and adjust seasonings, then use with your favorite fresh pasta or lasagna recipe.

Pasta Pomodoro

One of the easiest pasta dishes in the world is pasta pomodoro. Prepare the tomato sauce from this recipe. Cook some dried or fresh pasta noodles per directions, and then top with tomato sauce and grated Parmigiano-Reggiano, Grana Padano, or Pecorino Romano. Serve immediately and enjoy!

12 lasagna noodles

3 tablespoons extra-virgin olive oil

1 medium white onion, chopped

2 cloves garlic, minced

1½ pounds Italian sausage

4 cups Easy Fresh Tomato Sauce (page 223)

2 cups fresh ricotta

½ cup fresh goat cheese, crumbled

1¼ cups Parmigiano-Reggiano, finely grated

1 large egg, lightly beaten

½ teaspoon kosher salt

¼ teaspoon freshly ground black pepper

1 pound fresh mozzarella, thinly sliced

Italian Sausage with Fresh Mozzarella Lasagna

The inspiration for this recipe comes from The Barefoot Contessa, Ina Garten. She uses sweet Italian turkey sausage and a slightly different tomato sauce. Both are flavorful and delicious.

1. Boil a large, heavy pot of water and cook lasagna noodles for 8–11 minutes until just done. Rinse, drain, coat with 1 tablespoon olive oil, and set aside.

2. Meanwhile, in a large sauté pan, heat 2 tablespoons olive oil, add chopped onions, and sauté until soft and almost transparent. Add garlic and sauté a few minutes more until aromas are blended, then add crumbled Italian sausage and sauté until sausage is cooked through. Then add 4 cups of Easy Fresh Tomato Sauce.

3. In a small bowl, combine ricotta, goat cheese, 1 cup of Parmigiano-Reggiano, egg, salt, and pepper.

4. Heat oven to 375°F. In a 9" × 13" greased baking dish, layer noodles, mozzarella slices, cheese-and-egg mixture, and sausage-and-tomato-sauce mixture. Repeat, and then sprinkle with remaining ¼ cup Parmigiano-Reggiano. Bake for 30–45 minutes, until lasagna is browned and bubbly.

Shepherd's Pancetta and Cheese Lasagna

Make this lasagna on a bleak winter day, when everyone is pining for spring. You'll forget about the dreary weather the minute these aromas fill your house.

1. Heat a large, heavy pot of boiling water and cook lasagna noodles for 8–11 minutes until just done. Rinse, drain, coat with 1 tablespoon olive oil and set aside.

2. Meanwhile, in a large sauté pan, heat 2 tablespoons olive oil, add chopped onions, and sauté until soft and almost translucent. Add garlic and sauté a few minutes more until aromas are blended, then add chopped pancetta and sauté until pancetta is cooked through. Drain on paper towels, then return to pan, add zucchini, sauté for 10 minutes, and then add 4 cups of Easy Fresh Tomato Sauce.

3. In a small bowl, combine ricotta, goat cheese, grated Pecorino Stagionato, egg, salt, and pepper.

4. Heat oven to 375°F. In a 9" × 13" greased baking dish, layer noodles, mozzarella slices, cheese and egg mixture, and pancetta, zucchini, and tomato sauce mixture. Repeat, and then sprinkle with grated Parmigiano-Reggiano. Bake for 30–45 minutes, until lasagna is browned and bubbly.

Serves 8 to 10

- 12 lasagna noodles
- 3 tablespoons extra-virgin olive oil
- 1 medium white onion, chopped
- 2 cloves garlic, minced
- ½ pound pancetta, chopped into small cubes
- 4 large zucchini, chopped into small cubes
- 4 cups Easy Fresh Tomato Sauce (page 223)
- 2 cups fresh ricotta
- ½ cup fresh goat cheese, crumbled
- 1 cup Pecorino Stagianato, coarsely grated
- 1 large egg, lightly beaten
- ½ teaspoon kosher salt
- ¼ teaspoon freshly ground black pepper
- 1 pound fresh mozzarella, thinly sliced
- ¼ cup Parmigiano-Reggiano, finely grated

12 lasagna noodles

3 tablespoons extra-virgin olive oil

12 baby or 5 large leeks, cleaned and chopped into 1-inch squares

4 large zucchini, chopped into ½-inch pieces

5 cloves garlic, minced

3 cups Triple-Cream Cheese Sauce (page 213)

¼ pound whole-milk mozzarella, coarsely grated

¼ pound fontina, coarsely grated

1 pint fresh ricotta

¾ cup Parmigiano-Reggiano, finely grated

Freshly grated nutmeg

Zucchini and Leek Lasagna

This is a light entrée or side dish that is especially good during the holidays, when everyone is eating large, heavy meals. Gruyere, Asiago, and Emmental can all be used as substitutes for fontina.

1. Heat a large, heavy pot of boiling water and cook lasagna noodles for 8–11 minutes until just done. Rinse, drain, coat with 1 tablespoon olive oil, and set aside.

2. Meanwhile, in a large sauté pan, heat 2 tablespoons olive oil, add chopped leeks, and sauté for about 20 minutes until leeks begin to turn soft. Add chopped zucchini and garlic and cook another 10 minutes. Leeks should be very soft and golden.

3. Prepare 3 cups of Triple-Cream Cheese Sauce, remove from heat, and add grated mozzarella and fontina.

4. In a small bowl, combine ricotta and Parmigiano-Reggiano.

5. Heat oven to 375°F. Meanwhile, in a 9" × 13" greased baking dish, layer noodles, leek-and-zucchini mixture, ricotta and Parmigiano-Reggiano mixture, and cheese sauce. Repeat, and then cover with foil and bake for 30 minutes. Remove foil, sprinkle with freshly grated nutmeg, and bake for 15 minutes more, or until lasagna is browned and bubbly.

Rich and Creamy Seafood Lasagna

This makes a delicious and decadent lunch. Serve with a Sauvignon Blanc or an Extra-Brut Champagne, a fresh butter lettuce salad, and end with bowl of ripe strawberries.

Serves 8 to 10

12 lasagna noodles

3 tablespoon extra-virgin olive oil

1 bunch fresh spinach

2 cups fresh ricotta

2 cups Triple-Cream Cheese Sauce (page 213)

½ cup white onion, finely chopped

2 cloves garlic, minced

½ pound fresh scallops, cleaned coarsely chopped

1 pound fresh rock shrimp, cleaned

¼ cup Grana Padano, grated

1. Heat a large, heavy pot of boiling water and cook lasagna noodles for 8–11 minutes until just done. Rinse, drain, coat with 1 tablespoon olive oil, and set aside.

2. Wash and steam fresh spinach until limp. Cool, then chop into small pieces and combine with fresh ricotta.

3. Prepare Triple-Cream Cheese Sauce per recipe.

4. In a medium-size sauté pan, heat 2 tablespoons olive oil, add chopped onions, and simmer until translucent. Add minced garlic, simmer until aromas have blended, then add scallops and rock shrimp. Cook until scallops are done, three to five minutes.

5. Heat oven to 375°F. Meanwhile, in a 9" × 13" greased baking dish, layer noodles, seafood mixture, ricotta-and-spinach mixture, and sauce. Repeat, and then cover with foil and bake for 30 minutes. Remove foil, sprinkle with Grana Padano, and bake for 15 minutes more, or until cheese is browned and bubbly and lasagna is cooked through.

Cheese Platters and Plates

17

Entertain with Cheese

Entertaining is such a wonderful opportunity for cheese fanatics who are hard pressed to think about any other menu item until they've decided on the cheese. Cheese easily fits into every meal, pairs well with a delightful range of sweet and savory flavors, melts and grills spectacularly, and makes a very fine cooking ingredient. When you want to showcase cheese all by itself, however, plates and platters are the best thing to do.

An Hors d'oeuvre Course

The French phrase *hors d'oeuvre* means "dishes separate from the main meal," and has become synonymous with appetizers. When thinking about cheese as an appetizer, there are a few things to consider. First, by definition, it isn't the main meal, and because of this, it should be a light course, with relatively light flavors. Second, it can prepare everyone's palates for the main meal, or be a hearty entrée for a light meal. If the cheese prepares the palate, the flavors should pique people's curiosity about the food and open their palates with bright grass, citrus, and herbal flavors. If it is a hearty entrée, then bolder, earthier flavors will satisfy people's palates and allow them to enjoy a light salad or bowl of soup.

The recipes for "A Platter from France," "An American Artisan Platter," and "A Milky Trio" at the end of this chapter all make good light appetizer platters. For bolder tastes, go to "A Classic Antipasto Platter" or "A Platter from Spain."

An In-Between Course

For the most part, we think of serving cheese at the beginning or end of a meal, but stop and think for a moment about how certain cheeses enhance other tastes. Remember the pecorinos and Asiagos with roasted vegetables? How about the Gruyeres with potatoes, and fresh chèvre with salmon? Just because cheese is an excellent ingredient doesn't mean it can't be served as an accompaniment or as a transition between two courses. For example, if you are serving a first course of fresh spring greens followed by salmon, think about putting a plate of fresh chèvres on the table and invite people to taste the chèvres along with their salad and salmon. The lemony tang of the chèvres will pair beautifully with the grassy brightness of the greens while preparing everyone's palates for the salmon, and quite frankly, it's the easiest course you'll prepare for the meal. Likewise, a few semihard buttery cheeses pair well with soup, and piquant blues certainly spice up a salad and steak.

FACT

There are cheese professionals out there who can help you arrange a tasting party. Ask about cheese-tasting parties at your local cheese counter. Or, if you have a local culinary school, give them a call and see if they have a referral for someone who can help you plan your party. By hiring a professional, all you have to do is enjoy the tasting, along with your guests!

A Dessert Course

Sweet and hearty flavors finish our palates and give us a sense of contentment with the meal. When serving a cheese course for dessert, think about any flavors from the meal you want to lengthen. For example, a main course of juicy chicken is lovely followed by a bowl of French vanilla ice cream. This is because the creamy sweetness of ice cream finishes the chicken flavor; it completes it. Likewise, a rich platter of triple-cream cheeses will finish chicken beautifully, as will a combination of triple-cream bloomy-rind cheese, farmstead Cheddar, and rich blue cheeses. The heavy, bold flavors of a roast can be completed by a combination of washed-rind cheese, aged sheep's-milk cheese, and bold blue cheeses. On the lighter side, a meal of quiche and salad would be nicely completed by a natural-rind goat cheese, a semisoft medium-aged sheep's-milk cheese, and a young Gouda. There are literally hundreds of possible combinations, but you get the idea. The dessert is the end of the meal, and as you choose cheeses for a dessert course, choose those that complement the flavors of the meal and add enough sweetness to satisfy everyone's palate.

Host a Cheese-Tasting Party

What in the world could be more fun than a cheese-tasting party? You've come all this way, learning how cheese helped civilize the world; how animal milks are different in fat content, protein content, and taste; and how cheese is made and classified. You've learned where to buy cheese and how to buy cheese. You've learned the art of tasting cheese, which countries make which cheeses, all about cheese nutrition, how to keep cheese, how to pair it, and how to cut it. Finally, it's time to share. So, without any more fussing around, here's all you need to know to host a great cheese-tasting party.

Rule One: Have Fun

The first and foremost rule is to have fun, because the only way you and your friends will be open to the aesthetics of cheese tasting is if your minds are lively and open. Just as our palates open up to new flavors when they encounter the brightness of citrus and herbs, our minds open up to new experiences when we are excited and happy. Laughing is required.

Rule Two: Give Everyone a Cheese Language

It's one thing to taste something new; it's another thing to recognize the taste as being similar to something else, and it's quite another thing to be able to describe it. So give your guests a leg up by printing copies of the Cheese Notes chart that follows, or if you're feeling ambitious, make one of your own, using your own words. Be sure to write the names of the cheeses you are tasting on the charts for your guests. They'll want to remember them! As your guests sample each cheese, they can use this chart to circle the cheese's qualities as they discover them.

Cheese Notes

Cheese Name:					
Rind	*Paste Color*	*Paste Texture*	*Aroma*	*Flavor*	*Mouthfeel*
No Rind	Bright White	Soft	Milky	Sweet	Light
Natural	Bone White	Spreadable	Fruity	Tangy	Creamy
White	Cream	Flaky	Nutty	Lactic	Crumbly
Ash	Beige	Medium	Sweet	Nutty	Smooth
Orange	Yellow	Spongy	Herbal	Citrus	Granular
Soft	Orange	Rubbery	Spicy	Salty	Runny
Medium	Blue	Granular	Pungent	Grassy	Oily
Hard	Blotchy	Crumbly	Farmyard	Herbs	Greasy
Wax	Veined	Hard	Ammonia	Vegetable	Coating

Rule Three: Choose the Cheese

The best place to buy cheese for a tasting party is at a place where you can taste the cheeses first. Tasting the cheese will give you a good sense of the breadth of flavors and aromas, and how they complement each other. You'll want to select at least six and up to twelve cheeses (more than that, and everyone's palates will be overloaded). Choose cheeses that range from mild to strong and that represent different texture, rind, milk, and cheese-making categories. Beyond this, you can select cheese by any number of criteria: new and seasonal cheeses, cheeses from certain countries, cheeses from certain milks, Old World versus New World cheese, washed-curd cheeses, bandage-wrapped cheeses. You get the idea; just about every aspect of cheese making presents a way to experience a variety of different cheese.

Rule Four: Pair the Drinks

This is perhaps the trickiest part of a cheese tasting, because people tend to drink what they know and like. Fortunately, you can use the guide-lines in Chapters 11 and 12 to pair your cheeses with a selection of juice, wine, spirits, or beer. Put as many glasses out per guest as you expect to pour, let them know what they'll be drinking with each cheese, and provide plenty of ice water to allow everyone to clear their palates between different kinds of cheeses and drinks.

FACT

Professional cheese tasters always want to see the rind because cheese can be classified by rind type. The rind indicates the method of aging. A healthy cheese will have a healthy rind, so professional tasters also look for rinds that have the appropriate moisture and/or mold types appropriate to the cheese. Then they'll smell both the cheese and the rind before they taste a single morsel. Train yourself to look at the rind first, then the paste, then smell and taste.

Rule Five: Pair the Food

Cheese tasting alone will fill some people, especially if the cheeses are rich, but most likely you'll want to provide some other food to balance the cheese and satisfy appetites. Use ideas from Chapter 14 and from the platter recipes at the end of this chapter to pair cheeses with fruit, nuts, honey, jam, chutneys, and vegetables. You'll certainly want to serve crackers, sliced bread, or both, but remember, both should be as bland and mild as possible. Don't serve sesame-covered crackers unless you feel they enhance the flavors of a particular cheese, and don't serve a sourdough baguette unless you want the acid of it to balance a cheese. Plain crackers or a sliced sweet baguette will let the cheeses speak for themselves.

Rule Six: Prepare Cheese Plates

Let all the cheeses come to room temperature (you'll need an hour for hard cheeses, and twenty to thirty minutes for soft cheeses). Ideally, everyone should taste all parts of each cheese, and so it's best to prepare slices, ahead of time, on a plate for each guest. Each slice should have some rind, the outer edge of the cheese just underneath the rind, and a good sampling of the middle.

Arrange the slices on individual plates in a logical pattern, such as approximating the numbers of a clock, and use a garnish of some sort (for example, an edible leaf), to mark the starting cheese. Make sure you arrange the cheeses in order of mild to strong. Many cheeses are strong enough in aroma, flavor, or mouthfeel that they wipe one's palate out. That is, once you've tasted them, you'll have difficulty tasting anything else. Because of this, it's important to taste cheeses in order of mild to strong, with mild being cheeses that have light aromas and light tastes, and strong being cheeses with pungent aromas, bold tastes, or both.

Finally, put a generous pile of napkins at each place, and encourage people to use their fingers to test texture. (Fingerbowls are nice too).

QUESTION?

Why not put wedges of cheese out for people to help themselves?
If you pass wedges around for everyone to slice before tasting, you run the risk of people selecting only certain parts of the cheese. They may shy away from the rind, or take a large chunk from the middle, leaving the next person with mostly rind. After the tasting, put the remaining wedges on the table so people can help themselves.

Rule Seven: Prime Their Palates

Remember the first time you could distinguish a forward taste from a finish taste? And your delight in recognizing the lemony finish on fresh chèvre? This delight is what you want your guests to experience, and two things will help them get there. First, serve only mild-tasting (bland) appetizers and, if you can get away with it, plain water before you get to the cheese. Second, before the tasting begins, have people taste some other things, to give them an idea of the flavors and aromas they might sense in the cheese: lemon juice, orange juice, green apples, unsalted butter, plain yogurt, whole milk, almonds, cashews, walnuts, whole-wheat toast, mushrooms, and wheat grass, if you can find it. You don't need to use all of these, just a few to give your guests a sense of how different flavors show up on their tongues. Have everyone take small sips or bites and then talk about what they smell and taste. If you can get everyone to taste the same thing at the same time, even better!

Rule Eight: Look, Feel, Smell, Taste

Just as you would taste cheese at the cheese counter, have your guests go through the steps of looking, feeling, smelling, and tasting. Go in order of mild cheese to strong cheese, and have everyone look at the rind, the paste, and the layers of aging, and talk about how each is made. Have them feel the cheese to get a sense of its resilience and texture. Then have them smell the cheese. Finally, have everyone put a small piece of cheese on the tips of their tongues, then move the cheese slowly back in their mouths, noting where and when certain flavors pop up. Then they can chew. After each piece is swallowed, ask them to inhale and note the aromas and tastes at the end.

Platter How-To's

Whether you're preparing a plate or platter, or hosting a cheese-tasting party, you need to know how much to buy and serve, and then how to present the cheese in its best light.

Generally speaking, 3 ounces, or a little under ¼ pound of cheese per person, will suffice for appetizers, desserts, and cheese courses. In addition, you should take into account the heartiness and quantity of other foods. If there are lots of other appetizer or dessert choices, serve about 2 ounces per person. However, if you are serving more than one cheese, assume every-one will have a piece of each cheese, and be sure there are about 3 ounces of each cheese per person.

Cheese platters are a great way to present several varieties of cheeses at one time: mild to strong, soft to hard, no rind to wax rind, different milk types, or cheeses from certain regions or countries. Regardless, the platter should be arranged to emphasize variety and show off the full spectrum of colors, textures, and shapes.

Starting with the platter, choose one that promotes the cheese. For exam-ple, a dark platter highlights white and cream-colored cheeses. A white platter serves as a nice backdrop for a variety of different cheese colors. Rustic cheeses present well on a straw mat, and a clear glass platter or cake stand serves small crottins or Chevrots quite well. Wood platters or cutting boards always make nice cheese presentations, as do marble or slate platters. The size of the platter is important, too. A large platter with small pieces of cheese suggests small portions and restrained tasting. A platter just large enough for the cheese to fit on may look crowded and out of balance, or it can appear pleasingly abundant. A platter with room for each cheese but not much other space lets the cheese speak for itself, without comment from too little or too much space. Whatever you choose, it's good to choose something that allows cheese to shine.

Arrange cheeses in a pattern suggested by the cheeses' shapes. For example, three cheeses, one round, one stocky triangular wedge, and one slender wedge, can be grouped as if they were the points of a triangle, which allows each shape some room of its own. Closer together, the round cheese can be framed by the different wedges. If you have several large squares of cheese, cut a few into smaller squares or triangles before plating to provide a nice balance of shapes.

Garnishes are terrific on a cheese platter. Fresh, bright green leaves placed partway under cheese look lovely, as do fresh, edible flowers along the sides. You can also put small mounds of jams, preserves, or chutneys; small piles of figs or grapes; a pleasing row of vegetables; some olives; or nuts on a platter.

Depending on the cheese, you'll want to put crackers or sliced baguettes on the platter or on a tray near it. If the cheeses are soft and runny, put the crackers and bread on a separate plate. If the cheeses are firm, the crackers and bread can be on the same plate.

With platters, think about the weather and how long the cheese will be out. Soft cheeses do best when left out for short periods of time in temperate weather. Hard cheeses can withstand higher temperatures and be left out much longer before losing too much moisture. And highly pungent cheeses will begin to take over a room if left out too long. Finally, to keep the flavors of each cheese true, make sure each cheese has a knife of its own.

A Platter from France

Serves 12

¾ pound Brie de Meaux

¾ pound Saint Nectaire

¾ pound Fourme d'Ambert

½ cup cracked French green olives

1 sweet baguette

Lemon leaves for garnish

These French cheeses are stars of three cheese-making techniques. A soft bloomy-rind Brie with tones of earthy mushrooms pairs well with the light pungency of a semisoft, washed-rind Saint Nectaire. Contrast comes from the crisp, clean, blue called Fourme d'Ambert.

Bring all cheeses to room temperature. Arrange them on a platter, with separate knives for each cheese. Put olives in a low bowl that can be placed on the same platter or next to it. Slice the baguette and arrange in a bread basket or bowl, and complete the platter with a garnish of lemon leaves. Don't forget to put out an empty bowl for olive pits!

A Classic Antipasto Platter

Serves 12

¾ pound Pecorino Renero

¾ pound Taleggio

¾ pound aged Gorgonzola

¼ pound thinly sliced air-cured prosciutto

¼ pound Toscano salami

¼ pound mortadella

½ cup pepperoncini

¼ cup sun-dried tomatoes

¼ cup Italian Cerignola olives

1 sour baguette, rustic baguette, or Italian long bread

Nothing completes an Italian meal like an antipasto platter. The cheeses and meats combine beautifully with pepperoncini, sun-dried tomatoes, and olives. This platter combines cheeses made of medium-aged sheep's milk, a soft-washed rind, and hearty blue molds.

Bring all cheeses to room temperature. Slice the Pecorino Renero into triangles, then arrange the cheeses and sliced meats on a platter with several knives. Garnish with pepperoncinis, sun-dried tomatoes, and olives. Slice the baguette and arrange in a bread basket or bowl, and serve!

An American Artisan Platter

Use this as a foundation to create platters made from local, artisanal cheeses and fresh fruit. This platter combines a complex, tangy, aged cow's-milk cheese, an ash-layered goat's-milk cheese in a bloomy rind, and a sharp, bright cow's-milk blue.

Bring all cheeses to room temperature. Slice figs lengthwise in quarters. Arrange cheeses on a platter, using the sliced figs and flowers for garnish. The crackers can be on the same plate or on a plate to the side, and don't forget to provide a knife for each cheese.

Serves 12

¾ pound Bellwether Carmody Reserve

¾ pound Humboldt Fog

¾ pound Pt. Reyes Farmstead Blue

6 fresh figs

A few nasturtium flowers for garnish

Olive-oil crackers or stone-ground wheat crackers

A Platter from Spain

There's lots of flavor and heat on this platter. Place complementary flavors next to each other to give your guests hints of which to combine.

Bring all cheeses to room temperature. On a platter, arrange the Nevat near a small dish of boquerones, the Roncal near the piquillo peppers, and the Marcona almonds near the La Serena. Slice the baguette and put in a basket, lined with a colorful napkin, and serve.

Boquerones

You'll find boquerones in specialty food stores or delicatessens. They are anchovies that have been marinated in olive oil, salt, and sherry vinegar. Boquerones are standard fare in tapas bars in Spain. Once you've tried them, you'll see how different they are from unmarinated anchovies.

Serves 12

¾ pound Nevat

¾ pound Roncal

¾ pound La Serena

½ cup Marcona almonds

⅓ pound boquerones

¼ cup piquillo peppers

1 sweet baguette

A Creamy Platter

Serves 12

¾ pound Brebiou
¾ pound Brillat Savarin
¾ pound Saint Agur
¼ cup alfalfa honey
Table water crackers

Who doesn't enjoy cheeses rich in cream? Try this platter of creamy sheep's-milk, triple-cream cow's-milk, and luscious blue cheese for your next decadent dessert course. A small dish of honey adds just the right touch.

Bring all cheeses to room temperature (none of these will take much more than twenty minutes). Put honey in a small dish with a spoon, and arrange with cheese and crackers on a platter, with an individual knife for each cheese. Enjoy!

A Milky Trio

Serves 12

2 Redwood Hill Camellia Rounds
¾ pound Petit Basque
¾ pound Bethmal ·
Lemon leaves for garnish
Whole wheat crackers

It's always fun to try cheeses made of cow, goat, and sheep's milk on the same plate. This platter combines a goat's-milk Camembert with a semihard sheep's-milk cheese and a washed-rind raw cow's-milk cheese. All are fairly light in taste, which makes it easy to taste the differences in the milks.

Bring all cheeses to room temperature, then arrange on a platter over lemon leaves. Arrange crackers on the platter, and serve.

The Cows and Goats of Caumont
Bethmal comes from Caumont, France, and is made in two forms, one from goat's milk, and one from cow's milk. Both use raw milk, and each wheel is washed in brine. Try to taste them side by side sometime. You'll find the difference startling.

A Goat's-Milk Platter

This is a lovely way to present three very different goat's-milk cheeses. This recipe calls for serving the cheeses on a straw mat. If you can't find one, use some raffia for garnish.

Bring all cheeses to room temperature, garnish with flowers, and then arrange on a platter over a straw mat. Arrange flat bread on the platter, and serve with separate knives for each cheese.

Serves 8

1 Chevrot

½ pound Drunken Goat

½ pound Midnight Moon

Fresh, edible flowers for garnish

Straw mat

Pumpernickel flat bread

American Artisanal Cheddars

These are delightfully complex cheeses that vary considerably in sharpness, creaminess, and texture. There are many American artisanal Cheddars you can substitute, but taste them first to be sure they complement each other.

1. Bring all cheeses to room temperature.

2. Toss apples in a bowl with lemon juice.

3. Arrange cheeses on a platter with apple slices and crackers, and serve.

Serves 12

¾ pound San Joaquin Gold cheese

¾ pound Shelburne Farms Cheddar

¾ pound Beecher's Flagship Cheddar

2 crisp apples, cored and sliced

½ teaspoon fresh lemon juice

Hearty whole wheat crackers

Italian Table Cheeses

Serves 12

¾ pound fresh Asiago cheese

¾ pound Piave cheese

¾ Fontina Val D'Osta cheese

2 dozen breadsticks

The Italians and French are known for keeping a plate of tasty cheeses to present at every meal. Nothing could be simpler, and once you taste these you might start doing the very same thing.

Bring cheeses to room temperature. Arrange large wedges of each cheese on a plate, and put the breadsticks in several tall water glasses or an empty vase. Serve at every opportunity.

A Basque Table Platter

Serves 12

¾ pound Ossau Iraty

¾ pound Garrotxa

¾ pound Bleu de Basque

½ cup French dry-cured olives

Rustic baguette

If you can't find any of the three cheeses listed in this recipe, substitute with a semihard sheep's-milk cheese, a semihard goat's-milk cheese, and a sheep's-milk blue from the Basque country.

Bring all cheeses to room temperature. Arrange the cheeses on a platter with the olives and sliced baguette, with a knife for each cheese.

Earth and Mushroom Flavors

Next time you think hearty meal, think Basque cheese. These cheeses grew up next to big bowls of soup and steaming platters of beans. Whether you're serving lentils, black beans, or a bowl of hearty soup, hearty sheep's- and goat's-milk cheeses make gracious complements to elegant and simple meals.

A Platter from Greece

*This takes a little bit of preparation, but the results are wonderful.
If you can't find Manouri, you can use fresh ricotta instead.*

1. In a bowl, combine Manouri with crushed oregano, lemon juice, salt, and pepper until blended.

2. Bring Kasseri and Graviera to room temperature. Arrange cheeses, olives, and flatbread on a platter, garnish with the olive branch, and serve with individual knives for each cheese.

Serves 12

¾ pound Manouri

½ teaspoon dry Greek oregano

¼ teaspoon fresh lemon juice

Pinch of salt and pepper

¾ pound Kasseri

¾ pound Graviera

½ cup Thasos olives

Seeded flatbread

Olive branch for garnish

Goudas Galore

Have fun introducing your guests to these surprising Goudas. If you can't find them, ask your local cheese monger to recommend a young cow's-milk Gouda, a one-year-aged goat's-milk Gouda, and an eighteen-month-aged cow's-milk Gouda that can substitute.

Bring all cheeses to room temperature. Arrange cheese and cantaloupe on a platter, with a fork for the cantaloupe and knives for each cheese. Garnish with salted almonds and serve.

Don't Forget the Goudas

So many people grow up eating small rounds of red-wax Gouda, they are surprised at the huge variety of Goudas available. Next time you're at a cheese counter, ask if they have any Goudas. Then ask to try the youngest one first, followed by medium-aged ones, then end with the oldest. This order will keep your palate fresh.

Serves 12

¾ pound Vlaskaas

¾ pound Balarina one-year-aged goat Gouda

¾ pound Old Amsterdam

¼ of a fresh cantaloupe, sliced into long strips

¼ cup roasted, salted almonds

Serves 12

¾ pound Lighthouse Blue
   Brie

¾ pound Cashel Blue

¾ pound Stilton

½ cup fig jam

The Blues

Put on some jazz, pour some port, and let these cheeses sing.

Bring cheeses and fig jam to room temperature. Put the fig jam in a bowl, arrange cheeses and individual knives on a platter around the bowl, and serve.

Serves 12

1 heirloom tomato

¾ pound mozzarella
   bocconcinis

¾ pound fresh sheep's-milk
   ricotta

¾ pound cow's- or sheep's-
   milk Crecenza

Hearty, seeded crackers

A Fresh Course

Fresh cheeses aren't just for cooking anymore. They make elegant, light appetizer platters, too.

Slice tomato and arrange with cheese on a large-enough plate so the cheeses don't run together. Arrange crackers on a separate plate or serving dish. Serve with individual knives for each cheese.

Preview to Spice

Next time you serve hot and spicy curry, try serving this plate of cheeses along with it. The fruitiness of each cheese mellows out the spice and enhances the roundness of all the flavors.

Bring cheeses to room temperature, and then thinly slice about a quarter of a pound of each cheese. Arrange cheeses and dates on platter and serve with the meal.

Serves 12

¾ pound Ewephoria

¾ pound Pleasant Ridge Reserve

¾ pound Roaring Forties Blue

½ cup Medjhool dates

Washed-Rind Bliss

The trick to combining washed-rind cheese is going from mild to strong. Here, the light flavors of reblechon serve as a springboard to the goat Bethmal, and the goat Bethmal sets your taste buds up for the Epoisse. Small slices of pear, in between, cleanse the palate.

Bring cheeses to room temperature and thinly slice the pears. Put each cheese and some sliced pears on individual plates (one cheese per plate), and serve with a knife for each cheese.

Serves 12

¾ pound reblechon

¾ pound goat Bethmal

¾ pound Epoisse

2 Bosc pears

Chapter 18

Let Cheese Be Your Travel Guide

Next time you plan a trip, why not plan it around cheese? It's not such an outrageous thing to consider. People plan trips around sightseeing, museums, stores, wineries, and breweries all the time. When you return, not only will you have some great stories to tell, but also you'll have become acquainted with a whole new assortment of cheese!

Cheese Country

The best place to look for cheese is where it's made or sold in abundance. For example, you could fill months (no doubt years) sampling artisanal cheeses in France, but perhaps only a few hours sampling imported cheeses in Alaska. The first rule of thumb, then, is to head straight for cheese country. With a little research and planning, your trip will be successful.

Do a Little Research

Start with countries where cheese is abundant: Holland, Denmark, Norway, France, Germany, Switzerland, Italy, Spain, England, the United States, and Australia. Then think about what kind of cheese you most want to try.

FACT

When traveling for cheese, go places where you can find ones you are most curious about or want to try. Are you delighted with bloomy- and natural-rind chèvres? Then head for northern California, Vermont, or the Loire Valley. Or, do you want to try a dozen different Goudas? Then head straight to Holland.

Food tours are becoming more popular every day. To find a good cheese tour, check the Internet under "cheese tours" and browse the listings, but be sure to carefully check the tour's reputation, reliability, and refund policy. Check with travel agencies, and ask your fellow food friends or local cheese monger for recommendations. The foodie network is spectacular!

Local visitors bureaus and Chambers of Commerce are also good resources, and don't forget about travel guides. They often include places to eat and places to tour, and they'll know if there are any cheese-making operations open to the public. Use travel guides to help you find cheese shops, cheese festivals, and specialty food shops.

Take a Cheese Class

Places like Artisanal Premium Cheese in New York offer regular classes on cheese appreciation, cheese tasting, and pairing cheese with beverages and other foods. Many specialty food stores like The Pasta Shop in Oakland, and Murray's in New York also offer classes. Perhaps you will be in the area for another reason, and if so, take advantage of the opportunity to take a cheese class. Or, if you're really a devoted cheese lover, plan an entire trip around a cheese class and make sure you take the time to visit specialty food shops and cheese makers in the area you're visiting.

As mentioned previously, when signing on for a guided tour, follow the three R's: reputation, reliability, and refund policy. Word of mouth is one of the best ways to find good tours, so ask your friends who love to travel. They may not have taken a food tour, but they may know a reputable tour company that can help you find food tours.

Plan Ahead

Whether you are on a tour or driving yourself, it's good to have a map along. Good directions will keep you from getting lost and discouraged. If you're on a tour, you can use the map to see where you are (this is particularly good if you'd like to return on your own at another time). And, when you return home, you'll be able to see where you were. It makes the trip that much more memorable.

Be Comfortable and Cool

Nothing ruins a good gastronomic experience faster than tight-fitting clothes, heat, and sore feet. Plan ahead by dressing in climate-appropriate clothes that are comfortable. Take along a bottle of water that you can refill as you go. Wear comfortable shoes, and if you'll be touring creameries or farms, wear shoes that can get wet and muddy.

Take a Camera

Cheese country is always picturesque. There are pastures, animals, barns, cheese makers, and cheese, all of which make for spectacular photos. If you're visiting a city, cheese displays make gorgeous photos. You don't want to miss any of it, so be prepared to take as many pictures as you want.

ALERT!

Avoid wearing cologne or perfume while on a cheese tour. People on any food- or-beverage tasting tour need all their olfactory senses to concentrate on what they are tasting. If you wear cologne or perfume, it will distract your fellow travelers from being able to taste and smell the cheese.

Visiting Cheese Makers

Up until recently, most of the cheese tours you could take were of large-scale operations where the machinery was most of what you saw. Farmstead and artisan cheese makers throughout the world have heard your pleas. And while many are too small to offer tours on a regular basis (they have their hands full making cheese), more and more are opening up for seasonal tours and casual drop-in visitors. Through American artisanal cheese guilds, you'll find your way to the American creameries and farms open to tours.

California Artisan Cheese Guild and California Milk Advisory Board

Newly formed in 2006, the California Artisan Cheese Guild is busy developing a map of artisan and farmstead cheese makers, complete with information on visiting days and hours. Check their Web site, *www.cacheeseguild .org,* for updates. In the meantime, the California Milk Advisory Board's Web site, *www.realcaliforniacheese.com,* lists cow's-milk farmstead cheese makers along with contact information.

I Love Cheese.com

The founders of I Love Cheese.com are wise to the pull of artisanal and farmstead cheese. On *www.ilovecheese.com*, you can find maps to creameries on the East Coast, in the Midwest, on the West Coast, and in the Southern United States.

Maine Cheese Guild

The Maine Cheese Guild publishes a map on their Web site, *www .mainecheeseguild.org*, showing all the places in Maine you can buy cheese. The locations of twenty dairies are shown, as well as those of five specialty food stores.

Ohio Farmstead-Artisan Cheese Guild

Also a newly formed guild, the Web site of the Ohio Farmstead-Artisan Cheese Guild has recently launched their Web site. Check *www. ohcheeseguild.com* for updates, contact information, and guides to local creameries.

Pacific Northwest Cheese

Cheese events and creameries throughout Oregon and Washington are tracked on Pacific Northwest Cheese's Web site, *www.pnwcheese.typepad .com*.

Southern Cheesemakers' Guild

The Southern Cheesemakers' Guild publishes information on cheese-making dairies throughout the southern United States. The dairies and creameries are grouped by milk type and information on directions, visiting hours, and phone numbers is all there; see *www.southerncheese.com*.

Vermont Cheese Council

The Vermont Cheese Council recognizes thirty-nine artisan and farm-stead cheese makers on their brochure and map, "Vermont Cheesemakers." Phone numbers, visiting hours, and information on tours are all listed on the map, which can be found at *www.vtcheese.com*. And don't miss the Web site's virtual tour!

Wisconsin Milk Marketing Board

The Wisconsin Milk Marketing Board publishes a guide to artisanal and farmstead dairies in Wisconsin and a map, "A Traveler's Guide to Wisconsin Cheese, Beer and Wine." This is a terrific resource for travelers. On one side is a map of Wisconsin with all the food sites to see, and the opposite side provides names, directions, tour information, phone numbers, and hours. It also includes wineries and specialty food stores.

Make the Foodie Rounds

Admit it. You love cheese; you've read a book about it. You will now spend more time than anyone can imagine in pursuit of cheese. Do you know what this means? You're well on your way to foodiedom. But don't worry, that's all part of the fun, and now, whenever you travel, you'll find yourself in pursuit of fabulous food. It's all good.

Specialty Food Stores

Here's a chance to visit all those wonderful food stores you've been hearing about. If you're headed to New York, make a beeline to Dean & Deluca, Fairway Market, and Murray's. If you're in San Francisco visit Cowgirl Creamery at the farmers' market in the Ferry Building (if you're there on a Saturday morning, you'll be dazzled by the local produce!), or one of the two Pasta Shops in Berkeley and Oakland. In Portland? Visit one of almost a dozen New Seasons Markets and Steve's Cheese shops. You get the idea. Fabulous food stores are out there, and a visit to one of them is sure to be delightful to any cheese lover.

Wineries and Breweries

Wineries and breweries are also a great place to locate cheese. Aim for ones with restaurants or picnic areas; it's likely they'll offer cheese on the menu or for sale by the piece or the pound. More than likely, the cheeses will be local and paired with some of the wine or beer.

Farmers' Markets

If you're in a new town on a weekend, head for the local farmers' market to find some cheese. Not only will you have a chance to taste new and interesting cheeses, you might get to meet the cheese maker at the market. Stop and taste, have a chat, and enjoy the local scene. It's always a treat.

In the Produce Section

Is the town you're visiting short on specialty food stores, farmers' markets, and wineries? Then find out where the best produce is sold, and see if you can find some cheese there. Retailers know that people interested in fresh produce are likely to be interested in gourmet cheese, and if there is any local cheese to be sold, it could be there or in meat markets.

Cheese on a Picnic

Few people can resist the pull of an afternoon in the sun accompanied by good food and friends. Picnics are the perfect place for cheese, and now that you know about all these wonderful varieties, let them join the picnic too.

Picnic Baskets

Picnic baskets seem to have been made with cheese in mind. They provide just the right environment to bring your cheese to room temperature, and usually are equipped with cutting board, knives, and handy spots to pack cheese accompaniments.

The best way to pack cheese for a picnic is in a zip-top plastic storage bag. The bags keep cheeses to themselves (they are awfully generous with their aroma), and the humidity that collects in the bags is good for maintaining cheese moisture. They also make cleanup easy. If you have leftover cheese (a slim possibility), you can repack it in the same bags. If you don't have any zip-top bags handy, then wrap cheese in plastic wrap, thin foil, or wax paper.

Know you're going on a picnic today? Take an early walk to the bakery, market, or coffee shop, and pick up a fresh baguette. Pack it along with a serrated knife, and you'll have the perfect cheese partner. If you tend toward the savory, choose a sourdough baguette. If you lean toward sweet, choose a sweet baguette.

Best Cheeses for a Picnic

The easiest way to choose cheeses for a picnic is to pair them with other foods and drinks. For example, if you are having sliced ham, roast beef, and salami, you'll want three cheeses that complement these meats well. Gruyere is always great with ham, a soft sheep's-milk Brebiou will be all you need to add to roast beef, and sharp Cheddar never fails a good salami.

Picnicking with vegetarians? Then pack cheeses for eating and dips. Carrots and herbed Le Roule make a delightful match, as will fresh spring radishes and triple-cream cheese. Then add a hearty table cheese like Beaufort or Comte that can be eaten all alone. Finally, take a lesson from the monks, and pack a washed-rind cheese full of earthy pungency and goodness.

Pack ice if the day is warm, or if you're taking along a soft or semisoft cheese. And though it's always nice for each cheese to have its own knife, go a little rustic for the outdoors and let the flavors meld. After all, the very definition of picnic is simple and fun.

Wine and Cheese Kits

No discussion of picnics would be complete without mention of insulated wine and cheese kits. They are usually made of canvas, with insulation to keep wine and cheese cool and safe, and come complete with corkscrew, knife, forks, cutting board, acrylic wineglasses, plates, and napkins.

You can also make your own wine and cheese kit. Buy an insulated, zippered cooler, large enough for a bottle of wine, some cheese, and a log of salami or two. Stock it with plastic forks, napkins, and acrylic wineglasses and plates. Keep ice packs in your freezer. Then, when you are ready, put the ice packs in with the cheese and wine, and you're good to go!

Traveling with Cheese

Once your family and friends know you've become a tyrophile they'll always expect you to bring cheese. Not to mention, you'll feel somewhat bereft if you end up in a place where no one's ever heard of real Parmigiano-Reggiano. Here are a few tips to make sure all your travels are well accompanied by good cheese.

Cheese as Traveling Companion

Almost all train stations, bus stations, and airports in Europe sell abundant and varied types of cheese because Europeans are used to taking cheese to eat on trips. You don't need a shop at the train station or airport to make this happen. Buy some cheese ahead of time, and then watch the countryside go by while you munch on your favorite cheese. Some activities that lend themselves to cheese snacking include:

- **Boating:** Going on a long cruise? Pack a wheel of rich and nutty Gouda. The sailors of early days certainly did this. Why don't you? It will keep beautifully and provide a rustic, wholesome part of your daily meals.
- **Bicycling:** Cheese is the perfect power food to energize your next bike trip. Pack a hard cheese (see the list that follows) that doesn't need refrigeration to enjoy on a break with fresh, cool water, and a piece of fruit.
- **Hiking:** Crumbled Parmigiano-Reggiano mixed with cranberries and almonds makes the perfect trail mix. See the recipe on page 174.
- **Skiing:** The Swiss have known for hundreds of years that active winter sports need a boost from cheese. Take a couple of ounces of Gruyere the next time you hit the slopes. It's the perfect pick-me-up when you're feeling tired and cold.

Now you're ready to head out in search of new cheese. But you know it's going to be a long journey, and perhaps several hours or days before you reach your first destination. You'd better take a little cheese along, just in case.

Top Ten Road-Tested Cheeses

Here's a top ten list of cheeses that can handle all sorts of things. They need little or no refrigeration (as long as it's not too hot and you keep them out of the sun), they are fantastically delicious, and they'll give you important vitamins, calcium, and energy to keep you in top shape for the road.

- Grana Padano
- Parmigiano-Reggiano
- Piave
- San Joaquin Gold
- Mimolette
- Ewephoria
- Prima Donna
- Old Amsterdam
- Beemster X.O.
- Saenkaenter

How to Keep Your Cheese Happy

Invest in a couple of collapsible, soft-sided, insulated coolers and several cold packs you can keep in your freezer. Wrap the cold packs in cheese paper or butcher paper, then with some plastic wrap. This will keep the cheese from getting freezer burn. Then arrange the cheese in the cooler with an icepack or two, and you'll have no cheese worries for the day.

Sealed plastic containers make great cheese-traveling partners. They contain aromas while allowing cheese to breathe. Dan Strongin, of Edible Solutions says to look for containers with ribbed bottoms, then place a paper towel underneath the cheese and seal. The paper towel helps create humidity, which keeps the moisture in. Tupperware makes one of the best bottom-ribbed, sealed containers for cheese.

Mini Field Guide to Cheese

Whether you're looking for a good cheese to eat or finding one to pair with a meal or drink, it's always nice to have a good list as a reference and starting point. This Mini Field Guide of almost 200 cheeses will get you started. Use it as a guide to keep a list of all the new cheeses you find, too.

Appenzeller

(AH-pen-zeller)
Name-controlled, Switzerland
Raw cow's milk
Classifications: Semihard, brushed rind
Aged: At least sixty days
Fat: 45 percent
Description: Small eyes, smooth paste, ivory to ochre colored
Aroma: Fruity, nutty, sweet, spicy
Mouthfeel: Smooth, clean
Flavors: Light fruit, tangy, nutty, long finish
Pairings: Full-bodied Chardonnay, Beaujolais, Cabernet Sauvignon, Merlot

Ardrahan

(ARR-dra-han)
Burns family, Ireland
Cow's milk
Classifications: Semisoft, washed rind
Aged: Two months
Description: Farmstead, brownish-orange rind with beige-straw-colored paste
Aroma: Very pungent, earthy, and salty
Mouthfeel: Creamy and full coating
Flavors: Savory, smoky, and milky
Pairings: Riesling, fruity Syrah, full-body Rioja

Asiago

(ah-see-AH-go)
D.O.C. Controlled, Italy
Cow's milk
Classifications: Semisoft to hard
Aged: Two to nine months
Fat: 30–45 percent
Description: Loose texture, soft to hard, ivory colored
Aroma: Milky to spicy

Mouthfeel: Creamy to granular
Flavors: Lactic, tangy, citrus, salty
Pairings: Chardonnay, Gewurztraminer, Riesling, Barbera, Sangiovese

Banon
(BAN-awe)
Various Producers, France
Cow's, goat's, or sheep's milk
Classifications: Soft, leaf-wrapped
Aged: Less than thirty days
Fat: 45 percent
Description: Fresh chèvre wrapped in wine, or Cognac-dipped chestnut leaves
Aroma: Fresh, herbal
Mouthfeel: Creamy, smooth
Flavors: Tangy, citrus, grassy
Pairings: Cognac, Chenin Blanc, Pinot Noir

Beaufort
(BOW-for)
A.O.C. Controlled, France
Raw cow's milk
Classifications: Semihard, brushed rind
Aged: Six to eighteen months
Fat: 50 percent
Description: Smooth paste, creamy texture, melts well
Aroma: Mildly sweet and fruity
Mouthfeel: Light, creamy, smooth
Flavors: Lactic, sweet, fruity
Pairings: Pinot Noir, Riesling, full-body Chardonnay, dry Champagne, Syrah, porter

Beecher's Flagship
(BEE-chers)
Beecher's Cheese, America
Cow's milk
Classifications: Semihard, Cheddar
Description: Smooth ivory paste, breaks well
Aroma: Milky, tangy, spicy
Mouthfeel: Creamy, smooth

Flavors: Sweet, tangy, lactic, salty
Pairings: Pale ale

Beemster X.O.
(BEAM-ster)
Cheeseland, U.S. and Holland
Cow's milk
Classifications: Wax-coated Gouda
Aged: Twenty-six months
Description: Hard, irregular eyes, granular, butterscotch color
Aroma: Nutty, sweet, spicy, candy
Mouthfeel: Crumbly, granular, thick
Flavors: Sweet, tangy, nutty, caramel, butterscotch
Pairings: Porter, sweet stout, Scotch, whiskey, Cognac

Besace de Berger
(be-SACH-de-burg-er)
Le Chèvrefeuille, France
Goat's milk
Classifications: Soft, ash-coated
Aged: Less than sixty days
Description: Small, tall, ash-covered domes over bone-white paste
Aroma: Light tang
Mouthfeel: Smooth, flaky, and creamy
Flavors: Goat butter, grassy, tangy, and creamy
Pairings: Fruity Champagne, Sauvignon Blanc, Lambic beer

Bethmal
(BET-mall)
Jean Faup, France
Raw goat's or cow's milk
Classifications: Semisoft, washed rind
Aged: At least sixty days
Fat: 45–50 percent
Description: Orange-red rind, smooth, lightly open ivory paste
Aroma: Light pungency
Mouthfeel: Smooth, soft

Flavors: Creamy with a surprising, rustic tang
Pairings: Riesling, wheat lager beer

Bianco Sottobosco

(bee-AN-ko-so-toe-BOWS-GO)
Italy
Cow's milk
Classifications: Semihard, natural rind
Description: Small cylinders studded with black truffles
Aroma: Earthy, buttery, truffles
Mouthfeel: Dry, crumbly, then soft
Flavors: Mushrooms, truffles, cream, butter
Pairings: Sangiovese, Zinfandel

Black Diamond Cheddar

Canada
Cow's milk
Classifications: Semihard, Cheddar
Aged: Three to four years
Description: White Cheddar surrounded by black wax
Aroma: Sharp and lactic
Mouthfeel: Crumbly then creamy
Flavors: Milky, salty, sharp
Pairings: Full-bodied Chardonnay, Riesling, almost any beer

Bocconcini di Pura Capra

Italy
Goat's milk
Classifications: Soft, natural rind
Aged: Less than sixty days
Fat: 45 percent
Description: Small rounds of natural rind, moist paste
Aroma: Slight tang
Mouthfeel: Smooth, light
Flavors: Light cream with delightful tang
Pairings: Port, fino sherry

Brebiou

(bre-BEE-ough)
France
Sheep's milk
Classifications: Soft, natural rind
Aged: Less than sixty days
Fat: 50 percent
Description: Smooth, cream-colored rind, creamy paste, layered aging
Aroma: Light cream
Mouthfeel: Very smooth, gentle coating
Flavors: Nutty whipped cream
Pairings: Gewurtzraminer, dark lager

Brie De Meaux

(BREE-du-mow)
A.O.C. Controlled, France
Cow's milk
Classifications: Soft, bloomy rind
Aged: Less than sixty days
Fat: 45–60 percent
Description: Large 14" wheels; light, thin, bloom; butterscotch-colored paste
Aroma: Sharp, pungent, spicy, mushrooms
Mouthfeel: Creamy, smooth, coating
Flavors: Lactic, beefy, salty, pungent, mushroom
Pairings: Sauvingnon Blanc, Champagne, Lambic beer, Pilsner

Brillat Savarin

(bree-AT-sav-ar-EEN)
France
Cow's milk
Classifications: Soft, bloomy rind
Aged: Less than sixty days
Fat: 75 percent
Description: Triple cream, thick pillowy bloomy rind, white paste, layered aging
Aroma: Lightly pungent and salty
Mouthfeel: Silky and light
Flavors: Whipped cream with a delightful kick

Pairings: Champagne, Riesling, Sauvignon Blanc, Madiera, Kirsch, port, Oloroso sherry

Brin d'Amour
(BRIN-d-ah-more)
France
Raw sheep's milk
Classifications: Semisoft, herb coated
Fat: 45 percent
Description: Coated in rosemary, savory, and juniper berries
Aroma: Herbal, lactic
Mouthfeel: Smooth, creamy, lightly coating
Flavors: Herbs, butter, salt, cream
Pairings: Sauvignon Blanc, Riesling, Oloroso sherry, light Syrah, or a Martini

Bucheret
(boo-cher-EH)
Redwood Hill, America
Goat's milk
Classifications: Soft, bloomy rind
Aged: Less than sixty days
Description: Natural and bloomy rind, small cylinders, layered aging of white paste
Aroma: Light tang
Mouthfeel: Smooth, light
Flavors: Cream, butter, lemony tang, light fruit
Pairings: Sauvignon Blanc, complex Pinot Noir, Chardonnay

Bucheron
(boo-cher-ON)
France
Goat's milk
Classifications: Soft, bloomy rind
Aged: Less than sixty days
Fat: 45–50 percent
Description: Logs of bloomy rind over white paste with layered aging
Aroma: Light tang
Mouthfeel: Smooth, light

Flavors: Cream, butter, lemony tang, light fruit
Pairings: Sauvignon Blanc, complex Pinot Noir, Chardonnay

Buratta
(burr-at-TA)
Italy
Cow's milk
Classifications: Fresh, soft
Aged: Less than thirty days
Fat: 75–85 percent
Description: Mascarpone surrounded by fresh mozzarella
Aroma: Mild, sweet
Mouthfeel: Very creamy
Flavors: Rich cream, sweet, very mild pungency
Pairings: Champagne, port

Buttermilk Blue
Roth Kase, America
Cow's milk
Classifications: Semisoft, blue
Aged: At least sixty days
Description: Farmstead, foil covered, with dense blue mottling and veins
Aroma: Sharp, piquant, and tangy
Mouthfeel: Crumbly then creamy
Flavors: Sharp fruity, salt
Pairings: Gewurztaminer, Riesling

Cabot Vintage Cheddar
Cabot Creamery, America
Cow's Milk
Classifications: Semihard, Cheddar
Aged: Two years
Fat: 9 grams/ounce
Description: Artisanal Cheddar wrapped in purple wax
Aroma: Sharp, tangy, fruity
Mouthfeel: Crumbly then creamy
Flavors: Milky, fruity, spicy, and sharp
Pairings: Sangiovese, almost all beers, whiskey

Cadi Urgelia

(CAHDEE-er-hey-LEE-A)
Cadi, N.A. (Distr), Spain
Cow's milk
Classifications: Semisoft, washed rind
Aged: Forty-five days
Fat: 50 percent
Description: Washed rind, soft creamy white paste with loose texture
Aroma: Salty, mildly pungent
Mouthfeel: Smooth, clean
Flavors: Lightly pungent, roasted tomatoes with salt
Pairings: Pinot Noir

Camembert de Normandie

(kam-em-BARE-du-nor-mahn-DEE)
A.O.C. Controlled, France
Cow's milk
Classifications: Soft, bloomy rind
Aged: Less than sixty days
Fat: 45 percent
Description: Light bloom, straw-colored paste
Aroma: Mushrooms, garlic, and truffle
Mouthfeel: Smooth, creamy, lightly coating
Flavors: Mild with hint of mushroom, earthiness
Pairings: Sweet Chardonnay, Lambic beer

Camembert, Camellia

Redwood Hill, America
Goat's milk
Classifications: Soft, bloomy rind
Aged: Less than sixty days
Fat: 45 percent
Description: Farmstead, thin bloomy rind over small disks of bone-white paste
Aroma: Mushrooms, sweet tang
Mouthfeel: Smooth, clean
Flavors: Mild, light tang
Pairings: Champagne, Lambic beer

Cantal

(kahn-TALL)
A.O.C. Controlled, France
Raw cow's milk
Classifications: Semihard, natural rind
Fat: 45 percent
Description: Forty to eighty pound wheels, colorful, thin paper wrapping
Aroma: Milky, sweet, light
Mouthfeel: Smooth to crumbly, light
Flavors: Mild and complex, sweet, milky, citrus, fruit
Pairings: Chenin Blanc, mild ale, Lambic beer

Capricho de Cabra

(ka-PREE-cho-duh-KA-bra)
Montesinos, Spain
Goat's milk
Classifications: Soft, fresh
Aged: Fresh
Fat: 45 percent
Description: Fresh chèvre shaped in a large log
Aroma: Bright, fresh, tangy
Mouthfeel: Crumbly, then creamy
Flavors: Bright, lemony, tangy, creamy
Pairings: Chenin Blanc, Pinot Gris

Capricious

Achadinha Cheese, America
Goat's milk
Classifications: Hard
Aged: Two months
Description: Farmstead, pillow-shaped, light gray-tan rind, rubbed in olive oil, light straw-colored paste
Aroma: Tangy, earthy
Mouthfeel: Creamy, coating
Flavors: Rustic tang and earthiness, bold flavors
Pairings: Syrah, most beer

Carmody

Bellwether Farms, America

Cow's milk
Classifications: Semisoft, wax-coated
Aged: Less than three months
Description: Farmstead, deep yellow wax or natural rind over loosely textured cream-yellow paste
Aroma: Light butter, hint of lemon
Mouthfeel: Creamy, soft
Flavors: Light cream, slight lemon tang
Pairings: Chardonnay, Beaujolais, mild ale

Carmody Reserve

Bellwether Farms, America
Raw cow's milk
Classifications: Semisoft, wax-coated
Aged: Three months
Description: Farmstead, deep yellow wax or natural rind over loosely textured cream-yellow paste
Aroma: Butter and cream
Mouthfeel: Creamy
Flavors: Sweet, slightly tangy, almost effervescent, and nutty
Pairings: Chardonnay, Beaujolais, Pinot Noir, medium ale, lagers

Cashel Blue

(cash-L)
J&L Grubb Ltd, Ireland
Cow's milk
Classifications: Semisoft, blue
Aged: Six to twelve months
Description: Farmstead, foil wrapped, dense blue mottling and veining, yellow-cream paste
Aroma: Sharp, saline
Mouthfeel: Light cream
Flavors: Butter, cream, piquant blue
Pairings: Full-bodied Chardonnay, port, Madeira

Cabichou

(SHAH-bee-shoe)
A.O.C. Controlled, France
Goat's milk
Classifications: Semisoft, ladled

Aged: Less than sixty days
Fat: 45 percent
Description: Small light bloomy-rind cylinders, white paste, layered aging
Aroma: Mild, nutty, sweet
Mouthfeel: Very creamy, light
Flavors: Light milk, bright tang, bright butter
Pairings: Pinot Blanc, Sauvignon Blanc

Chaource

(shah-ORCE)
A.O.C. Controlled, France
Cow's milk
Classifications: Soft, bloomy rind
Aged: Less than sixty days
Fat: 50 percent
Description: Small light bloomy-rind cylinders, white paste, layered aging
Aroma: Mild pungency, tangy
Mouthfeel: Light and creamy
Flavors: Creamy tang, mild pungency, light mushroom, and earthiness
Pairings: Champagne

Cheshire

(CHESH-er)
Neal's Yard, England
Cow's milk
Classifications: Semihard, bandage wrapped
Fat: 45 percent
Description: Farmstead, resembles light Cheddar, crumbly texture, buff to light orange colored
Aroma: Tangy and salty
Mouthfeel: Crumbly, light
Flavors: Lactic, tangy, mild
Pairings: Light Chardonnay, Viognier, Riesling, Beaujolais, Merlot, Pale Ale

Chevrot

(shev-ROW)
Various Producers, France
Goat's milk

Classifications: Soft, natural rind
Aged: Less than sixty days
Fat: 50 percent
Description: Small, rounded cylinders, white paste, layered aging
Aroma: Bright, light spice, milky
Mouthfeel: Light, crumbly, smooth
Flavors: Sweet tang, light cream, lemon, bright
Pairings: Pinot Gris

Chipotle Cheddar

(chip-OT-lay)
Bravo Farms, America
Cow's milk
Classifications: Semihard Cheddar
Description: Tall, thin blocks, rust-colored veining
Aroma: Spicy, milky
Mouthfeel: Light, crumbly
Flavors: Spicy, roasted, cream
Pairings: porter, dark lager

Coeur du Berry

(core-dew-berry)
Fromagerie Jacquin, France
Goat's milk
Classifications: Soft, fresh, and ash-coated
Aged: Less than sixty days
Fat: 45 percent
Description: Heart-shaped, fresh, or ash-covered with bone-white paste
Aroma: Slight tang
Mouthfeel: Very creamy
Flavors: Lactic tang, hint of grass and citrus
Pairings: Champagne

Colby

Various producers, America
Cow's milk
Classifications: Semisoft, pressed
Fat: 50 percent
Description: Similar to Cheddar, but looser texture
Aroma: Mild cheese

Mouthfeel: Crumbly, then creamy
Flavors: Milky, sweet, salty
Pairings: Delicatessen meats, fruit

Cold-pack Cheese

Various producers, America
Cow's milk
Classifications: Soft, processed
Description: Very smooth, usually packed in containers
Aroma: Sharp, metallic
Mouthfeel: Cloying
Flavors: Varied

Comte

(kon-TAY)
A.O.C. Controlled, France
Raw cow's milk
Classifications: Semihard, natural rind
Aged: Twelve to eighteen months
Fat: 45 percent
Description: Large wheels, small scattered eyes, light granules, yellow-cream paste
Aroma: Spicy, fruity, full aroma
Mouthfeel: Creamy, sometimes crumbly, smooth, mild coating
Flavors: Fruit, salt, nuts (cashews), lemon, grass
Pairings: Chardonnay, Chenin Blanc, Gewurtzraminer, Riesling, Beaujolais, Syrah, porter

Cone de Port Aubry

(CONE-de-port-AWE-bry)
The Peterson Company (Imp), France
Goat's milk
Classifications: Soft, bloomy, mold-ripened
Fat: 45 percent
Description: Large Hershey Kiss shapes covered in ash and bloomy rind with layered aging paste
Aroma: Herbal, tangy
Mouthfeel: Silky
Flavors: Cream, sweet milk, citrus tang, hint of grass
Pairings: Champagne

Constant Bliss
Jasper Hills, America
Raw cow's milk
Classifications: Soft, triple-cream bloomy rind
Fat: 75 percent
Description: Pyramids of bloomy rind over layers of bone-white aged paste
Aroma: Sharp, full
Mouthfeel: Silky
Flavors: Sharp, almost tannic at times, with whipped cream
Pairings: Champagne, Gewurtzraminer

Cream Cheese
Various producers, various countries
Cow's milk
Classifications: Fresh
Aged: Less than thirty days
Fat: 33 percent
Description: Usually packed in small tubs or in foil
Aroma: Mild, sweet
Mouthfeel: Mildly coating
Flavors: Sweet cream

Crème Fraiche
Various producers, various countries
Cow's milk
Classifications: Fresh
Aged: Made daily
Description: Usually packed in small tubs
Aroma: Mild, sweet
Mouthfeel: Mildly coating
Flavors: Sweet cream

Crottin de Chavignol
(crow-TAH-du-shah-veen-YOLE)
A.O.C. Controlled, France
Goat's milk
Classifications: Soft, natural rind
Aged: Minimum of ten days
Fat: 45 percent

Description: Small natural-rind buff-colored mound with flaky white paste and layered aging
Aroma: Bright, light
Mouthfeel: Flaky, then creamy and lightly coating
Flavors: Tang, sharpness, then creamy bright and lemony
Pairings: Pinot Gris, Sauvingnon Blanc, Champagne

Drunken Goat
Queso de Murcia al Vino, Spain
Goat's milk
Classifications: Semisoft, wine washed
Fat: 10 grams/ounce
Description: Immersed in red wine
Aroma: Light tang, clean
Mouthfeel: Smooth, creamy
Flavors: Light tang, creamy, hint of wine
Pairings: Red Riojas, fino sherry

Durrus
(dur-rus)
Ireland
Raw cow's milk
Classifications: Semisoft, washed rind
Aged: Three to five weeks
Description: Artisan, orange-beige rind with creamy orange paste
Aroma: Light fruit, some pungency
Mouthfeel: Smooth and light
Flavors: Sweet and tangy with a hint of fermented fruit
Pairings: Gewurztraminer, Riesling, Sauternes

Emmental
(EM-en-TAHL)
Name-Controlled, Switzerland
Cow's milk
Classifications: Semihard, wax-coated
Aged: Two months to two years
Fat: 45 percent
Description: Large wheels, large eyes, yellow-beige paste

Aroma: Light spice, fruit, cooked milk
Mouthfeel: Smooth, no coating, light
Flavors: Mild fruitiness, light tang, mild cream
Pairings: Sweet Chardonnay, wheat ale

English Sage Derby

Tuxford & Terbutt, England
Cow's milk
Classifications: Semihard, Cheddar, with dried sage
Fat: 9 grams/ounce
Aroma: Creamy, sharp, herbal
Mouthfeel: Smooth
Flavors: Sharp Cheddar with mild sage
Pairings: Pale ale

Epoisse

(eh-PWOSS)
A.O.C. Controlled, France
Cow's milk
Classifications: Soft, washed rind
Aged: Five to six weeks
Fat: 45 percent
Description: Washed in wine or brandy; small, bright rust-colored rounds; straw-colored paste
Aroma: Very pungent, earthy, and salty
Mouthfeel: Very smooth, creamy, lightly coating
Flavors: Transformative, spicy and salty to creamy fruit and nuts
Pairings: Cabernet Sauvignon, Sauternes, complex Viognier, Cognac

Ewe-F-O

(you-f-o)
Cypress Grove, America
Sheep's milk
Classifications: Rubbed
Aged: Six months
Description: Hard, rubbed rind with light straw, loose-textured paste
Aroma: Nutty and sweet
Mouthfeel: Creamy and oily
Flavors: Roasted nuts, rich butter

Pairings: Pilsner, wheat beer

Ewephoria

(you-for-ee-a)
Cheeseland, U.S., and Holland
Sheep's milk
Classifications: Wax-coated Gouda
Aged: Ten months
Description: Hard, wax-coated, pink to orange granular, dry paste
Aroma: Candy and nuts
Mouthfeel: Crumbly, then creamy
Flavors: Sweet, salt, fruit, light nuts, toffee
Pairings: Whiskey, almost all beer

Explorateur

(ex-plore-ah-TOUR)
Various producers, France
Cow's milk
Classifications: Soft, bloomy rind
Aged: Less than sixty days
Fat: 75 percent
Description: Triple cream, thick pillowy bloomy rind, white paste, layered aging
Aroma: Sharp, pungent, milky
Mouthfeel: Silky
Flavors: Rich ice cream with an end kick
Pairings: Champagne

Feta

(fet-a)
Various producers, various countries
Sheep's and goat's milk
Classifications: Fresh, brine cured
Aged: Less than thirty days
Fat: 6–7 grams/ounce
Description: Crumbly, white, packed in brine
Aroma: Salty, sharp
Mouthfeel: Crumbly
Flavors: Salty, tang, creamy

Fiore Sardo

(fee-or-eh-sar-do)

Various producers, Sardinia

Sheep's milk

Classifications: Semihard, natural, or wax-coated

Aged: Eight months or more

Description: Medium-size cylinders, pale yellow paste, slightly uneven texture

Aroma: Sharp, milky, hint of herbs

Mouthfeel: Creamy and buttery

Flavors: Milky, fruity, warm nuts, and melted butter

Pairings: Sangiovese, Zinfandel

Fiscalini Bandage-Wrapped Cheddar

Fiscalini Farms, America

Cow's milk

Classifications: Semihard, bandage wrapped

Aged: At least sixty days

Description: Farmstead, large wrapped wheels, with pale yellow paste and some fractures

Aroma: Sharp, fruity tang

Mouthfeel: Crumbly, creamy, and smooth

Flavors: Rich, tangy Cheddar with long butter notes

Pairings: Chardonnay, pale ale

Fiscalini San Joaquin Gold

Fiscalini Farms, America

Raw cow's milk

Classifications: Semihard, natural rind

Aged: At least sixty days

Fat: 9 grams/ounce

Description: Farmstead, large wheels with gray-brown rind and soft yellow granular paste

Aroma: Sharp, salty, fruity

Mouthfeel: Dry, granular

Flavors: Rich, salty, long finish of fruit and nuts

Pairings: Chardonnay, pale ale

Fleure Verte

France

Goat's milk

Classifications: Soft, fresh

Aged: Fresh

Fat: 45 percent

Description: Petal-shaped wheel of fresh chèvre covered in tarragon and red peppercorns

Aroma: Light, tangy, herbal, peppery

Mouthfeel: Creamy, clean

Flavors: Herbal, pepper, lemony tang

Pairings: Sauvignon Blanc, dry Riesling, Pinot Noir

Fog Lights

Cypress Grove, America

Goat's milk

Classifications: Soft, bloomy ash rind

Description: Pyramids, about two inches high

Aroma: Light, tangy

Mouthfeel: Creamy, clean

Flavors: Bright, cream, slightly herbal

Pairings: Sauvignon Blanc, Champagne

Fontina d'Aosta

(fawn-TEEN-ah-D-OHS-tah)

D.O.C. Controlled, Italy

Cow's milk

Classifications: Semihard, brushed rind

Fat: 45–50 percent

Description: Reddish-brown rind, reddish-beige paste, scattered, small eyes

Aroma: Pungent spiciness, light fruit

Mouthfeel: Supple

Flavors: Bright earthiness, fruit, somewhat heady

Pairings: Barbaresco or Barolo, Sangiovese

Fourme d'Ambert

(FORM-dome-BEAR)

A.O.C. Controlled, France

Cow's milk

Classifications: Semisoft, blue

Fat: 45 percent

Description: Foil covered, tall round cylinders, heavy green mottling, light green to cream paste

Aroma: Mildly pungent earthiness

Mouthfeel: Smooth, light granularity

Flavors: Bright, sharp blue with creaminess
Pairings: port, Oloroso sherry

Fresh Chèvre
Various producers, various countries
Goat's milk
Classifications: Soft, fresh
Aged: Fresh
Fat: 45 percent
Description: All sizes and shapes in various packages
Aroma: Light farmyard and tang
Mouthfeel: Smooth and creamy
Flavors: Bright, sharp, citrus

Fromage d'Affinois
(fro-mage-de-af-in-wah)
France
Cow's milk
Classifications: Soft, bloomy rind
Aged: Less than sixty days
Fat: 55–60 percent
Description: Brie-style rind with oozing, cream-yellow paste
Aroma: Tangy, milky
Mouthfeel: Silky
Flavors: Whipped cream and fresh mushrooms
Pairings: Pinot Noir, Chardonnay, Riesling

Gariotin
(gare-ee-oh-tan)
France
Goat's milk
Classifications: Soft, natural rind
Fat: 45 percent
Description: Small natural-rind buff-colored mound with flaky white paste and layered aging
Aroma: Pungent farmyard
Mouthfeel: Flaky, then creamy and lightly coating
Flavors: Light farmyard, earthiness, citrus, and salt
Pairings: Chardonnay, figs

Garrotxa
(ga-rrroat-CHA)
Cabra, Spain
Goat's milk
Classifications: Semi-soft, mold rind
Aged: Twenty days or more
Description: Velvety suede rind with creamy white, smooth paste
Aroma: Earthy and light
Mouthfeel: Creamy, slightly crumbly
Flavors: Subtle mushrooms, hint of tang, full roundness
Pairings: Sauvignon Blanc, light Chardonnay, white Riojas, Zinfandel

Gjetost
(yeah-toast)
Various producers, Norway
Carmelized whey
Classifications: Semihard, whey
Description: Small, caramel-colored blocks
Aroma: Sweet, toasted
Mouthfeel: Sticky
Flavors: Caramel, toasted milk

Gorgonzola
(gore-gone-ZOH-lah)
D.O.C. Controlled, Italy
Cow's milk
Classifications: Semisoft, blue
Aged: Three to five months
Fat: 48 percent
Description: Dense blue veining, uneven paste, rustic
Aroma: Assertive, earthy, pungent
Mouthfeel: Creamy, with light granularity
Flavors: Tangy, earthy, spicy, and very full
Pairings: Cabernet Sauvignon, Madeira

Gorgonzola, Dolce Latte
(gore-gone-ZOH-lah-DOHL-che-LOTTE)
D.O.C. Controlled, Italy

Cow's milk
Classifications: Semisoft, blue
Aged: Three to five months
Fat: 45 percent
Description: Uneven blue striations, creamy paste, foil covered
Aroma: Assertive, earthy sweetness
Mouthfeel: Very creamy, light crunch, light coating
Flavors: Sweet, earthy, spicy
Pairings: Sweet stout

Grafton Cheddar

Grafton Village Cheese Co., America
Cow's milk
Classifications: Semihard, Cheddar
Aged: Thirty to thirty-six months
Description: Naturally ripened, extra aged
Aroma: Sharp, lactic, hint of citrus
Mouthfeel: Crumbly, then creamy
Flavors: Sharp Cheddar, spicy, lactic, full-flavored
Pairings: Chardonnay, Riesling, or Gerwurtzraminer, pale ale, whiskey

Grana Padano

(gran-a-pa-DA-NO)
D.O.C. Controlled, Italy
Raw cow's milk
Classifications: Natural rind, Grana
Aged: Fourteen months to three years
Description: Large wheels, oiled rinds and granular, straw-colored paste
Aroma: Mild, salty
Mouthfeel: Granular
Flavors: Salt, fruit, sharp, and flavorful
Pairings: Fruity Champagne, Chardonnay, Sauvignon Blanc, Lambic beer

Graviera Fresca

(grav-ee-era-fresca)
Mt. Vikos, Crete
Sheep's and goat's milk
Classification: Semihard

Description: Large, cream-colored wheels with natural or light clear wax rind
Aroma: Mild and tangy
Mouthfeel: Very smooth and creamy
Flavors: Sweet, tangy, nutty, and buttery

Gruyere

(gree-YAIR)
Name-Controlled, Switzerland
Raw cow's milk
Classifications: Semihard, brushed rind
Aged: Four months or more
Fat: 45 percent
Description: Large wheels, brushed brown rind, smooth, lightly eyed, dense cream-yellow paste
Aroma: Nuts and fruit
Mouthfeel: Smooth, lightly coating
Flavors: Roasted nuts, ripe fruit, rich butter, very complex
Pairings: Champagne, Pinot Noir, Riesling, Sangiovese, Zinfandel, coffee, malted barley beer, porter, Kahlua

Gubbeen

(goo-BEAN)
Gubbeen House, Ireland, with Neal's Yard, England
Cow's milk
Classifications: Semisoft, washed rind
Description: Farmstead, low orange-beige wheels with yellow-cream, smooth paste
Aroma: Lightly pungent and salty
Mouthfeel: Smooth, light with some cream coating
Flavors: Fruity, robust, earthy, and pungent
Pairings: Gewurztraminer, Riesling, Viognier

Haloumi

(hah-loom-ee)
Various producers, Greece
Sheep's milk
Classifications: Semisoft, pasta filata
Aged: Less than thirty days
Fat: 40 percent

Description: Flavored with Mint
Aroma: Mild
Mouthfeel: Rubbery, light
Flavors: Nutty and buttery

Harley Farms Chèvre

Harley Farms, America
Goat's milk
Classifications: Fresh, smooth
Fat: 45 percent
Description: Farmstead, fresh chèvre flavored and decorated with fruit, nuts, and edible flowers
Aroma: Fresh, herbal
Mouthfeel: Creamy and smooth
Flavors: Lemony tang, herbal, floral
Pairings: Sauvignon Blanc

Havarti

Various producers, various countries
Cow's milk
Classifications: Semisoft, rindless
Aged: Less than thirty days
Fat: 60 percent
Description: Commodity-style cheese produced in large quantities, rindless, loose open texture
Aroma: Light and lactic
Mouthfeel: Rubbery, light
Flavors: Mild, slightly tangy, milky

Hoja Santa

(OH-ha-SAN-ta)
America
Goat's milk
Classifications: Soft, leaf-wrapped
Description: Wrapped in Hoja Santa leaves
Aroma: Minty, tangy
Mouthfeel: Creamy
Flavors: Mint, sassafrass, lemony tang
Pairings: Gin, vodka

Humboldt Fog

(hum-bolt-fog)
Cypress Grove, America
Goat's milk
Classifications: Soft, bloomy ash rind
Aged: Two months
Fat: 7 grams/ounce
Description: Farmstead, morning and evening milk, separated by vegetable ash and rolled in ash
Aroma: Light farmyard and tang
Mouthfeel: Creamy and smooth
Flavors: Cream, sweet lemon, and long finish
Pairings: Sauvignon Blanc, light Pinot Noir

Iberico

Spain
Cow's, goat's, and sheep's milk
Classifications: Semihard
Aged: Two months or more
Fat: 9 grams/ounce
Description: Paprika or oil rubbed
Aroma: Light, sweet, mild
Mouthfeel: Light cream
Flavors: Gentle mix of sweet, cream, nuts, butter
Pairings: Riesling, wheat beer

Ibores

(ee-BORE-es)
Spain
Goat's milk
Classifications: Semihard, spice rubbed
Aged: Two to three months
Fat: 10 grams/ounce
Description: Artisanal cheese, oiled or rubbed with paprika, bone-white, smooth paste
Aroma: Piquant and spicy
Mouthfeel: Smooth and creamy
Flavors: Salty, tangy, light citrus and spice
Pairings: Rioja reds, Sauvignon Blanc, Pinot Noir

Idiazabal

(ee-dee-AHH-za-ball)
D.O. Controlled, Spain
Raw sheep's milk
Classifications: Semihard, rubbed or wax coated
Aged: Two to four months
Fat: 45–50 percent
Description: Hard, yellow-orange rind, light straw-colored paste with loose texture
Aroma: Smokey tang
Mouthfeel: Crumbly, creamy, lightly oily
Flavors: Smoky; spicy; tang, followed by nuts and butter
Pairings: Oloroso sherry, or a martini

Jarlsberg

(yarls-berg)
Various producers, various countries
Cow's milk
Classifications: Semisoft, pressed
Description: Large wheels with wax coating and large, multiple eyes
Aroma: Fruity
Mouthfeel: Rubbery, light
Flavors: Fruity, light, and lactic
Pairings: Wheat beer, Pilsner, sweet stout

Keen's Cheddar

Neal's Yard, England
Raw cow's milk
Classifications: Semihard, bandage wrapped
Description: Farmstead, large bandage-wrapped wheels with creamy yellow paste and traces of blue veining
Aroma: Sharp, musty, earthy
Mouthfeel: Crumbly, then creamy
Flavors: Sharp Cheddar, rich butter, hint of blue, and long finish
Pairings: Chardonnay, Riesling, or Gerwurtzraminer, pale ale, whiskey

La Tur

(la-tour)
Italy
Cow's, goat's, and sheep's milk
Classifications: Soft, natural rind
Description: Small, thin natural rind over moist cream-colored paste
Aroma: Light pungency
Mouthfeel: Very creamy
Flavors: Piquant, complex, tangy, lactic, salty
Pairings: Champagne

Laguiole

(lie-YOLE)
A.O.C. Controlled, France
Raw cow's milk
Classifications: Semihard, natural rind
Aged: Four to nine months
Fat: 45 percent
Description: Tall, large cylinders with light brown rind, lemon-yellow paste
Aroma: Bright, grassy, hints of milky citrus
Mouthfeel: Crumbly, lightly coating
Flavors: Unusual blend of cream and citrus; bright, delicate, and long finish of light butter
Pairings: Pale ale, Lambic beer

Lancashire

(LANK-a-sure)
Neal's Yard, England
Raw cow's milk
Classifications: Semihard, bandage wrapped
Aged: Four to eight months
Fat: 45 percent
Description: Medium-size cylinders, pale yellow paste, slightly uneven texture
Aroma: Light sharpness, hint of cream
Mouthfeel: Light and crumbly
Flavors: Creamy tang with milk and mild nut tones
Pairings: Merlot, British ale, pale ale

Laughing Cow

Laughing Cow Company, various countries
Cow's milk
Classifications: Processed cheese product
Description: Foil-wrapped cubes of processed cheese
Aroma: Light
Mouthfeel: Slick
Flavors: Varied

Le Roule

(lay-rue)
France
Cow's milk
Classifications: Soft, herb coated
Aged: Fresh
Description: Fresh herbs rolled with cream cheese
Aroma: Light, herbal
Mouthfeel: Creamy
Flavors: Sweet, herbal
Pairings: Whole-wheat cracker, baguette

L'Edel de Cleron

(LAY-del-de-CLER-on)
France
Cow's milk
Classifications: Soft, bloomy rind
Aged: Less than sixty days
Fat: 55 percent
Description: Small rounds surrounded by bark, with creamy oozing paste
Aroma: Mushrooms, cream
Mouthfeel: Smooth, sometimes chalky
Flavors: Light earthy mushrooms and whipped cream
Pairings: Champagne

Leyden

(LIE-den)
Holland
Cow's milk
Classifications: Semisoft, Gouda
Fat: 40 percent
Description: Young Gouda studded with caraway, cumin seeds, or both
Aroma: Spicy, mildly pungent
Mouthfeel: Smooth, lightly coating
Flavors: Caraway, cumin, or a combination; vegetables and cream
Pairings: Ham, pastrami, and smoked turkey

Lighthouse Blue Brie

King Island Dairy, Australia
Cow's milk
Classifications: Semisoft, blue
Description: Blue cheese and Brie style combined
Aroma: Full, musty, mushroomy
Mouthfeel: Very creamy
Flavors: Rich, creamy, tangy, and flavorful
Pairings: Pinot Noir, Sauternes

Lincolnshire Poacher

England
Cow's milk
Classifications: Semihard, bandage wrapped
Description: Gray-brown rind over cream-yellow, flaky texture paste
Aroma: Mild
Mouthfeel: Creamy
Flavors: Mild fruit, grass, butter
Pairings: Chardonnay, Gewurtzraminer, pale ale

Lingot

(LYNN-go)
France
Goat's milk
Classifications: Soft, natural rind
Description: Small bricks of natural-rind chèvre, layered aging
Aroma: Pungent farmyard
Mouthfeel: Very creamy
Flavors: Lactic, nutty, and tangy
Pairings: Gewurtzraminer, Pinot Gris, Riesling, Chardonnay, Beaujolais

Livarot

(LEE-vah-row)
A.O.C. Controlled, France
Cow's milk
Classifications: Soft, washed rind
Aged: One to three months
Fat: 40–45 percent
Description: Small, orange disks with straw-colored paste
Aroma: Spicy and pungent
Mouthfeel: Smooth and creamy to rubbery
Flavors: Mild to strong, beefy and nutty mushrooms
Pairings: Gewurztraminer, Riesling, Pinot Gris, Oloroso sherry

Mahon

(ma-HONE)
D.O. Controlled, Spain
Cow's milk
Classifications: Semihard, bandage wrapped
Aged: Two weeks to two years
Fat: 45 percent
Description: Pillow shaped, light gray rind, layered aging, light straw-colored paste
Aroma: Saffron, light tangy pungency
Mouthfeel: Smooth and lightly coating
Flavors: Bright, nutty, rich milk with a definite tang
Pairings: Pinot Noir, Oloroso sherry, port

Majorero

(MAH-or-ER-oh)
Spain
Goat's milk
Classifications: Semisoft, rindless
Aged: Two months
Description: An almost all-white cheese with thin, clear wax and smooth paste
Aroma: Light tang
Mouthfeel: Smooth and clean
Flavors: Long complex taste, light at first; opens to light nuts, hints of milk, sweetness
Pairings: Chenin Blanc, Pinot Gris, fino sherry

Manchego

(mahn-CHE-go)
D.O. Controlled, Spain
Sheep's milk
Classifications: Semihard, rubbed or wax coated
Aged: Sixty days to three years
Fat: 45 percent
Description: Wax or rubbed rind, sometimes with basket-weave design, loosely textured, light straw-colored rind
Aroma: Nutty, buttery, almost sweet
Mouthfeel: Rich and creamy
Flavors: Heavy butter, hazelnuts, sun-ripened fruit
Pairings: Merlot, red Riojas, sherries, Sauternes, Chardonnays, Pinot Noir

Maroilles

(mah-WALL)
A.O.C. Controlled, France
Cow's milk
Classifications: Semisoft, washed rind
Aged: Less than sixty days
Fat: 45–50 percent
Description: Rustic rust-colored rind, creamy straw-colored paste
Aroma: Pungent, salty, with hints of farmyard
Mouthfeel: Smooth, coating, and creamy
Flavors: Salty, creamy, pungent
Pairings: Gewurztraminer

Mascarpone

(mahs-car-PONE)
Various producers, Italy
Cow's milk
Classifications: Soft, fresh
Aged: One to two weeks
Fat: 70–75 percent
Description: Usually sold in half-pint tubs. Creamy and white.
Aroma: Mild
Mouthfeel: Silky and creamy
Flavors: Sweet cream with a light kick

Pairings: Cognac, Kirsch, rum

Maytag Blue

Maytag Cheese, America
Cow's milk
Classifications: Semisoft, blue
Description: Foil wrapped, dense blue mottling and veining
Aroma: Sharp
Mouthfeel: Creamy
Flavors: Piquant, tangy, sharp
Pairings: Port, Zinfandel

Midnight Moon

Cypress Grove, America
Goat's milk
Classifications: Wax-coated Gouda
Aged: One year
Description: Black wax around bone-white, dense paste
Aroma: Clean and nutty
Mouthfeel: Very creamy
Flavors: Nuts, fresh butter, bright citrus, followed by sweet tang
Pairings: Pinot Noir, Oloroso sherry, whiskey, light ales, lager

Mimolette

(MEE-moh-LET)
France
Cow's milk
Classifications: Natural rind
Aged: Eighteen months
Fat: 45 percent
Description: Looks like a cantaloupe; bright orange, smooth paste with scattered eyes
Aroma: Very subtle aromas
Mouthfeel: Almost dry, slightly granular
Flavors: Wait for these flavors; they pop up at the end: salt, sharpness, and hints of bold cream and fruit
Pairings: Cabernet Sauvignon, porter

Mobay

Carr Valley Cheese Company, America
Goat's and sheep's milk
Classifications: Semisoft, natural rind
Description: Artisanal cheese, made in two halves, with ash in the center and outside. One-half goat, one-half sheep.
Aroma: Light, nutty
Mouthfeel: Creamy
Flavors: Tang, nuts, butter, light
Pairings: Wheat beer, Pilsner, sweet stout

Montasio

(mohn-TAH-zee-yo)
Italy
Cow's milk
Classifications: Semisoft, soft ripened
Aged: Two months to four years
Fat: 30–45 percent
Description: Large, flat wheels with gray-beige rind and light straw paste
Aroma: Mild and sweet
Mouthfeel: Light
Flavors: Light tang with tones of butterscotch
Pairings: Merlot

Montbriac

(mohn-bree-ACK)
Les Caves de L'Ance, France
Cow's milk
Classifications: Soft, ash coated
Aged: Less than sixty days
Fat: 55 percent
Description: Small flat discs covered in ash and bloomy rind, creamy white paste
Aroma: Mild, earthy
Mouthfeel: Light and creamy
Flavors: Subtle and lightly flavorful with cream, salt, and slight earthiness
Pairings: Pinot Blanc

Monte Enebro

(MON-te-hen-EH-bro)
Queserias del Tietar, S.I., Spain
Goat's milk
Classifications: Soft, bloomy ash rind
Aged: Three weeks
Fat: 55 percent
Description: Farmstead, flat ash-covered logs with bone-white finely textured paste and layered aging
Aroma: Sharp, piquant, and tangy
Mouthfeel: Very smooth, light cream
Flavors: Salty, tangy, and bright
Pairings: Gewurztraminer, Riesling, Sauternes

Monterey Jack

Various producers, America
Cow's milk
Classifications: Semisoft, pressed
Fat: 50 percent
Description: Large wheels, rindless, smooth cream-colored paste with some loose texture
Aroma: Mild
Mouthfeel: Slightly rubbery
Flavors: Sweet, creamy, light
Pairings: Sweet Chardonnay

Montgomery's Cheddar

Neal's Yard, England
Raw cow's milk
Classifications: Semihard, bandage wrapped
Aged: Fourteen months
Description: Large wheels, gray-brown rind underneath bandage, cream-yellow, smooth paste with some blue fractures
Aroma: Full, musty, mushroomy
Mouthfeel: Crumbly, then creamy
Flavors: Nutty, buttery, not terribly sharp, full-flavored Cheddar
Pairings: Chardonnay, Cabernet Sauvignon, Zinfandel, pale ale, porter

Morbier

(MORE-bee-yay)
France
Raw cow's milk
Classifications: Semisoft, washed rind
Fat: 45 percent
Description: Made in layers of two milkings, with vegetable ash in the middle. Pinkish-orange rind.
Aroma: Light pungency and straw
Mouthfeel: Smooth, creamy, light
Flavors: Light apricot and hint of cashews, salty, and bright
Pairings: Wheat beer, Pilsner, sweet stout

Mozzarella di Bufala

D.O.C. Controlled, Italy
Water buffalo's or cow's milk, or both
Classifications: Soft, fresh
Description: Soft, round globes, packed in brine
Aroma: Fresh, slightly salty from brine
Mouthfeel: Very creamy, light
Flavors: Light and creamy
Pairings: Dark lager

Mozzarella, Fresh

Various producers, various countries
Cow's milk
Classifications: Soft, fresh
Description: Soft, round globes, packed in brine
Aroma: Fresh, slightly salty from brine
Mouthfeel: Very creamy, light
Flavors: Light and creamy

Mt. Tam

Cowgirl Creamery, America
Cow's milk
Classifications: Soft, bloomy rind
Aged: Less than sixty days
Fat: 75 percent
Description: Pillowy bloom over small mounds of cream-colored paste
Aroma: Heady, mushrooms, grass

Mouthfeel: Very creamy
Flavors: Rich mushroom, butter, and cream
Pairings: Champagne, Gewürztraminer

Muenster, Alsace
(MUN-ster)
A.O.C. Controlled, France
Cow's milk
Classifications: Soft, washed rind
Aged: Less than thirty days
Fat: 45–50 percent
Description: Soft, light orange rind and creamy paste
Aroma: Lightly pungent and salty
Mouthfeel: Very creamy and smooth
Flavors: Fruit, nuts, salt, and cream with a hint of pungency
Pairings: Gewurztraminer, Riesling, Pinot Gris, Pinot Noir, Oloroso sherry

Myzithra
Various producers, Greece
Sheep's milk
Classifications: Hard, pressed whey curd
Description: Pressed, bone-white, and granular
Aroma: Mild, salty
Mouthfeel: Dry, crumbly
Flavors: Salty, bright

Nancy's Camembert
Old Chatham Sheepherding, America
Sheep's milk
Classifications: Soft, bloomy rind
Aged: Less than sixty days
Fat: 75 percent
Description: Fluffy white bloomy rind, white paste with layered aging
Aroma: Tangy sweet butter
Mouthfeel: Silky butter
Flavors: Whipped cream and butter with a delightful kick
Pairings: Champagne

Old Amsterdam
Holland
Cow's milk
Classifications: Wax-coated Gouda
Aged: Eighteen months
Fat: 11 grams/ounce
Description: Large Gouda wheel, black wax, toffee-colored paste with irregular eyes and fissures
Aroma: Caramel, butterscotch
Mouthfeel: Dry, crumbly, coating
Flavors: Candy tones, caramel, toffee, butterscotch, and nuts
Pairings: Beer, Cognac

Ossau Iraty
(OH-so-EAR-ah-tee)
A.O.C. Controlled, France
Sheep's milk
Classifications: Semisoft, natural rind
Aged: One hundred twenty days
Fat: 45 percent
Description: Rounded, mottled white, and brown rind; cream-beige paste, smooth
Aroma: Earthy, nutty, piquant
Mouthfeel: Creamy and smooth, melting
Flavors: Light fruit and nuts upfront, then deeper, roasted butter and hazlenuts at the end
Pairings: Merlot, Pinot Noir, Zinfandel, sherry, dark lager, Cognac

Parmigiano-Reggiano
(par-me-JON-oh-reg-ee-AHN-o)
D.O.C. Controlled, Italy
Raw cow's milk
Classifications: Natural rind, grana
Aged: Three years
Fat: 28–32 percent
Description: Large seventy- to eighty-pound wheels, deep straw-colored rind and paste, granular and prone to fractures
Aroma: Salty, sweet
Mouthfeel: Dry, granular, then creamy

Flavors: Fruit, salt
Pairings: Sangiovese, Cabernet Sauvignon

Pasteurized Process
Various producers, America
Classifications: Processed cheese
Fat: 43–50 percent
Description: Processed from different types of cheese
Aroma: Varies
Mouthfeel: Rubbery
Flavors: Varies

Pau
Spain
Goat's milk
Classifications: Semisoft, mold rind
Aged: Two to three months
Fat: 55 percent
Description: Small wheels, mottled straw–colored, with buff-colored, creamy paste
Aroma: Farmyard
Mouthfeel: Creamy
Flavors: Light farmyard, earthiness, citrus, and salt
Pairings: Red Riojas, sherries, Sauternes, Chardonnays, Pinot Noir

Pecorino al Tartufo
(peh-ko-REEN-o-al-tar-TOO-foe)
Various producers, Italy
Sheep's milk
Classifications: Semihard, wax coated
Description: Unpressed, wax coated, light yellow paste, studded with black truffles
Aroma: Truffles, butter, and nuts
Mouthfeel: Very creamy
Flavors: Truffles, butter, nuts
Pairings: Sangiovese

Pecorino Antico
(peh-ko-REEN-o-AN-tee-co)
Various producers, Italy

Sheep's milk
Classifications: Semi hard, Wax coated
Description: Medium aged, unpressed, wax coated, light yellow paste
Aroma: Rich in butter
Mouthfeel: Creamy
Flavors: Spicy, buttery, and nutty
Pairings: Chardonnay, Pinot Noir, Merlot, fino sherry, wheat beer

Pecorino Fresco
(peh-ko-REEN-o-fres-co)
Various producers, Italy
Sheep's milk
Classifications: Semisoft, wax coated
Description: Young, unpressed, wax coated, light yellow paste
Aroma: Light
Mouthfeel: Creamy
Flavors: Light, creamy butter with mild nuts
Pairings: Pinot Grigio

Pecorino Renero
(peh-ko-REEN-o-ren-ER-o)
Various producers, Italy
Sheep's milk
Classifications: Semihard, wax coated
Description: Medium aged, unpressed, wax coated, light yellow paste
Aroma: Butter and cream
Mouthfeel: Crumbly then creamy
Flavors: Spicy, buttery, nutty, and rich
Pairings: Pinot Grigio, Pinot Noir, Merlot, Sangiovese, fino sherry

Pecorino Romano
(peh-ko-REEN-o-row-MAHN-o)
D.O.C. Controlled, Italy
Sheep's milk
Classifications: Semihard, wax coated
Fat: 45 percent

Description: Large, tall cylinders usually coated with thin wax or paper, bone white, granular paste
Aroma: Salt, pepper, sharp
Mouthfeel: Dry, crumbly
Flavors: Salt, cream, pepper, and mild nuts
Pairings: Usually a cooking cheese; shave over pasta, lasagna, vegetables, etc.

Pecorino Stagianato

(peh-ko-REEN-o-stah-gee-o-NOT-o)
D.O.C. Controlled, Italy
Sheep's milk
Classifications: Semihard, wax coated
Description: Very aged, unpressed, wax coated, light yellow paste, almost a grana
Aroma: Sharp
Mouthfeel: Very dry
Flavors: Tangy, buttery, and full-flavored
Pairings: Merlot, Sangiovese

Pecorino Toscano

(peh-ko-REEN-o-toe-SKAH-no)
D.O.C. Controlled, Italy
Sheep's milk
Classifications: Semihard, wax coated
Aged: One month to two years
Fat: 45–50 percent
Description: Wax or rubbed rind, ivory colored, smooth paste
Aroma: Light nuts and butter
Mouthfeel: Smooth, creamy, olive oil
Flavors: Piquant butter and nuts with olives
Pairings: Merlot, wheat beer

Peilloute

(pay-YOU-tay)
France
Goat's milk
Classifications: Soft, bloomy rind
Aged: Less than sixty days
Fat: 45 percent

Description: Brie-style cheese with creamy bone-colored paste
Aroma: Light, tangy
Mouthfeel: Very smooth
Flavors: Light, fruity, slight tang
Pairings: Champagne, Chenin Blanc, Kirsch

Pepato

(pep-a-TO)
Italy
Sheep's milk
Classifications: Semihard, wax coated
Description: Unpressed, wax coated, light yellow paste, studded with peppercorns
Aroma: Slight tang, mild
Mouthfeel: Crumbly, then creamy
Flavors: Pepper, soft butter, light tang
Pairings: Sangiovese, Zinfandel, or a martini

Petit Basque

France
Sheep's milk
Classifications: Semisoft, natural rind
Fat: 45 percent
Description: Small cylinders, reddish-brown wax, cream-beige paste, smooth
Aroma: Earthy, nutty, piquant
Mouthfeel: Creamy and smooth, melting
Flavors: Light fruit and nuts
Pairings: Chardonnay, Pinot Noir, sherry, dark lager, wheat beer

Piave

(pe-ah-VEY)
Italy
Cow's milk
Classifications: Natural rind, grana
Aged: One to twelve months
Fat: 51 percent
Description: Medium wheels, clear wax rind over hard, granular, butter-colored paste
Aroma: Fruity, sweet

Mouthfeel: Dry, granular
Flavors: Fruit, citrus, sweet
Pairings: Pinot Noir, Merlot, Sangiovese, Sauternes, Lambic beer, steam beer

Pierre Robert
(pe-ERR-row-BEAR)
France
Cow's milk
Classifications: Soft, bloomy rind
Aged: Less than sixty days
Fat: 75 percent
Description: Triple cream; thick, pillowy, bloomy rind; white paste; layered aging
Aroma: Hint of tang, luscious cream
Mouthfeel: Silky and smooth
Flavors: Salt, butter, and toast
Pairings: Champagne, Pinot Gris, Riesling

Pleasant Ridge Reserve
Uplands Cheese, Inc., America
Raw cow's milk
Classifications: Semihard, natural rind
Aged: At least sixty days
Description: Farmstead, pressed, natural rind, deep yellow, smooth paste
Aroma: Fruity, roasted nuts
Mouthfeel: Creamy
Flavors: Heavy fruit, complex
Pairings: Lambic beer, lager, Sangiovese, Zinfandel

Pont l'Eveque
(PAWN-lay-VECK)
A.O.C. Controlled, France
Cow's milk
Classifications: Semisoft, washed rind
Aged: Less than sixty days
Fat: 50 percent
Description: Reddish-brown rind, reddish-beige paste, scattered, small eyes
Aroma: Pungent, salty, with hints of farmyard
Mouthfeel: Smooth, creamy, light coating

Flavors: Mushroom earthiness, sharp, tangy, and pungent
Pairings: Chenin Blanc, Reisling, Lambic beer

Prima Donna
Cheeseland, U.S. and Holland
Cow's milk
Classifications: Wax-coated Gouda
Aged: Six to fifteen months
Fat: 47 percent
Description: Not technically a Gouda, but a large wheel, red or blue wax covered, golden paste, irregular eyes
Aroma: Nutty and sweet
Mouthfeel: Creamy, mildly coating
Flavors: Nuts, roasted butter, butterscotch
Pairings: Sangiovese, Zinfandel, Cognac, Pilsner, most beer

Provolone
(pro-voh-LOH-neh)
D.O.C. Protected
Cow's milk
Classifications: Semisoft, pasta filata
Fat: 45 percent
Description: Usually rindless, all sizes and shapes, light straw–colored, very smooth paste
Aroma: Very mild with hint of tang
Mouthfeel: Rubbery, light
Flavors: Very mild, slightly oily, sharp when aged
Pairings: Beaujolais

Pt. Reyes Blue
Pt. Reyes Farmstead, America
Raw cow's milk
Classifications: Semisoft, blue
Aged: Two to six months
Description: Farmstead, foil-wrapped over cream-white paste, with mottled blue-green striations
Aroma: Piquant, sharp, spicy
Mouthfeel: Very creamy

Flavors: Sharp, full flavored, creamy milk, fresh blue, piquant
Pairings: Reisling, Zinfandel, Pinot Noir, Gewurztraminer, port

Pyrenees Peppercorns

Prairiol, Onetik, France
Cow's milk
Classifications: Semisoft, wax coated
Fat: 50 percent
Description: Black wax around bone-white, dense paste, studded with peppercorns
Aroma: Mild, sweet, peppery
Mouthfeel: Slightly creamy
Flavors: Mild, sweet, peppery
Pairings: Sangiovese, Zinfandel

Queso Al Romero

(Keh-so-al-rome-ER-o)
Don Enrique, Spain
Sheep's milk
Classifications: Semisoft, herb wrapped
Aged: Twenty days to six months
Description: Rosemary coated over buff-colored, loose texture paste
Aroma: Herbal, olive oil
Mouthfeel: Creamy
Flavors: Rosemary, butter, nuts, olive oil
Pairings: Sangiovese, Syrah

Queso Cabrero

(KEH-so-CAB-rer-o)
Bodega Goat Cheese, Spain
Goat's milk
Classifications: Hard, natural rind
Aged: Two to three months
Description: Farmstead, organic, wheels rubbed with Zinfandel, creamy white paste
Aroma: Grassy tang
Mouthfeel: Crumbly, creamy
Flavors: Fruity, tangy, grassy
Pairings: Zinfandel

Queso de Cabra

(KEH-so-de-CAB-bra)
Rocinante, Spain
Goat's milk
Classifications: Semisoft, wax coated
Description: Pimento-colored wax over bone-white, finely textured paste
Aroma: Creamy tang
Mouthfeel: Creamy
Flavors: Creamy tang
Pairings: Pinot Grigio

Queso de la Serena

(KEH-so-de-la-SARE-en-ya)
Spain
Sheep's milk
Classifications: Soft, washed rind
Aged: Sixty days
Fat: 50 percent
Description: Small wheels, mottled straw–colored, with buff-colored, creamy paste
Aroma: Sharp, pungent, earthy, tangy
Mouthfeel: Smooth, lightly coating
Flavors: Grassy, tart, and heavenly cream
Pairings: Cabernet Sauvignon, port, Riesling, lager beer

Queso de Oro

(KEH-so-de-OR-o)
Bravo Farms, America
Cow's milk
Classifications: Semisoft, rindless
Aged: At least sixty days
Description: Rindless butter-yellow, smooth paste
Aroma: Mild
Mouthfeel: Lightly creamy
Flavors: Mild butter, milk, sweet
Pairings: Most beer

Queso Fresco
(KEH-so-FRES-co)
Various producers, Mexico and America
Cow's milk
Classifications: Soft, fresh
Description: Crumbly, white cheese, almost curd-like
Aroma: Mild
Mouthfeel: Crumbly
Flavors: Mildly sweet and tangy
Pairings: Most beer

Raclette, Swiss
(rah-CLETT)
Name-Controlled, Switzerland
Sheep's milk
Classifications: Semihard, brushed rind
Fat: 45 percent
Description: Large, round wheels, brushed rind with buff-colored, smooth paste
Aroma: Mild, piquant fruit
Mouthfeel: Smooth
Flavors: Flavor intensifies with heat, full, meaty, and fruity
Pairings: Kirsch

Reblechon
(ruh-blow-SHAW)
A.O.C. Controlled, France
Cow's milk
Classifications: Semisoft, washed rind
Aged: Four to five weeks
Fat: 50 percent
Description: Light orange to light brown rind, creamy, ivory paste with small irregular holes
Aroma: Lightly pungent and salty
Mouthfeel: Smooth and silky
Flavors: Earthy pungency with hints of ripe fruit
Pairings: Riesling, Beaujolais, Pinot Noir, Chardonnay

Red Hawk
Cowgirl Creamery, America
Cow's milk
Classifications: Semisoft, washed rind
Aged: One month
Fat: 75 percent
Description: Artisanal, organic milk, sunset-colored rind, small low domes of cream-colored, soft paste
Aroma: Pungent, strong
Mouthfeel: Very creamy
Flavors: Salt, heavy cream, pungent
Pairings: Syrah

Ricotta
Various producers
Various countries
Cow's, sheep's milk, or both
Classifications: Soft, fresh
Description: Usually packaged in small tubs, creamy white
Aroma: Fresh, milky
Mouthfeel: Smooth, slightly creamy
Flavors: Fresh butter, light cream, hint of grassiness

Ricotta Salata
(ree-COH-tah-sah-LAH-tah)
Various producers, Italy
Sheep's milk
Classifications: Hard, pressed whey curd
Fat: 45 percent
Description: Large, pressed, rindless wheels, bone-white and granular
Aroma: Light tang and salt
Mouthfeel: Dry, crumbly
Flavors: Salty, tangy, light butter

Roaring Forties Blue
King Island Dairy, Australia
Cow's milk
Classifications: Semisoft, blue
Aged: Four to five weeks

Description: Foil-wrapped, heavy blue mottling, light green tones
Aroma: Full and fruity
Mouthfeel: Creamy, sometimes granular
Flavors: Sweet, fruity, piquant
Pairings: Pinot Gris, rum

Robiola Bosina
Italy
Cow's, goat's, and sheep's milk
Classifications: Soft, natural rind
Aged: Less than sixty days
Fat: 57 percent
Description: Small flat squares, beige rind, creamy, oozing paste
Aroma: Light pungency
Mouthfeel: Silky and light
Flavors: Distinct pungency with creamy surround
Pairings: Pinot Gris

Rogue River Blue
Rogue River Creamery, America
Raw cow's milk
Classifications: Semisoft, leaf wrapped, blue
Aged: Eight to twelve months
Description: Wrapped in pear brandy grape leaves
Aroma: Heady, fruity, full
Mouthfeel: Very creamy, soft
Flavors: Piquant, fruity, milky
Pairings: Cabernet Sauvignon, Madeira, Sauternes, gin, vodka, sweet stout

Roncal
(roan-KAHL)
D.O. Controlled, Spain
Raw sheep's milk
Classifications: Semihard, rubbed or wax coated
Aged: Four months
Fat: 50 percent
Description: Hard, rubbed rind with light straw, loose-textured paste
Aroma: Nuts and olive oil

Mouthfeel: Creamy, olive oil, gently coating
Flavors: Rich butter, roasted nuts, warm olive oil, light fruit
Pairings: Merlot, Sauvignon Blanc, Zinfandel, port

Roquefort
(roke-FORE)
A.O.C. Controlled, France
Raw cow's milk
Classifications: Semisoft, blue
Fat: 45 percent
Description: Foil covered, short half or full cylinders, heavy blue-green mottling, light green to cream paste
Aroma: Piquant, spicy, and earthy
Mouthfeel: Very creamy and smooth
Flavors: Piquant butter, earthy tang, rich and complex
Pairings: Cabernet Sauvignon, Madeira, Sauternes

Saenkaenter
Holland
Cow's milk
Classifications: Wax-coated Gouda
Aged: Four years
Description: Aged large wheel with black wax rind over caramel-colored hard paste with irregular eyes
Aroma: Candy tones
Mouthfeel: Crumbly, coating
Flavors: Intense caramel, butterscotch
Pairings: Cognac, porter, Pilsner

Saint Nectaire
(SAN-neck-TARE)
A.O.C. Controlled, France
Cow's milk
Classifications: Semisoft, washed rind
Aged: Three to five weeks
Fat: 45 percent
Description: Orange-red rind, smooth, lightly open ivory paste
Aroma: Mild pungency, light fruit

Mouthfeel: Smooth
Flavors: Rustic fruit and cream
Pairings: Beaujolais, Pinot Noir

Sainte-Maure De Touraine
(SAINT-MORE-du-ter-RAN)
A.O.C. Controlled, France
Goat's milk
Classifications: Soft, natural and ash rind
Fat: 45–50 percent
Description: Log-shaped and natural or ash rind with a natural straw for a core. Bone-white, flaky paste
Aroma: Light, earthy, and tangy
Mouthfeel: Smooth and flaky
Flavors: Piquant lemon, hay, bright cream and tang
Pairings: Sauvignon Blanc

Scarmoza
Italy
Cow's milk
Classifications: Semisoft, smoked
Fat: 40–45 percent
Description: Braided mozzarella, smoked to light brown rind
Aroma: Smoky
Mouthfeel: Smooth
Flavors: Smoky cream
Pairings: Bock beer

Selles-sur-Cher
(SELL-sir-SHAIR)
A.O.C. Controlled, France
Goat's milk
Classifications: Soft, bloomy ash rind
Aged: Less than sixty days
Fat: 45 percent
Description: Small, flat, ash-coated disks with bone white paste
Aroma: Light and goaty
Mouthfeel: Light and smooth, mild coating
Flavors: Bright, tangy, hint of farmyard
Pairings: Sauvignon Blanc

Shropshire Blue
(SHROP-sure)
Neal's Yard, England
Cow's milk
Classifications: Semisoft, blue
Fat: 45 percent
Description: Light rusty brown rind, tall cylinders, Cheddar-orange paste with intricate blue veining
Aroma: Sharp, deep, musty, with some tang
Mouthfeel: Smooth as butter
Flavors: Very complex, fruity tang, bright, sharp earth tones
Pairings: Port, Madeira, British ale, scotch, whiskey

Smoked Gouda
Various producers, various countries
Cow's milk
Classifications: Natural rind, Gouda
Fat: 8 grams/ounce
Description: Rust rind over lighter rust, smooth paste
Aroma: Smoky tang
Mouthfeel: Light rubber
Flavors: Sweet smokiness
Pairings: Bock beer

Sonoma Jack
Sonoma Cheese, America
Cow's milk
Classifications: Semisoft, rindless
Description: Mild yellow-cream paste
Aroma: Mild
Mouthfeel: Light cream
Flavors: Mild, creamy
Pairings: Pinot Noir, most ales, Pilsner

Saint Agur
France
Cow's milk
Classifications: Semisoft, blue
Description: Foil-wrapped densely mottled blue
Aroma: Fresh, piquant

Mouthfeel: Creamy
Flavors: Cream, piquant blue
Pairings: Port

St. Andre
France
Cow's milk
Classifications: Soft, bloomy rind
Fat: 75 percent
Description: Cake-like bloomy rind over dense, creamy-yellow paste
Aroma: Mild
Mouthfeel: Very creamy
Flavors: Full butter
Pairings: Champagne, port

St. George
Matos Cheese, America
Raw cow's milk
Classifications: Semihard, natural rind
Aged: Seven months
Description: Medium, buff-colored rind over very open texture; yellow paste
Aroma: Lemony tang
Mouthfeel: Crumbly
Flavors: Mild, tangy, bright
Pairings: Chardonnay, Sauvignon Blanc, wheat and Lambic beer

Stilton, Colston Bassett
(STILL-ton)
Neal's Yard, England
Cow's milk
Classifications: Semisoft, blue, natural rind
Fat: 55 percent
Description: Light rusty brown rind, tall cylinders, cream-yellow paste with intricate blue veining
Aroma: Sharp, deep, musty, with some tang
Mouthfeel: Smooth as butter
Flavors: Very complex, buttery brightness with sharp earth tones
Pairings: Port, Madeira, British ale, scotch, whiskey

Stracchino
(stra-KEE-no)
Various producers, various countries
Cow's milk
Classifications: Soft, natural rind
Aged: One to two weeks
Fat: 48 percent
Description: Low, flat, pale yellow squares with the texture of firm pudding
Aroma: Mild, milky sharpness
Mouthfeel: Smooth and light
Flavors: Mild lactic with hay tones to full fruity tang
Pairings: Chardonnay, Kirsch

Taleggio
(tah-LEDGG-ee-oh)
D.O.C. Controlled, Italy
Cow's milk
Classifications: Semisoft, washed rind
Fat: 48 percent
Description: Low, flat squares of mottled salmon-colored rind, creamy off-white paste
Aroma: Pungent and thick
Mouthfeel: Creamy and smooth
Flavors: Sharp fruit, salt, meaty
Pairings: Chenin Blanc, Gewurztraminer, Barbaresco or Barolo, Sangiovese, Syrah

Teleme
(tell-em-ee)
Peluso, America
Cow's milk
Classifications: Soft, rice-flour coated
Fat: 7 grams/ounce
Description: Flat squares coated in rice flour over cream-colored oozing paste
Aroma: Mild
Mouthfeel: Very creamy
Flavors: Mild creaminess, a hint of fruit; then a pungent, almost bitter finish
Pairings: Kirsch

Tete de Moine

(TET-du-MWAN)
Name-Controlled, Switzerland
Cow's milk
Classifications: Semisoft, brushed rind
Fat: 51 percent
Description: Low cylinders with brushed rind and yellow-gold smooth paste. Designed to be peeled in rounds from top.
Aroma: Bright and lightly pungent, similar to Swiss cheese
Mouthfeel: Smooth, light
Flavors: Fruit, nuts, cooked cream
Pairings: Wheat beer

Tomme Crayeuse

(TUM-cray-USE)
Schmidhauser, France
Cow's milk
Classifications: Soft, floral rind
Fat: 50 percent
Description: Fuzzy, floral rind with beige-brown paste, small holes in creamy paste
Aroma: Mild to full, earthy, vegetable, and grassy
Mouthfeel: Smooth with thick coating
Flavors: Light nuts; soft butter; earthy mushrooms; long, complex and milky finish
Pairings: Light Pinot Noir

Tomme de Ma Grand-Mere

(TUM-de-ma-GRAND-mare)
Chèvrechard, France
Goat's milk
Classifications: Soft, natural rind
Description: Large natural-rind chèvre
Aroma: Mild pungency
Mouthfeel: Smooth and creamy
Flavors: Bright tang, citrus, grassy
Pairings: Chardonnay, Chenin Blanc, Gewürztraminer, Riesling, Beaujolais, Syrah, porter

Tomme de Savoie

(TUM-du-sav-WAH)
France
Cow's milk
Classifications: Soft, floral rind
Fat: 20–40 percent
Description: Fuzzy, floral rind with beige-brown paste, small holes in creamy paste
Aroma: Mild to full, earthy, vegetable, and grassy
Mouthfeel: Smooth with thick coating
Flavors: Light nuts, earthy mushrooms, some brightness on the finish
Pairings: Light Pinot Noir

Tomme du Levezou

(TUM-du-leh-veh-ZOO)
France
Cow's milk
Classifications: Soft, floral rind
Fat: 50 percent
Description: Pale orange rind over loose-textured, cream-white paste
Aroma: Sharp and milky
Mouthfeel: Smooth and clean
Flavors: Lightly nutty and creamy
Pairings: Light Pinot Noir

Vacherin Fribourgeois

(vash-er-AHN-free-bore-ZHWAH)
France
Raw cow's milk
Classifications: Semisoft, brushed rind
Fat: 45 percent
Description: Light reddish-brown rind, lightly pink and yellow paste, smooth and dense
Aroma: Light to full pungency, sharp and fruity
Mouthfeel: Smooth, not coating
Flavors: Pungent, raw nuts
Pairings: Bordeaux, Merlot, Riesling

Vacherin Mont d'Or
(vash-er-AHN-mon-d-ORE)
A.O.C. Controlled, France
Cow's milk
Classifications: Soft, washed rind
Aged: Less than sixty days
Fat: 45 percent
Description: Small orange discs with bits of bloomy white rind, surrounded by strip of bark, with smooth, cream-colored paste
Aroma: Heady and earthy
Mouthfeel: Silky and smooth
Flavors: Sauteed mushrooms with an aromatic kick
Pairings: Champagne, Viognier, Syrah

Valdeon
(val-dee-ON)
Leon, Spain
Cow's and goat's milk
Classifications: Semisoft, leaf wrapped, blue
Aged: Two months or more
Fat: 45 percent
Description: Usually wrapped in leaves; paste is heavily mottled and blue veined
Aroma: Tangy, fruity, and salty
Mouthfeel: Creamy, granular
Flavors: Powerful fruit, tang, mustiness, and sharpness
Pairings: Beaujolais, full-body Chardonnay

Valencay
(VAL-on-SAY)
France
Goat's milk
Classifications: Soft, bloomy ash rind
Aged: Less than sixty days
Fat: 45 percent
Description: Small, pyramid shaped; coated with ash and bloomy rind; flaky, bone-white paste with layered aging
Aroma: Light tang
Mouthfeel: Smooth, flaky, and creamy coating

Flavors: Flinty tang, lemon, finishes on light cream
Pairings: Chenin Blancs to Beaujalois

Vella Dry Jack
Vella Cheese, America
Cow's milk
Classifications: Semihard, spice rubbed
Aged: Seven months to two years
Description: Cocoa, black pepper, vegetable oil rind over deep yellow, flaky, hard paste
Aroma: Bright and tangy
Mouthfeel: Creamy
Flavors: Herbal, buttery, mild
Pairings: Sangiovese, Zinfandel

Velveeta
Kraft, America
Cow's milk
Classifications: Semisoft, processed
Description: Processed and preserved cheese food
Aroma: Tangy and slightly chemical
Mouthfeel: Slick
Flavors: Mild, sweet

Vlaskaas
Cheeseland, United States and Holland
Cow's milk
Classifications: Wax-coated Gouda
Aged: Five months
Fat: 9 grams/ounce
Description: Large-wheeled Gouda with wax rind, bright straw-colored paste with scattered eyes
Aroma: Mild
Mouthfeel: Smooth, almost plastic
Flavors: Piquant creaminess
Pairings: Chenin Blanc, light ale, Lambic beer, steam beer

Wensleydale
(WHENZ-slee-dale)
Hawe's Creamery, England
Cow's milk

Classifications: Semihard, Cheddar
Fat: 40–45 percent
Description: Light gray rind and light cream-yellow, flaky texture paste
Aroma: Butter and cream
Mouthfeel: Smooth, crumbly, light coating
Flavors: Light, creamy butter with some lemon tang
Pairings: Dry white wines, mild ale

Westcombe Cheddar

Neal's Yard, England
Cow's milk
Classifications: Semihard, bandage wrapped
Aged: Twelve to fourteen months
Description: Gray-brown rind over bright orange, flaky texture paste
Aroma: Mild
Mouthfeel: Smooth, crumbly, light coating
Flavors: Mild sharpness, salty and sweet
Pairings: Pale ale, steam beer, lager beer

Zamorano

(zam-orrr-AN-yo)
D.O. Controlled, Spain
Raw sheep's milk
Classifications: Semihard, wax coated
Aged: Three months to one year
Description: Dark green basket-weave wax rind, light straw-colored paste with loose texture
Aroma: Tangy nuts and butter
Mouthfeel: Smooth, coating, buttery
Flavors: Complex nuts and butter, with a hint of olives
Pairings: Cabernet Sauvignon, Syrah, Zinfandel, Madeira, fino sherry

Cheese Resources

Use the resources in this appendix to do more reading about cheese, track down specialty food and cheese stores, order cheese and cheese supplies by mail, and learn about cheese associations.

Specialty Food and Cheese Stores

The following stores, listed by state, are noted for their excellent cheese selections.

Arizona

AJ's Fine Foods
Phoenix
(602) 230-7015
⌦ *www.ajsfinefoods.com*

Chez Eynard Ltd
Phoenix
(602) 260-2433

Two Sisters Gourmet Foods
Phoenix
(602) 955-5369

California

Andronico's Market
Locations in Northern California
(510) 524-2696
⌦ *www.andronicos.co m*

Artisan Cheese Gallery
Studio City
(818) 505-0207

Artisan Cheese Shop
San Francisco
(415) 929-8610

Bristol Farms
Locations in Southern California
El Segundo
(310) 726-1300

The Cheese Board
Berkeley
(510) 549-3183

The Cheese Course
Healdsburg
(707) 433-4998

The Cheese Shop
Carmel
(831) 625-2272

The Cheese Store of Beverly Hills
Beverly Hills
(310) 278-2855
☞ *www.cheesestorebh.com*

Cowgirl Creamery
Ferry Building Plaza
San Francisco

Oakville Grocery
(Several locations)
Oakville
(707) 944-8802
☞ *www.oakvillegrocery.com*

The Pasta Shop
(Two locations)
Berkeley and Oakland
(510) 547-4005

Rainbow Grocery
San Francisco
(415) 863-0620

River Cafe & Cheese Shop
Santa Cruz

Tomales Bay Foods
Point Reyes Station
(415) 633-9335

Colorado
The Truffle, Inc.
Denver
(303) 322-7363

Wild Oats
(Several locations)
Boulder
(303) 440-5220

Connecticut
Darien Cheese and Fine Foods
Darien
(203) 655-4344

The Good Food Store
Darien
(203) 655-7355

Say Cheese Too!
West Hartford
(860) 233-7309

Florida
Miami Epicure Market
Miami Beach
(305) 672-1861

Georgia
Star Provisions
Atlanta
(404) 365-0410

Illinois
Caputo Cheese Market
1931 N. 15th Ave.
Melrose Park, IL 60160
(708) 450-0074

Dominick's Finer Foods
(Several locations)
(708) 429-5443

Don's Finest Foods
Lake Forest
(847) 234-2700

Indiana
The Cheese Shop
Indianapolis
(317) 846-6885

Kentucky
Party Source
(Several locations)
Bellevue
(859) 291-4007

Louisiana
The Wine & Cheese Shop
Baton Rouge
(225) 926-8847

Maine
Horton's Naturally Smoked
Portland
(207) 228-2056

Maryland
Sutton Place Gourmet
Bethesda
(310) 564-6006

The Wine Source
3601 Elm Avenue
Baltimore, MD 21211
(410) 467-7777

Massachusetts
Fine Wine Cellars of Chestnut Hill
Boston
(617) 232-1020

Fromaggio Kitchen, Inc.
(Two locations)
Cambridge
(617) 354-4650

The Richmond Store Grocers
Richmond
(413) 698-8698

Savenor's Market
Boston
(617) 236-7979

University Wine Shop
Cambridge
(617) 547-4258

Wasik's Cheese Shop
Wellesley
(781) 237-0916

Michigan
Zingerman's Delicatessen & Creamery
Ann Arbor
(734) 663-3354
www.zingermans.com

Minnesota
Kowalski's Market
(Several locations)
Woodbury
(651) 578-8800

Lunds & Byerly's
(Several locations)
Minneapolis
(612) 825-2440
✆ www.lundsmarket.com

Surdyk's
Minneapolis
(612) 379-2323
✆ www.surdyks.com

Missouri
The Better Cheddar
(Two locations)
Kansas City
(816) 561-8204

Provisions Gourmet Market
St. Louis
(314) 989-0020

The Wine & Cheese Place
(Three locations)
St. Louis
(314) 962-8150

The Wine Merchant, Ltd.
20 S. Hanley
Clayton, MO 63105
(800) 770-VINO (8466)
✆ www.winemerchantltd.com

Nebraska
Broadmoor Market
Omaha
(402) 391-0312

Nevada
Valley Cheese & Wine
Henderson
(702) 341-8191
✆ www.valleycheeseandwine.com

New Jersey
Gary's Wine & Marketplace
(Three locations)
Madison
(973) 822-0200
✆ www.garysmarket.com

New Mexico
Juan Tabo Wild Oats Natural Marketplace
Albuquerque
(505) 275-6660

Tesuque Village Market
Tesuque
(505) 988-8848

New York
Artisanal
New York
(212) 673-2600

Balducci's
(Two locations)
New York
(212) 653-8320

Citarella
(Several locations)
New York
(212) 874-0383
✆ www.citarella.com

Dean & Deluca
Manhattan
(212) 431-1691
✍ *www.deandeluca.com*

Fairway Market
(Several locations)
New York
(212) 595-1888

Ideal Cheese Shop
New York
(212) 688-7579
✍ *www.idealcheese.com*

Murray's
New York
(888) 692-4339
✍ *www.murrayscheese.com*

Wegmans Food Markets
(Several locations)
Rochester
(585) 328-2550

Zabar's
New York
(212) 787-2000

North Carolina

City Beverage
Winston-Salem
(336) 722-2774

Dean & Deluca
Charlotte
(704) 643-6868

Fowler's Gourmet
Durham
(919) 683-2555

The Fresh Market
(Several locations)
Raleigh
(919) 828-7888

Ohio

Annemarie's Dairy
Cleveland
(216) 344-9333

The Cheese Shoppe
Cleveland
(216) 771-6349

Jungle Jim's
Cincinnati
(513) 829-1919

The Kroger Company
(Several locations)
Cincinnati
(513) 762-4877

West Point Market
Akron
(330) 864-2151

Oregon

Foster & Dobbs Authentic Foods
Portland
(503) 284-1157
✍ *www.fosteranddobbs.com*

New Seasons Market
(Eight locations)
Portland
✍ *www.newseasonsmarket.com*

Pastaworks
Portland
(503) 232-1010
✍ www.pastaworks.com

Steve's Cheese
Portland
(503) 222-6014

Zupan's Market
(Several locations)
Portland
(503) 203-5962
✍ www.zupans.com

Pennsylvania
DiBruno Bros.
Philadelphia
(215) 922-2876
✍ www.dibruno.com

Downtown Cheese
Philadelphia
(215) 351-7412

Pittsburgh Cheese Terminal
Pittsburgh
(412) 434-5800

South Carolina
O'Hara & Flynn Wine & Cheese
(Two locations)
Charleston
(843) 534-1916

Tennessee
Corner Market
Nashville
(615) 352-6772

Texas
Central Market
(Seven locations)
(800) 360-2552

Utah
Tony Caputo's Market & Deli
Salt Lake City
(801) 582-7758

Vermont
Cheese Traders
Burlington, Vermont
(800) 540-4261

Sugarbush Farms
Woodstock, Vermont
(800) 281-1757

Virginia
The Cheese Shop
Williamsburg
(757) 229-6754

Warwick Cheese Shoppe
Newport News
(757) 599-3985
✍ www.warwickcheese.com

Washington
Beecher's Cheese
Seattle
(206) 605-2915

Larry's Market
Seattle
(206) 527-5333

Madison Market Co-op
Seattle

Metropolitan Market
Seattle, WA
✎ *www.metropolitan-market.com*

Washington, D.C.
Cowgirl Creamery
(866) 433-7834 or (202) 393-6880
✎ *www.cowgirlcreamery.com*

Dean & Deluca
Washington
(202) 342-2500
✎ *www.deandeluca.com*

Wisconsin
Jim's Cheese Pantry
410 Portland Rd.,
Waterloo, WI 53594
(800) 345-3571
✎ *www.jimscheesepantry.com*

Maple Leaf Cheese and Chocolate Haus
554 1st Street and Hwy 39
New Glarus, WI 53574
(608) 527-2000
✎ *www.wischeese.com*

Meister Cheese Company
1050 Industrial Drive
Muscoda, WI 53573
(608) 739-3134
✎ *www.meistercheese.com*

Roth Kase Cheese Factory & Alp and Dell Cheese Store
W5676 Rolling Acres Lane

Monroe, WI 53566
(608) 328-3355

Specialty Cheese Company, Inc.
455 S. River St.
Lowell, WI 53557
(920) 927-3888
✎ *www.specialcheese.com*

Zimmerman Cheese, Inc.
N6853 Hwy 78
South Wayne, WI 53566
(608) 968-3414

Nationwide
Whole Foods Stores

Internet Order Cheese and Cheese Supplies

Here are some great places for you to order cheese and cheese supplies.

Artisanal Premium Cheese
✎ *www.artisanalcheese.com*

Cowgirl Creamery
✎ *www.cowgirlcreamery.com/index.html*

Dean & Deluca
✎ *www.deandeluca.com*

Murray's Cheese
✎ *www.murrayscheese.com*

NapaStyle
✎ *www.napastyle.com*

The Pasta Shop

✍ *www.markethallfoods.com*

Williams Sonoma

✍ *www.williams-sonoma.com*

Great Books on Cheese

Enjoy all of the following books on cheese.

Barthelemy, Roland, and Arnaud Sperat-Czar. *Cheeses of the World* (New York: Hachette Press, 2001).

Boisard, Pierre. *Camembert* (Berkeley: University of California Press, 1992).

Brennan, Ethel, and Georgeane Brennan. *Goat Cheese* (San Francisco: Chronicle Books, 1997).

Carroll, Ricki. *Home Cheese Making* (North Adams, MA: Storey Publishing, 2002).

Chenel, Laura, and Linda Siegfried. *American Country Cheese* (Berkeley, CA: Aris Books, 1989).

Dorling Kindersley. *French Cheeses* (New York: Dorling Kindersley Press, 1996).

Eekhof-Stork, Nancy. *The World Atlas of Cheese* (Amsterdam, The Netherlands: Paddington Press Ltd, 1976).

Fletcher, Janet. *The Cheese Course* (San Franscisio: Chronicle Books, 2000).

The Giacomini Family. *The Blue Course* (Point Reyes, CA: Point Reyes Farmstead Cheese Company, 2004).

Harbutt, Juliet. *Cheese.* (Minocqua: WI: Willow Creek Press, 1999).

———. *The Cheese Lover's Kitchen Handbook* (London: Southwater, an imprint of Anness Publishing Ltd., 2000).

Jenkins, Steve. *Cheese Primer* (New York: Workman Publishing, 1996).

Kindstedt, Paul, et al. *American Farmstead Cheese* (White River Jct., VT: Chelsea Green Publishing, 2005).

Lambert, Paula. *The Cheese Lover's Cookbook & Guide* (New York: Simon & Schuster, 2000).

McCalman, Max, and David Gibbons. *Cheese.* (New York: Clarkson Potter, 2005).

———. *The Cheese Plate* (New York: Clarkson Potter 2002.)

Michelson, Patricia. *The Cheese Room* (New York: Penguin Books, 2001).

Ridgeway, Judy. *The Cheese Companion.* (Philadelphia: Running Press, 1999).

Slow Food Group. *Italian Cheese* (Bra, Italy: Slow Food Group, 1999–2000).

Teubner, Christian. *The Cheese Bible* (New York: Penguin Books, 1998).

Werlin, Laura. *The All American Cheese and Wine Book* (New York: Stuart, Tabori & Chang, 2003).

———. *Great Grilled Cheese.* (New York: Stewart, Tabori & Chang, 2004).

———. *The New American Cheese.* (New York: Stuart, Tabori & Chang, 2000).

Index

THE EVERYTHING SERIES!

BUSINESS & PERSONAL FINANCE

Everything® Accounting Book
Everything® Budgeting Book
Everything® Business Planning Book
Everything® Coaching and Mentoring Book
Everything® Fundraising Book
Everything® Get Out of Debt Book
Everything® Grant Writing Book
Everything® Guide to Personal Finance for Single Mothers
Everything® Home-Based Business Book, 2nd Ed.
Everything® Homebuying Book, 2nd Ed.
Everything® Homeselling Book, 2nd Ed.
Everything® Improve Your Credit Book
Everything® Investing Book, 2nd Ed.
Everything® Landlording Book
Everything® Leadership Book
Everything® Managing People Book, 2nd Ed.
Everything® Negotiating Book
Everything® Online Auctions Book
Everything® Online Business Book
Everything® Personal Finance Book
Everything® Personal Finance in Your 20s and 30s Book
Everything® Project Management Book
Everything® Real Estate Investing Book
Everything® Retirement Planning Book
Everything® Robert's Rules Book, $7.95
Everything® Selling Book
Everything® Start Your Own Business Book, 2nd Ed.
Everything® Wills & Estate Planning Book

COOKING

Everything® Barbecue Cookbook
Everything® Bartender's Book, $9.95
Everything® Cheese Book
Everything® Chinese Cookbook
Everything® Classic Recipes Book
Everything® Cocktail Parties and Drinks Book
Everything® College Cookbook
Everything® Cooking for Baby and Toddler Book
Everything® Cooking for Two Cookbook
Everything® Diabetes Cookbook
Everything® Easy Gourmet Cookbook
Everything® Fondue Cookbook
Everything® Fondue Party Book
Everything® Gluten-Free Cookbook
Everything® Glycemic Index Cookbook
Everything® Grilling Cookbook

Everything® Healthy Meals in Minutes Cookbook
Everything® Holiday Cookbook
Everything® Indian Cookbook
Everything® Italian Cookbook
Everything® Low-Carb Cookbook
Everything® Low-Fat High-Flavor Cookbook
Everything® Low-Salt Cookbook
Everything® Meals for a Month Cookbook
Everything® Mediterranean Cookbook
Everything® Mexican Cookbook
Everything® No Trans Fat Cookbook
Everything® One-Pot Cookbook
Everything® Pizza Cookbook
Everything® Quick and Easy 30-Minute, 5-Ingredient Cookbook
Everything® Quick Meals Cookbook
Everything® Slow Cooker Cookbook
Everything® Slow Cooking for a Crowd Cookbook
Everything® Soup Cookbook
Everything® Stir-Fry Cookbook
Everything® Tex-Mex Cookbook
Everything® Thai Cookbook
Everything® Vegetarian Cookbook
Everything® Wild Game Cookbook
Everything® Wine Book, 2nd Ed.

GAMES

Everything® 15-Minute Sudoku Book, $9.95
Everything® 30-Minute Sudoku Book, $9.95
Everything® Blackjack Strategy Book
Everything® Brain Strain Book, $9.95
Everything® Bridge Book
Everything® Card Games Book
Everything® Card Tricks Book, $9.95
Everything® Casino Gambling Book, 2nd Ed.
Everything® Chess Basics Book
Everything® Craps Strategy Book
Everything® Crossword and Puzzle Book
Everything® Crossword Challenge Book
Everything® Crosswords for the Beach Book, $9.95
Everything® Cryptograms Book, $9.95
Everything® Easy Crosswords Book
Everything® Easy Kakuro Book, $9.95
Everything® Easy Large Print Crosswords Book
Everything® Games Book, 2nd Ed.
Everything® Giant Sudoku Book, $9.95
Everything® Kakuro Challenge Book, $9.95
Everything® Large-Print Crossword Challenge Book

Everything® Large-Print Crosswords Book
Everything® Lateral Thinking Puzzles Book, $9.95
Everything® Mazes Book
Everything® Movie Crosswords Book, $9.95
Everything® Online Poker Book, $12.95
Everything® Pencil Puzzles Book, $9.95
Everything® Poker Strategy Book
Everything® Pool & Billiards Book
Everything® Sports Crosswords Book, $9.95
Everything® Test Your IQ Book, $9.95
Everything® Texas Hold 'Em Book, $9.95
Everything® Travel Crosswords Book, $9.95
Everything® Word Games Challenge Book
Everything® Word Scramble Book
Everything® Word Search Book

HEALTH

Everything® Alzheimer's Book
Everything® Diabetes Book
Everything® Health Guide to Adult Bipolar Disorder
Everything® Health Guide to Controlling Anxiety
Everything® Health Guide to Fibromyalgia
Everything® Health Guide to Postpartum Care
Everything® Health Guide to Thyroid Disease
Everything® Hypnosis Book
Everything® Low Cholesterol Book
Everything® Massage Book
Everything® Menopause Book
Everything® Nutrition Book
Everything® Reflexology Book
Everything® Stress Management Book

HISTORY

Everything® American Government Book
Everything® American History Book, 2nd Ed.
Everything® Civil War Book
Everything® Freemasons Book
Everything® Irish History & Heritage Book
Everything® Middle East Book

HOBBIES

Everything® Candlemaking Book
Everything® Cartooning Book
Everything® Coin Collecting Book
Everything® Drawing Book
Everything® Family Tree Book, 2nd Ed.
Everything® Knitting Book
Everything® Knots Book
Everything® Photography Book

Everything® Quilting Book
Everything® Scrapbooking Book
Everything® Sewing Book
Everything® Soapmaking Book, 2nd Ed.
Everything® Woodworking Book

HOME IMPROVEMENT

Everything® Feng Shui Book
Everything® Feng Shui Decluttering Book, $9.95
Everything® Fix-It Book
Everything® Home Decorating Book
Everything® Home Storage Solutions Book
Everything® Homebuilding Book
Everything® Organize Your Home Book

KIDS' BOOKS

All titles are $7.95
Everything® Kids' Animal Puzzle & Activity Book
Everything® Kids' Baseball Book, 4th Ed.
Everything® Kids' Bible Trivia Book
Everything® Kids' Bugs Book
Everything® Kids' Cars and Trucks Puzzle
     & Activity Book
Everything® Kids' Christmas Puzzle
     & Activity Book
Everything® Kids' Cookbook
Everything® Kids' Crazy Puzzles Book
Everything® Kids' Dinosaurs Book
Everything® Kids' First Spanish Puzzle and
     Activity Book
Everything® Kids' Gross Cookbook
Everything® Kids' Gross Hidden Pictures Book
Everything® Kids' Gross Jokes Book
Everything® Kids' Gross Mazes Book
Everything® Kids' Gross Puzzle and
     Activity Book
Everything® Kids' Halloween Puzzle
     & Activity Book
Everything® Kids' Hidden Pictures Book
Everything® Kids' Horses Book
Everything® Kids' Joke Book
Everything® Kids' Knock Knock Book
Everything® Kids' Learning Spanish Book
Everything® Kids' Math Puzzles Book
Everything® Kids' Mazes Book
Everything® Kids' Money Book
Everything® Kids' Nature Book
Everything® Kids' Pirates Puzzle and Activity Book
Everything® Kids' Presidents Book
Everything® Kids' Princess Puzzle and Activity Book
Everything® Kids' Puzzle Book
Everything® Kids' Riddles & Brain Teasers Book
Everything® Kids' Science Experiments Book
Everything® Kids' Sharks Book
Everything® Kids' Soccer Book
Everything® Kids' States Book
Everything® Kids' Travel Activity Book

KIDS' STORY BOOKS

Everything® Fairy Tales Book

LANGUAGE

Everything® Conversational Japanese Book with
     CD, $19.95
Everything® French Grammar Book
Everything® French Phrase Book, $9.95
Everything® French Verb Book, $9.95
Everything® German Practice Book with CD,
     $19.95
Everything® Inglés Book
**Everything® Intermediate Spanish Book with
     CD, $19.95**
**Everything® Learning Brazilian Portuguese
     Book with CD, $19.95**
Everything® Learning French Book
Everything® Learning German Book
Everything® Learning Italian Book
Everything® Learning Latin Book
**Everything® Learning Spanish Book with
     CD, 2nd Edition, $19.95**
Everything® Russian Practice Book with CD, $19.95
Everything® Sign Language Book
Everything® Spanish Grammar Book
Everything® Spanish Phrase Book, $9.95
Everything® Spanish Practice Book
     with CD, $19.95
Everything® Spanish Verb Book, $9.95
Everything® Speaking Mandarin Chinese Book
     with CD, $19.95

MUSIC

Everything® Drums Book with CD, $19.95
**Everything® Guitar Book with CD, 2nd
     Edition, $19.95**
Everything® Guitar Chords Book with CD, $19.95
Everything® Home Recording Book
Everything® Music Theory Book with CD, $19.95
Everything® Reading Music Book with CD, $19.95
Everything® Rock & Blues Guitar Book
     with CD, $19.95
**Everything® Rock and Blues Piano Book
     with CD, $19.95**
Everything® Songwriting Book

NEW AGE

Everything® Astrology Book, 2nd Ed.
Everything® Birthday Personology Book
Everything® Dreams Book, 2nd Ed.
Everything® Love Signs Book, $9.95
Everything® Numerology Book
Everything® Paganism Book
Everything® Palmistry Book
Everything® Psychic Book
Everything® Reiki Book

Everything® Sex Signs Book, $9.95
Everything® Tarot Book, 2nd Ed.
Everything® Toltec Wisdom Book
Everything® Wicca and Witchcraft Book

PARENTING

Everything® Baby Names Book, 2nd Ed.
Everything® Baby Shower Book
Everything® Baby's First Year Book
Everything® Birthing Book
Everything® Breastfeeding Book
Everything® Father-to-Be Book
Everything® Father's First Year Book
Everything® Get Ready for Baby Book
Everything® Get Your Baby to Sleep Book, $9.95
Everything® Getting Pregnant Book
Everything® Guide to Raising a One-Year-Old
Everything® Guide to Raising a Two-Year-Old
Everything® Homeschooling Book
Everything® Mother's First Year Book
**Everything® Parent's Guide to Childhood
     Illnesses**
Everything® Parent's Guide to Children
     and Divorce
Everything® Parent's Guide to Children
     with ADD/ADHD
Everything® Parent's Guide to Children
     with Asperger's Syndrome
Everything® Parent's Guide to Children
     with Autism
Everything® Parent's Guide to Children with
     Bipolar Disorder
**Everything® Parent's Guide to Children with
     Depression**
Everything® Parent's Guide to Children
     with Dyslexia
**Everything® Parent's Guide to Children with
     Juvenile Diabetes**
Everything® Parent's Guide to Positive Discipline
Everything® Parent's Guide to Raising a
     Successful Child
Everything® Parent's Guide to Raising Boys
Everything® Parent's Guide to Raising Girls
Everything® Parent's Guide to Raising Siblings
Everything® Parent's Guide to Sensory
     Integration Disorder
Everything® Parent's Guide to Tantrums
Everything® Parent's Guide to the Strong-Willed
     Child
Everything® Parenting a Teenager Book
Everything® Potty Training Book, $9.95
Everything® Pregnancy Book, 3rd Ed.
Everything® Pregnancy Fitness Book
Everything® Pregnancy Nutrition Book
Everything® Pregnancy Organizer, 2nd Ed., $16.95
Everything® Toddler Activities Book
Everything® Toddler Book

Everything® Tween Book
Everything® Twins, Triplets, and More Book

PETS

Everything® Aquarium Book
Everything® Boxer Book
Everything® Cat Book, 2nd Ed.
Everything® Chihuahua Book
Everything® Dachshund Book
Everything® Dog Book
Everything® Dog Health Book
Everything® Dog Obedience Book
Everything® Dog Owner's Organizer, $16.95
Everything® Dog Training and Tricks Book
Everything® German Shepherd Book
Everything® Golden Retriever Book
Everything® Horse Book
Everything® Horse Care Book
Everything® Horseback Riding Book
Everything® Labrador Retriever Book
Everything® Poodle Book
Everything® Pug Book
Everything® Puppy Book
Everything® Rottweiler Book
Everything® Small Dogs Book
Everything® Tropical Fish Book
Everything® Yorkshire Terrier Book

REFERENCE

Everything® American Presidents Book
Everything® Blogging Book
Everything® Build Your Vocabulary Book
Everything® Car Care Book
Everything® Classical Mythology Book
Everything® Da Vinci Book
Everything® Divorce Book
Everything® Einstein Book
Everything® Enneagram Book
Everything® Etiquette Book, 2nd Ed.
Everything® Inventions and Patents Book
Everything® Mafia Book
Everything® Philosophy Book
Everything® Pirates Book
Everything® Psychology Book

RELIGION

Everything® Angels Book
Everything® Bible Book
Everything® Buddhism Book
Everything® Catholicism Book
Everything® Christianity Book
Everything® Gnostic Gospels Book
Everything® History of the Bible Book
Everything® Jesus Book

Everything® Jewish History & Heritage Book
Everything® Judaism Book
Everything® Kabbalah Book
Everything® Koran Book
Everything® Mary Book
Everything® Mary Magdalene Book
Everything® Prayer Book
Everything® Saints Book, 2nd Ed.
Everything® Torah Book
Everything® Understanding Islam Book
Everything® World's Religions Book
Everything® Zen Book

SCHOOL & CAREERS

Everything® Alternative Careers Book
Everything® Career Tests Book
Everything® College Major Test Book
Everything® College Survival Book, 2nd Ed.
Everything® Cover Letter Book, 2nd Ed.
Everything® Filmmaking Book
Everything® Get-a-Job Book, 2nd Ed.
Everything® Guide to Being a Paralegal
Everything® Guide to Being a Personal Trainer
Everything® Guide to Being a Real Estate Agent
Everything® Guide to Being a Sales Rep
Everything® Guide to Careers in Health Care
Everything® Guide to Careers in Law Enforcement
Everything® Guide to Government Jobs
Everything® Guide to Starting and Running a Restaurant
Everything® Job Interview Book
Everything® New Nurse Book
Everything® New Teacher Book
Everything® Paying for College Book
Everything® Practice Interview Book
Everything® Resume Book, 2nd Ed.
Everything® Study Book

SELF-HELP

Everything® Dating Book, 2nd Ed.
Everything® Great Sex Book
Everything® Self-Esteem Book
Everything® Tantric Sex Book

SPORTS & FITNESS

Everything® Easy Fitness Book
Everything® Running Book
Everything® Weight Training Book

TRAVEL

Everything® Family Guide to Cruise Vacations
Everything® Family Guide to Hawaii
Everything® Family Guide to Las Vegas, 2nd Ed.
Everything® Family Guide to Mexico
Everything® Family Guide to New York City, 2nd Ed.
Everything® Family Guide to RV Travel & Campgrounds
Everything® Family Guide to the Caribbean
Everything® Family Guide to the Walt Disney World Resort®, Universal Studios®, and Greater Orlando, 4th Ed.
Everything® Family Guide to Timeshares
Everything® Family Guide to Washington D.C., 2nd Ed.

WEDDINGS

Everything® Bachelorette Party Book, $9.95
Everything® Bridesmaid Book, $9.95
Everything® Destination Wedding Book
Everything® Elopement Book, $9.95
Everything® Father of the Bride Book, $9.95
Everything® Groom Book, $9.95
Everything® Mother of the Bride Book, $9.95
Everything® Outdoor Wedding Book
Everything® Wedding Book, 3rd Ed.
Everything® Wedding Checklist, $9.95
Everything® Wedding Etiquette Book, $9.95
Everything® Wedding Organizer, 2nd Ed., $16.95
Everything® Wedding Shower Book, $9.95
Everything® Wedding Vows Book, $9.95
Everything® Wedding Workout Book
Everything® Weddings on a Budget Book, $9.95

WRITING

Everything® Creative Writing Book
Everything® Get Published Book, 2nd Ed.
Everything® Grammar and Style Book
Everything® Guide to Magazine Writing
Everything® Guide to Writing a Book Proposal
Everything® Guide to Writing a Novel
Everything® Guide to Writing Children's Books
Everything® Guide to Writing Copy
Everything® Guide to Writing Research Papers
Everything® Screenwriting Book
Everything® Writing Poetry Book
Everything® Writing Well Book